Valencia, Spain

Sandra Wilkins

Contents

Articles

Attractions

Transportation

References

Overview of Spain

History of Spain

Transition to Democracy
Modern Spain
Topics
Economic History
Military History
Spain Portal

The **history of Spain** spans from prehistoric Iberia, through the rise and fall of a global empire, to the recent history of Spain as a member of the European Union.

Modern humans entered the Iberian Peninsula about 32,000 years ago. Different populations and cultures followed over the millennia, including the Iberians, the Tartessians, Celts and Celtiberians, Phoenicians, Greeks, Carthaginians, Romans, Suebi and Visigoths. In 711, the Moors, a Berber and Arab army, invaded and conquered nearly the entire peninsula. During the next 750 years, independent Muslim states were established, and the entire area of Muslim control became known as Al-Andalus. Meanwhile the Christian kingdoms in the north began the long and slow recovery of the peninsula, a process called the *Reconquista*, which was concluded in 1492 with the fall of Granada.

The Kingdom of Spain was created in 1492 with the unification of the Kingdom of Castile and the Kingdom of Aragon. In this year also was the first voyage of Christopher Columbus to the New World, beginning the development of the Spanish Empire. The Inquisition was established and Jews and Muslims who refused to convert were expelled from the country.

For the next three centuries Spain was the most important colonial power in the world. It was the most powerful state in Europe and the foremost global power during the 16th century and the greater part of the 17th century. Spanish literature and fine arts, scholarship and philosophy flourished during this time. Spain established a vast empire in the Americas, stretching from California to Patagonia, and colonies in the western Pacific. Financed in part by the riches pouring in from its colonies, Spain became embroiled in the religiously charged wars and intrigues of Europe, including, for example, obtaining and losing possessions in today's Netherlands, Italy, France, and Germany, and engaging in wars with France, England, Sweden, and the Ottomans in the Mediterranean Sea and northern Africa. Spain's European wars, however, led to economic damage, and the latter part of the 17th century saw a gradual decline of power under an increasingly neglectful and inept Habsburg regime. The decline culminated in the War of Spanish Succession, which ended with the relegation of Spain from the position of a leading western power, to that of a secondary one, although it remained (with Russia) the leading colonial power.

The eighteenth century saw a new dynasty, the Bourbons, which directed considerable efforts towards the renewal of state institutions, with some success, finishing in a successful involvement in the American War of Independence. However, as the century ended, a reaction set in with the accession of a new monarch. The end of the eighteenth and the start of the nineteenth centuries saw turmoil unleashed throughout Europe by the French Revolutionary and Napoleonic Wars, which finally led to a French occupation of much of the continent, including Spain. This triggered a successful but devastating war of independence that shattered the country and created an opening for what would ultimately be the successful independence of Spain's mainland American colonies. Shattered by the war, Spain was destabilised as different political parties representing "liberal", "reactionary" and "moderate" groups throughout the remainder of the century fought for and won short-lived control without any being sufficiently strong to bring about lasting stability. Nationalist movements emerged in the last significant remnants of the old empire (Cuba and the Philippines) which led to a brief war with the United States and the loss of the remaining old colonies at the end of the century.

Following a period of growing political instability in the early twentieth century, in 1936 Spain was plunged into a bloody civil war. The war ended in a nationalist dictatorship, led by Francisco Franco which controlled the Spanish government until 1975. Spain was officially neutral during World War II, although many Spanish volunteers fought on both sides. The post-war decades were relatively stable (with the notable exception of an armed independence movement in the Basque Country), and the country experienced rapid economic growth in the 1960s and early 1970s. The death of Franco in 1975 resulted in the return of the Bourbon monarchy headed by Prince Juan Carlos. While tensions remain (for example, with Muslim immigrants and in the Basque region), modern Spain has seen the development of a robust, modern democracy as a constitutional monarchy with popular King Juan Carlos, one of the fastest-growing standards of living in Europe, entry into the European Community, and the 1992 Summer Olympics.

Early history

Main article: Prehistoric Iberia

The earliest record of hominids living in Europe has been found in the Spanish cave of Atapuerca; fossils found there are dated to roughly 1.2 million years ago. Modern humans in the form of Cro-Magnons began arriving in the Iberian Peninsula from north of the Pyrenees some 35,000 years ago. The most conspicuous sign of prehistoric human settlements are the famous paintings in the northern Spanish cave of Altamira, which were done ca. 15,000 BC and are regarded as paramount instances of cave art. Furthermore, archeological evidence in places like Los Millares in Almería and in El Argar in Murcia suggests developed cultures existed in the eastern part of the Iberian Peninsula during the late Neolithic and the Bronze Age.

The seafaring Phoenicians, Greeks and Carthaginians successively settled along the Mediterranean Sea (modern day Cádiz) near Tartessos. Regarding Tartessos, it should also be mentioned that according to John Koch Cunliffe, Karl, Wodtko and other highly respected scholars, Celtic culture may well have developed first in far Southern Portugal and Southwestern Spain, approximately 500 years prior to anything recorded in Central Europe. The Tartessian language from the southwest of Spain, written in a version of the Phoenician script in use around 825 BC, has been readily translated by John T. Koch as Celtic and is being accepted by a growing number of philologists and other linguists as the first Celtic language. In the 9th century BC, the first Greek colonies, such as Emporion (modern Empúries), were founded along the Mediterranean coast on the east, leaving the south coast to the Phoenicians. The Greeks are responsible for the name *Iberia*, apparently after the river Iber (Ebro in Spanish). In the 6th century BC, the Carthaginians arrived in Iberia, struggling first with the Greeks, and shortly after, with the newly arriving Romans for control of the Western Mediterranean. Their most important colony was Carthago Nova (Latin name of modern day Cartagena).

The native peoples whom the Romans met at the time of their invasion in what is now known as Spain were the Iberians, inhabiting from the southwest part of the Peninsula through the northeast part of it, and then the Celts, mostly inhabiting the north and northwest part of the Peninsula. In the inner part of the Peninsula, where both groups were in contact, a mixed, distinctive, culture was present, the one known as Celtiberian. The Celtiberian Wars or Spanish Wars were fought between the advancing legions of the Roman Republic and the Celtiberian tribes of Hispania Citerior from 181 to 133 BC.

Roman *Hispania*

Main article: Hispania

Further information: Roman conquest of Hispania

Hispania was divided: Hispania Ulterior and Hispania Citerior during the late Roman Republic; and, during the Roman Empire, Hispania Taraconensis in the northeast, Hispania Baetica in the south (roughly corresponding to Andalucia), and Lusitania in the southwest (corresponding to modern Portugal).

The base Celtiberian population remained in various stages of Romanisation, and local leaders were admitted into the Roman aristocratic class.

The Romans improved existing cities, such as Tarragona (*Tarraco*), and established others like Zaragoza (*Caesaraugusta*), Mérida (*Augusta Emerita*), Valencia (*Valentia*), León ("Legio Septima"), Badajoz ("Pax Augusta"), and Palencia. The peninsula's economy expanded under Roman tutelage. Hispania supplied Rome with food, olive oil, wine and metal. The emperors Trajan, Hadrian, Theodosius I, the philosopher Seneca and the poets Martial, Quintilian and Lucan were born in Spain. The Spanish Bishops held the Council at Elvira in 306.

The first Germanic tribes to invade Hispania arrived in the 5th century, as the Roman Empire decayed. The Visigoths, Suebi, Vandals and Alans arrived in Spain by crossing the Pyrenees mountain range. The Romanized Visigoths entered Hispania in 415. After the conversion of their monarchy to Roman Catholicism, the Visigothic Kingdom eventually encompassed a great part of the Iberian Peninsula after conquering the disordered Suebic territories in the northwest and Byzantine territories in the southeast.

The collapse of the Western Roman Empire did not lead to the same wholesale destruction of Western classical society as happened in areas like Roman Britain, Gaul and Germania Inferior during the Dark Ages, even if the institutions, infrastructure and economy did suffer considerable degradation. Spain's present languages, its religion, and the basis of its laws originate from this period. The centuries of uninterrupted Roman rule and settlement left a deep and enduring imprint upon the culture of Spain.

Germanic Occupation of Hispania (5th–8th centuries)

Further information: Kingdom of Toledo, Suebic Kingdom of Galicia, and Spania

After the decline of the Roman Empire, Germanic tribes invaded the former empire. Several turned sedentary and created successor-kingdoms to the Romans in various parts of Europe. Iberia was taken over by the Visigoths after 410.

In the Iberian peninsula, as elsewhere, the Empire fell not with a bang but with a whimper. Rather than there being any convenient date for the "fall of the Roman Empire" there was a progressive "de-Romanization" of the Western Roman Empire in Hispania and a weakening of central authority, throughout the 3rd, 4th and 5th centuries. At the same time, there was a process of "Romanization" of the Germanic and Hunnic tribes settled on both sides of the *limes* (the fortified frontier of the Empire along the Rhine and Danube rivers). The Visigoths, for example, were converted to Arian Christianity around 360, even before they were pushed into imperial territory by the expansion of the Huns. In the winter of 406, taking advantage of the frozen Rhine, the (Germanic) Vandals and Sueves, and the (Sarmatian) Alans invaded the empire in force. Three years later they crossed the Pyrenees into Iberia and divided the Western parts, roughly corresponding to modern Portugal and western Spain as far as Madrid, between them. The Visigoths meanwhile, having sacked Rome two years earlier, arrived in the region in 412 founding the Visigothic kingdom of Toulouse (in the south of modern France) and gradually expanded their influence into the Iberian peninsula at the expense of the Vandals and Alans, who moved on into North Africa without leaving much permanent mark on Hispanic culture. The Visigothic Kingdom shifted its capital to Toledo and reached a high point during the reign of Leovigild.

Importantly, Spain never saw a decline in interest in classical culture to the degree observable in Britain, Gaul, Lombardy and Germany. The Visigoths tended to maintain more of the old Roman institutions, and they had a unique respect for legal codes that resulted in continuous frameworks and historical records for most of the period between 415, when Visigothic rule in Spain began, and 711, when it is traditionally said to end. The proximity of the Visigothic kingdoms to the Mediterranean and the continuity of western Mediterranean trade, though in reduced quantity, supported Visigothic culture. Arian Visigothic nobility kept apart from the local Catholic population. The Visigothic ruling class looked to Constantinople for style and technology while the rivals of Visigothic power and culture were the Catholic bishops— and a brief incursion of Byzantine power in Cordoba.

The period of rule by the Visigothic Kingdom saw the spread of Arianism briefly in Spain. In 587, Reccared, the Visigothic king at Toledo, having been converted to Catholicism put an end to dissension on the question of Arianism and launched a movement in Spain to unify the various religious doctrines that existed in the land. The Council of Lerida in 546 constrained the clergy and extended the power of law over them under the blessings of Rome.

The Visigoths inherited from Late Antiquity a sort of feudal system in Spain, based in the south on the Roman villa system and in the north drawing on their vassals to supply troops in exchange for protection. The bulk of the Visigothic army was

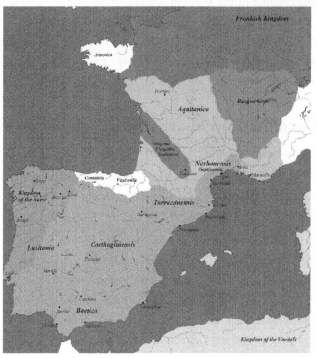

Greatest extent of the Visigothic Kingdom of Toulouse, c. 500, showing Territory lost after Vouille in light orange.

composed of slaves, raised from the countryside. The loose council of nobles that advised Spain's Visigothic kings and legitimized their rule was responsible for raising the army, and only upon its consent was the king able to summon soldiers.

The impact of Visigothic rule was not widely felt on society at large, and certainly not compared to the vast bureaucracy of the Roman Empire; they tended to rule as barbarians of a mild sort, uninterested in the events of the nation and economy, working for personal benefit, and little literature remains to us from the period. They did not, until the period of Muslim rule, merge with the Spanish population, preferring to remain separate, and indeed the Visigothic language left only the faintest mark on the modern languages of Iberia. The most visible effect was the depopulation of the cities as they moved to the countryside. Even while the country enjoyed a degree of prosperity when compared to the famines of France and Germany in this period, the Visigoths felt little reason to contribute to the welfare, permanency, and infrastructure of their people and state. This contributed to their downfall, as they could not count on the loyalty of their subjects when the Moors arrived in the 8th century.

Muslim Era—al-Andalus (8th–15th centuries)

Main articles: Muslim conquests, Umayyad conquest of Hispania, Al-Andalus, and Reconquista

The Arab Islamic conquest covered dominated most of North Africa by 640 AD. In 711 an Islamic Arab and Berber raiding party, led by Tariq ibn-Ziyad, was sent to Iberia to intervene in a civil war in the Visigothic Kingdom. Crossing the Strait of Gibraltar, they won a decisive victory in the summer of 711 when the Visigothic King Roderic was defeated and killed on July 19 at the Battle of Guadalete. Tariq's commander, Musa bin Nusair quickly crossed with substantial reinforcements, and by 718 the Muslims dominated most of the Iberian Peninsula. The advance into Western Europe was stopped in north-central France by the West Germanic Franks under Charles Martel at the Battle of Tours in 732.

Caliph Al-Walid I paid great attention to the expansion of an organized military, building the strongest navy in the Umayyad Caliphate (first Arab dynasty of Al-Andalus) era. It was this tactic that supported the ultimate expansion to Spain. Caliph Al-Walid I's reign is considered as the apex of Islamic power.[citation needed]

The rulers of Al-Andalus were granted the rank of Emir by the Umayyad Caliph Al-Walid I in Damascus. Emir Abd-ar-rahman I challenged the Abbasids. The Umayyad Caliphate, with origin in Hejaz, Arabian peninsula *or Emirate* was overthrown by the Abbasid Caliphate *or Emirate* (second Arab dynasty), some of the remaining Umayyad leaders escaped to Castile and declared Cordoba an independent emirate. Al-Andalus was rife with internal conflict between the Islamic Umayyad rulers and people and the Christian Visigoth-Roman leaders and people.

In the 10th century Abd-ar-rahman III, from Hejaz, Arabian peninsula, grandson of the last caliph of Damascus, Syria declared the Caliphate of Cordoba, effectively breaking all ties with the Egyptian and Syrian caliphs. The Caliphate was mostly concerned with maintaining its power base in North Africa, but these possessions eventually dwindled to the Ceuta province. The first navy of the Caliph of Cordoba *or Emir* was built after the humiliating Viking ascent of the Guadalquivir in 844 when they sacked Seville. In 942, pagan Magyars (present day Hungary) raided across Europe as far west as Al-Andalus. Meanwhile, a slow but steady migration of Christian subjects to the northern kingdoms in Christian Hispania was slowly increasing their power. Even so, Al-Andalus remained vastly superior to all the northern kingdoms combined in population, economy, culture and military might, and internal conflict between the Christian kingdoms contributed to keep them relatively harmless.

Al-Andalus coincided with *La Convivencia*, an era of religious tolerance and with the Golden age of Jewish culture in the Iberian Peninsula. (See: Emir Abd-ar-Rahman III 912 ; the Granada massacre 1066).

Muslim interest in the peninsula returned in force around the year 1000 when Al-Mansur (known as *Almanzor*), sacked Barcelona (985). Under his son, other Christian cities were subjected to numerous raids. After his son's death, the caliphate plunged into a civil war and splintered into the so-called "Taifa Kingdoms". The Taifa kings competed against each other not only in war, but also in the protection of the arts, and culture enjoyed a brief upswing. The Taifa kingdoms lost ground to the Christian realms in the north and, after the loss of Toledo in 1085, the Muslim rulers reluctantly invited the Almoravides, who invaded Al-Andalus from North Africa and established an empire. In the 12th century the Almoravid empire broke up again, only to be taken over by the Almohad invasion, who were defeated in the decisive battle of Las Navas de Tolosa in 1212.

Medieval Spain was the scene of almost constant warfare between Muslims and Christians. The Almohads, who had taken control of the Almoravids' Maghribi and Andalusian territories by 1147, far surpassed the Almoravides in fundamentalist outlook, and they treated the *dhimmis* harshly. Faced with the choice of death, conversion, or emigration, many Jews and Christians left. By the mid-13th century Emirate of Granada was the only independent Muslim realm in Spain, which would last until 1492.

The Kings of Aragón ruled territories that consisted of not only the present administrative region of Aragon but also Catalonia, and later the Balearic Islands, Valencia, Sicily, Naples and Sardinia (see Crown of Aragon). Considered by most to have been the first mercenary company in Western Europe, the Catalan Company proceeded to occupy the Duchy of Athens, which they placed under the protection of a prince of the House of Aragon and ruled until 1379.

Dynastic Union

As the *Reconquista* continued, Christian kingdoms and principalities developed. By the 15th century, the most important among these were the Kingdom of Castile (occupying a northern and central portion of the Iberian Peninsula) and the Kingdom of Aragon (occupying northeastern portions of the peninsula). The rulers of these two kingdoms were allied with dynastic families in Portugal, France, and other neighboring kingdoms. The death of Henry IV in 1474 set off a struggle for power between contenders for the throne of Castile, including Joanna La Beltraneja, supported by Portugal and France, and Queen Isabella I, supported by the Kingdom of Aragon, and by the Castilian nobility. Following the War of the Castilian Succession, Isabella retained the throne, and ruled jointly with her husband, King Ferdinand II.

Isabella of Castile and Ferdinand of Aragon were known as the "Catholic Monarchs" (Spanish: *los Reyes Católicos*), a title bestowed on them by Pope Alexander VI. They married in 1469 in Valladolid, uniting both crowns and effectively leading to the creation of the Kingdom of Spain, at the dawn of the modern era. They oversaw the final stages of the Reconquista of Iberian territory from the Moors with the conquest of Granada, conquered the Canary Islands and expelled the Jews and Muslims from Spain under the Alhambra decree. They authorized the expedition of Christopher Columbus, who became the first European to reach the New World since Leif Ericson, which led to an influx of wealth into Spain, funding the coffers of the new state that would prove to be a dominant power of Europe for the next two centuries.

Isabella ensured long-term political stability in Spain by arranging strategic marriages for each of her five children. Her firstborn, a daughter named Isabella, married Alfonso of Portugal, forging important ties between these two neighboring countries and hopefully to ensure future alliance, but Isabella soon died before giving birth to an heir. Juana, Isabella's second daughter, married into the Habsburg dynasty when she wed Philip the Handsome, the son of Maximilian I, King of Bohemia (Austria) and entitled to the crown of the Holy Roman Emperor. This ensured alliance with the Habsburgs and the Holy Roman Empire, a powerful, far-reaching territory that assured Spain's future political security. Isabella's first and only son, Juan, married Margaret of Austria, further maintaining ties with the Habsburg dynasty. Her fourth child, Maria, married Manuel I of Portugal, strengthening the link forged by her older sister's marriage. Her fifth child, Catherine, married Henry VIII, King of England and was mother to Queen Mary I.

If until the 13th century religious minorities (Jews and Muslims) had enjoyed quite some tolerance in Castilla and Aragon - the only Christian kingdoms where Jews were not restricted from any professional occupation - the situation of the Jews collapsed over the 14th century, reaching a climax in 1391 with large scale massacres in every major city, with the exception of Avilla. Over the next century, half of the estimated 200,000 Spanish Jews converted to Christianity (becoming "conversos"). The final step was taken by the Catholic Monarchs, who, in 1492, ordered the remaining Jews to convert or face expulsion from Spain. Depending on different sources, the number of Jews actually expelled is estimated to be anywhere from 40,000 to 120,000 people. Over the following decades, Muslims faced the same fate and about 60 years after the Jews, they were also compelled to convert ("moriscos") or be expelled. Jews and Muslims were not the only people to be persecuted during this time period. Gypsies also endured a tragic fate: all Gypsy males were forced to serve in galleys between the age of 18 and 26 - which was equivalent to a death sentence - but the majority managed to hide and avoid arrest.

The Spanish language and universities

In the 13th century, there were many languages spoken in the Christian sections of what is now Spain, among them Castilian, Aragonese, Catalan, Basque, Galician, Aranese and Leonese. But throughout the century, Castilian (what is also known today as Spanish) gained more and more prominence in the Kingdom of Castile as the language of culture and communication. One example of this is the *El Cid*. In the last years of the reign of Ferdinand III of Castile, Castilian began to be used for certain types of documents, but it was during the reign of Alfonso X that it became the official language. Henceforth all public documents were written in Castilian, likewise all translations were made into Castilian instead of Latin.

Furthermore, in the 13th Century many universities were founded in León and in Castile, some, like those of the leonese Salamanca and Palencia were among the earliest universities in Europe. In 1492, under the Catholic Monarchs, the first edition of the *Grammar of the Castilian Language* by Antonio de Nebrija was published.

Imperial Spain

Main article: Spanish Empire

See also: Habsburg Spain

The Spanish Empire was one of the first modern global empires. It was also one of the largest empires in world history. In the 16th century Spain and Portugal were in the vanguard of European global exploration and colonial expansion and the opening of trade routes across the oceans, with trade flourishing across the Atlantic between Spain and the Americas and across the Pacific between East Asia and Mexico via the Philippines. Conquistadors toppled the Aztec, Inca and Maya civilizations and laid claim to vast stretches of land in North and South America. For a time, the Spanish Empire dominated the oceans with its experienced navy and ruled the European battlefield with its fearsome and well trained infantry, the famous *tercios*: in the words of the prominent French historian Pierre Vilar, "enacting the most extraordinary epic in human history". Spain enjoyed a cultural golden age in the 16th and 17th centuries.

This American empire was at first a disappointment, as the natives had little to trade, though settlement did encourage trade. The diseases such as smallpox and measles that arrived with the colonizers devastated the native populations, especially in the densely populated regions of the Aztec, Maya and Inca civilizations, and this reduced economic potential of conquered areas.

In the 1520s large scale extraction of silver from the rich deposits of Mexico's Guanajuato began, to be greatly augmented by the silver mines in Mexico's Zacatecas and Bolivia's Potosí from 1546. These silver shipments re-oriented the Spanish economy, leading to the importation of luxuries and grain. They also became indispensable in financing the military capability of Habsburg Spain in its long series of European and North African wars, though, with the exception of a few years in the seventeenth century, Spain itself (Castile in particular) was by far the most important source of revenue. From the time beginning with the incorporation of the Portuguese empire in 1580 (lost in 1640) until the loss of its American colonies in the 19th century, Spain maintained the largest empire in the world even though it suffered fluctuating military and economic fortunes from the 1640s. Confronted by the new experiences, difficulties and suffering created by empire-building, Spanish thinkers formulated some of the first modern thoughts on natural law, sovereignty, international law, war, and economics; there were even questions about the legitimacy of imperialism — in related schools of thought referred to collectively as the School of Salamanca.

Spanish Kingdoms under the Habsburgs (16th–17th centuries)

Main article: Habsburg Spain

Spain's powerful world empire of the 16th and 17th centuries reached its height and declined under the Habsburgs. The Spanish Empire reached its maximum extent in Europe under Charles I of Spain, as he was also Emperor Charles V of the Holy Roman Empire.

Charles V became king in 1516, and the history of Spain became even more firmly enmeshed with the dynastic struggles in Europe. The king was not often in Spain, and as he approached the end of his life he made provision for the division of the Habsburg inheritance into two parts: on the one hand Spain, and its possessions in the Mediterranean and overseas, and the Holy Roman Empire itself on the other. The Habsburg possessions in the Netherlands also remained with the Spanish crown.

This was to prove a difficulty for his successor Philip II of Spain, who became king on Charles V's abdication in 1556. Spain largely escaped the religious conflicts that were raging throughout the rest of Europe, and remained firmly Roman Catholic. Philip saw himself as a champion of Catholicism, both against the Ottoman Turks and the heretics. In the 1560s, plans to consolidate control of the Netherlands led to unrest, which gradually led to the Calvinist leadership of the revolt and the Eighty Years' War. This conflict consumed much Spanish expenditure, and led to an attempt to conquer England – a cautious supporter of the Dutch – in the unsuccessful Spanish Armada, an early battle in the Anglo-Spanish War (1585–1604) and war with France (1590–1598).

Despite these problems, the growing inflow of American silver from mid 16th century, the justified military reputation of the Spanish infantry and even the navy quickly recovering from its Armada disaster, made Spain the leading European power, a novel situation of which its citizens were only just becoming aware. The Iberian Union with Portugal in 1580 not only unified the peninsula, but added that country's worldwide resources to the Spanish crown. However, economic and administrative problems multiplied in Castile, and the weakness of the native economy became evident in the following century: rising inflation, the ongoing aftermath of the expulsion of the Jews and Moors from Spain, and the growing dependency of Spain on the gold and silver imports, combined to cause several bankruptcies that caused economic crisis in the country, especially in heavily burdened Castile.

The coastal villages of Spain and of the Balearic Islands were frequently attacked by Barbary pirates from North Africa. Formentera was even temporarily left by its population. This occurred also along long stretches of the Spanish and Italian coasts, a relatively short distance across a calm sea from the pirates in their North African lairs. The most famous corsair was the Turkish Barbarossa ("Redbeard"). According to Robert Davis between 1 million and 1.25 million Europeans were captured by North African pirates and sold as slaves in North Africa and Ottoman Empire between the 16th and 19th centuries This was gradually alleviated as Spain and other Christian powers began to check Muslim naval dominance in the Mediterranean after the 1571 victory at Lepanto, but it would be a scourge that continued to afflict the country even in the next century.

The great plague of 1596-1602 killed 600,000 to 700,000 people, or about 10% of the population. Altogether more than 1,250,000 deaths resulted from the extreme incidence of plague in 17th century Spain.

Philip II died in 1598, and was succeeded by his son Philip III, in whose reign a ten year truce with the Dutch was overshadowed in 1618 by Spain's involvement in the European-wide Thirty Years' War. Government policy was dominated by favorites, but it was also the reign in which the geniuses of Cervantes and El Greco flourished.

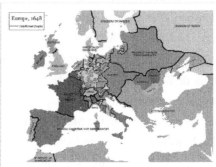

Map of Europe in 1648, after the Peace of Westphalia.

Philip III was succeeded in 1621 by his son Philip IV of Spain. Much of the policy was conducted by the minister Gaspar de Guzmán, Count-Duke of Olivares. In 1640, with the war in central Europe having no clear winner except the French, both Portugal and Catalonia rebelled.

Portugal was lost to the crown for good, in Italy and most of Catalonia, French forces were expelled and Catalonia's independence suppressed. In the reign of Philip's developmentally disabled son and successor Charles II, Spain was essentially left leaderless and was gradually being reduced to a second-rank power.

The Habsburg dynasty became extinct in Spain and the War of the Spanish Succession ensued in which the other European powers tried to assume control of the Spanish monarchy. King Louis XIV of France eventually "won" the War of Spanish Succession, and control of Spain passed to the Bourbon dynasty but the peace deals that followed included the relinquishing of the right to unite the French and Spanish thrones and the partitioning of Spain's European empire.

The Golden Age (*Siglo de Oro*)

Main article: Spanish Golden Age

The Spanish Golden Age (in Spanish, *Siglo de Oro*) was a period of flourishing arts and letters in the Spanish Empire (now Spain and the Spanish-speaking countries of Latin America), coinciding with the political decline and fall of the Habsburgs (Philip III, Philip IV and Charles II). The last great writer of the age, Sor Juana Inés de la Cruz, died in New Spain in 1695.

The Habsburgs, both in Spain and Austria, were great patrons of art in their countries. *El Escorial*, the great royal monastery built by King Philip II, invited the attention of some of Europe's greatest architects and painters. Diego Velázquez, regarded as one of the most influential painters of European history and a greatly respected artist in his own time, cultivated a relationship

Toledo by El Greco

with King Philip IV and his chief minister, the Count-Duke of Olivares, leaving us several portraits that demonstrate his style and skill. El Greco, a respected Greek artist from the period, settled in Spain, and infused Spanish art with the styles of the Italian renaissance and helped create a uniquely Spanish style of painting. Some of Spain's greatest music is regarded as having been written in the period. Such composers as Tomás Luis de Victoria, Luis de Milán and Alonso Lobo helped to shape Renaissance music and the styles of counterpoint and polychoral music, and their influence lasted far into the Baroque period.

Spanish literature blossomed as well, most famously demonstrated in the work of Miguel de Cervantes, the author of *Don Quixote de la Mancha*. Spain's most prolific playwright, Lope de Vega, wrote possibly as many as one thousand plays over his lifetime, over four hundred of which survive to the present day.

Enlightenment: Spain under the Bourbons (18th century)

Main article: Enlightenment Spain

Philip V, the first Bourbon king, of French origin, signed the *Decreto de Nueva Planta* in 1715, a new law that revoked most of the historical rights and privileges of the different kingdoms that formed the Spanish Crown, specially Crown of Aragon, unifying them under the laws of Castile, where the Cortes had been more receptive to the royal wish. Spain became culturally and politically a follower of absolutist France. The rule of the Spanish Bourbons continued under Ferdinand VI and Charles III. Great influence was exerted over Elisabeth of Parma on Spain's foreign policy. Her principal aim was to have Spain's lost territories in Italy restored. She eventually received Franco-British support for this after the Congress of Soissons.

Under the rule of Charles III and his ministers, Leopoldo de Gregorio, Marquis of Esquilache and José Moñino, Count of Floridablanca, Spain embarked on a program of enlightened despotism that brought Spain a new prosperity in the middle of the eighteenth century. Fearing that Britain's victory over France in the Seven Years War threatened the European balance of power, Spain allied themselves to France but suffered a series of military defeats and ended up having to cede Florida to the British at the Treaty of Paris. Despite being on the losing alongside France against the British in the Seven Years' War, Spain recouped most of her territorial losses in the American Revolutionary War, and gained an improved international standing.

An 18th century map of the Iberian Peninsula

However, the reforming spirit of Charles III was extinguished in the reign of his son, Charles IV, seen by some as mentally handicapped. Dominated by his wife's lover, Manuel de Godoy, Charles IV embarked on policies that overturned much of Charles III's reforms. After briefly opposing Revolutionary France early in the French Revolutionary Wars, Spain was

Attacking Spanish infantry (about 1740)

cajoled into an uneasy alliance with its northern neighbor, only to be blockaded by the British. Charles IV's vacillation, culminating in his failure to honour the alliance by neglecting to enforce the Continental System led to Napoleon I, Emperor of the French, invading Spain in 1808, thereby triggering Spain's War of Independence.

During most of the eighteenth century Spain had made substantial progress since its steady decline in the latter part of the 17th century, under an increasingly inept Habsburg dynasty. But despite the progress, it continued to lag in the political and mercantile developments then transforming other parts of Europe, most notably in the United Kingdom, France and the Low Countries. The chaos unleashed by the Napoleonic intervention would cause this gap to widen greatly.

Napoleonic Wars: War of Spanish Independence (1808–1814)

Main article: Peninsular War

See also: Spanish American wars of independence

Spain initially sided against France in the Napoleonic Wars, but the defeat of her army early in the war led to Charles IV's pragmatic decision to align with the revolutionary French. Spain was put under a British blockade, and her colonies—for the first time separated from their colonial rulers—began to trade independently with Britain. The defeat of the British invasions of the River Plate in South America emboldened an independent attitude in Spain's American colonies. A major Franco-Spanish fleet was annihilated, at the decisive Battle of Trafalgar in 1805, prompting the vacillating king of Spain to reconsider his alliance with France. Spain

The Third of May 1808 by Francisco Goya, showing Spanish resisters being executed by Napoleon's troops.

broke off from the Continental System temporarily, and Napoleon—aggravated with the Bourbon kings of Spain—invaded Spain in 1808 and deposed Ferdinand VII, who had just been on the throne forty-eight days after his father's abdication in March.

The Spanish people vigorously resisted Napoleon's move, and *juntas* were formed across Spain that pronounced themselves in favor of Ferdinand VII. Initially, the juntas declared their support for Ferdinand VII, and convened a "General and Extraordinary Cortes" for all the kingdoms of the Spanish Monarchy. The Cortes assembled in 1810 and took refuge at Cádiz. In 1812 the Cádiz Cortes created the first modern Spanish constitution, the Constitution of 1812 (informally named *La Pepa*).

The British, led by the Duke of Wellington, fought Napoleon's forces in the Peninsular War, with Joseph Bonaparte ruling as king at Madrid. The brutal war was one of the first guerrilla wars in modern Western history; French supply lines stretching across Spain were mauled repeatedly by Spanish guerrillas. The war in the Iberian Peninsula fluctuated repeatedly, with Wellington spending several years behind his fortresses in Portugal while launching occasional campaigns into Spain. The French were decisively defeated at the Battle of Vitoria in 1813, and the following year, Ferdinand VII was restored as King of Spain.

Spain in the nineteenth century (1814–1873)

Main article: Mid-nineteenth century Spain

Although the *juntas* that had forced the French to leave Spain had sworn by the liberal Constitution of 1812, Ferdinand VII openly believed that it was too liberal for the country. On his return to Spain, he refused to swear by it himself, and he continued to rule in the authoritarian fashion of his forebears.

Although Spain accepted the rejection of the Constitution, the policy was not warmly accepted in Spain's empire in the New World. Revolution broke out. Spain, nearly bankrupt from the war with France and the reconstruction of the country, was unable to pay her soldiers, and in 1819 was forced to sell Florida to the United States for 5 million dollars. In 1820, an expedition intended for the colonies (which, at the time, were on the verge of being lost themselves, to rebels and the Monroe Doctrine) revolted in Cadiz. When armies throughout Spain pronounced themselves in sympathy with the revolters, led by Rafael del Riego, Ferdinand relented and was forced to accept the liberal Constitution of 1812. Ferdinand himself was placed under effective house arrest for the duration of the liberal experiment.

The three years of liberal rule that followed coincided with a civil war in Spain that would typify Spanish politics for the next century. The liberal government, which reminded European statesmen entirely too much of the governments of the French Revolution, was looked on with hostility by the Congress of Verona in 1822, and France was authorized to intervene. France crushed the liberal government with massive force in the so-called Spanish expedition, and Ferdinand was restored as absolute monarch. The American colonies, however, were completely lost; in 1824, the last Spanish army on the American mainland was defeated at the Battle of Ayacucho in southern Peru.

A period of uneasy peace followed in Spain for the next decade. Having borne only a female heir presumptive, it appeared that Ferdinand would be succeeded by his brother, Infante Carlos of Spain. While Ferdinand aligned with the conservatives, fearing another national insurrection, he did not view the reactionary policies of his brother as a viable option. Ferdinand — resisting the wishes of his brother — decreed the Pragmatic Sanction of 1830, enabling his daughter Isabella to become Queen. Carlos, who made known his intent to resist the sanction, fled to Portugal.

Ferdinand's death in 1833 and the accession of Isabella (only three years old at the time) as Queen of Spain sparked the First Carlist War. Carlos invaded Spain and attracted support from reactionaries and conservatives in Spain; Isabella's mother, Maria Cristina of Bourbon-Two Sicilies, was named regent until her daughter came of age.

The insurrection seemed to have been crushed by the end of the year; Maria Cristina's armies, called "Cristino" forces, had driven the Carlist armies from most of the Basque country. Carlos then named the Basque general Tomás de Zumalacárregui his commander-in-chief. Zumalacárregui resuscitated the Carlist cause, and by 1835 had driven the Cristino armies to the Ebro River and transformed the Carlist army from a demoralized band into a professional army of 30,000 of quality superior to the government forces.

Zumalacárregui's death in 1835 changed the Carlists' fortunes. The Cristinos found a capable general in Baldomero Espartero. His victory at the Battle of Luchana (1836) turned the tide of the war, and in 1839, the Convention of Vergara put an end to the first Carlist insurrection.

Espartero, operating on his popularity as a war hero and his sobriquet "Pacifier of Spain", demanded liberal reforms from Maria Cristina. The Queen Regent, who resisted any such idea, preferred to resign and let Espartero become regent instead. Espartero's liberal reforms were opposed, then, by moderates; the former general's heavy-handedness caused a series of sporadic uprisings throughout the country from various quarters, all of which were bloodily suppressed. He was overthrown as regent in 1843 by Ramón María Narváez, a moderate, who was in turn perceived as too reactionary. Another Carlist uprising, the Matiners' War, was launched in 1846 in Catalonia, but it was poorly organized and suppressed by 1849.

Isabella II of Spain took a more active role in government after she came of age, but she was immensely unpopular throughout her reign. She was viewed as beholden to whoever was closest to her at court, and that she cared little for the people of Spain. In 1856, she attempted to form a pan-national coalition, the Union Liberal, under the leadership of Leopoldo O'Donnell who had already marched on Madrid that year and deposed another Espartero ministry. Isabella's plan failed and cost Isabella more prestige and favor with the people.

Isabella launched a successful war against Morocco, waged by generals O'Donnell and Juan Prim, in 1860 that stabilized her popularity in Spain. However, a campaign to reconquer Peru and Chile during the Chincha Islands War proved disastrous and Spain suffered defeat before the determined South American powers.

In 1866, a revolt led by Juan Prim was suppressed, but it was becoming increasingly clear that the people of Spain were upset with Isabella's approach to governance. In 1868, the Glorious Revolution broke out when the *progresista* generals Francisco Serrano and Juan Prim revolted against her, and defeated her *moderado* generals at the Battle of Alcolea. Isabella was driven into exile in Paris.

Revolution and anarchy broke out in Spain in the two years that followed; it was only in 1870 that the Cortes declared that Spain would have a king again. As it turned out, this decision played an important role in European and world history, for a German prince's candidacy to the Spanish throne and French opposition to him served as the immediate motive for the Franco-Prussian War. Amadeus of Savoy was selected, and he was duly crowned King of Spain early the following year.

Amadeus — a liberal who swore by the liberal constitution the Cortes promulgated — was faced immediately with the incredible task of bringing the disparate political ideologies of Spain to one table. He was plagued by internecine strife, not merely between Spaniards but within Spanish parties.

First Spanish Republic (1873–1874)

Main article: First Spanish Republic

Following the Hidalgo affair, Amadeus famously declared the people of Spain to be ungovernable, and fled the country. In his absence, a government of radicals and Republicans was formed that declared Spain a republic.

The republic was immediately under siege from all quarters — the Carlists were the most immediate threat, launching a violent insurrection after their poor showing in the 1872 elections. There were calls for socialist revolution from the International Workingmen's Association, revolts and unrest in the autonomous regions of Navarre and Catalonia, and pressure from the Roman Catholic Church against the fledgling republic.

The Restoration (1874–1931)

Main article: Spain under the Restoration

Although the former queen, Isabella II was still alive, she recognized that she was too divisive as a leader, and abdicated in 1870 in favor of her son, Alfonso, who was duly crowned Alfonso XII of Spain. After the tumult of the First Spanish Republic, Spaniards were willing to accept a return to stability under Bourbon rule. The Republican armies in Spain — which were resisting a Carlist insurrection — pronounced their allegiance to Alfonso in the winter of 1874–1875, led by Brigadier General Martinez Campos. The Republic was dissolved and Antonio Canovas del Castillo, a trusted advisor to the king, was named Prime Minister on New Year's Eve, 1874. The Carlist insurrection was put down vigorously by the new king, who took an active role in the war and rapidly gained the support of most of his countrymen.

A system of *turnos* was established in Spain in which the liberals, led by Práxedes Mateo Sagasta and the conservatives, led by Antonio Canovas del Castillo, alternated in control of the government. A modicum of stability and economic progress was restored to Spain during Alfonso XII's rule. His death in 1885, followed by the assassination of Canovas del Castillo in 1897, destabilized the government.

Cuba rebelled against Spain in the Ten Years' War beginning in 1868, resulting in the abolition of slavery in Spain's colonies in the New World. American interests in the island, coupled with concerns for the people of Cuba, aggravated relations between the two countries. The explosion of the USS *Maine* launched the Spanish-American War in 1898, in which Spain fared disastrously. Cuba gained its independence and Spain lost its remaining New World colony, Puerto Rico, which together with Guam and the Philippines were ceded to the United States for 20 million dollars. In 1899, Spain sold its remaining Pacific islands—the Northern Mariana Islands, Caroline Islands and Palau—to Germany and Spanish colonial possessions were reduced to Spanish Morocco, Spanish Sahara and Spanish Guinea, all in Africa.

The "disaster" of 1898 created the Generation of '98, a group of statesmen and intellectuals who demanded change from the new government. Anarchist and fascist movements were on the rise in Spain in the early twentieth century. A revolt in 1909 in Catalonia was bloodily suppressed.

Spain's neutrality in World War I allowed it to become a supplier of material for both sides to its great advantage, prompting an economic boom in Spain. The outbreak of Spanish influenza in Spain and elsewhere, along with a major economic slowdown in the postwar period, hit Spain particularly hard, and the country went into debt. A major worker's strike was suppressed in 1919.

Mistreatment of the indigenous population in Spanish Morocco led to an uprising and the loss of this North African possession except for the enclaves of Ceuta and Melilla in 1921. (See Muhammad Ibn 'Abd al-Karim al-Khattabi, Annual). In order to avoid accountability, King Alfonso XIII decided to support the dictatorship of General Miguel Primo de Rivera, ending the period of constitutional monarchy in Spain.

In joint action with France, the Moroccan territory was recovered (1925–1927), but in 1930 bankruptcy and massive unpopularity left the king no option but to force Primo de Rivera to resign. Disgusted with the king's involvement in his dictatorship, the urban population voted for republican parties in the municipal elections of April 1931. The king fled the country without abdicating and a republic was established.

Second Spanish Republic (1931–1939)

Main article: Second Spanish Republic

See also: Catholicism in the Second Spanish Republic

Under the Second Spanish Republic, women were allowed to vote in general elections for the first time. The Republic devolved substantial autonomy to the Basque Country and to Catalonia.

The first governments of the Republic, were center-left, headed by Niceto Alcalá-Zamora, and Manuel Azaña. Economic turmoil, substantial debt inherited from the Primo de Rivera regime, and fractious, rapidly changing governing coalitions led to serious political unrest. In 1933, the right-wing CEDA won power; an armed rising of workers of October 1934, which reached its greatest intensity in Asturias and Catalonia, was forcefully put down by the CEDA government. This in turn energized political movements across the spectrum in Spain, including a revived anarchist movement and new reactionary and fascist groups, including the Falange and a revived Carlist movement.

Spanish Civil War (1936–1939)

Main article: Spanish Civil War

In the 1930s, Spanish politics were polarized at the left and right of the political spectrum. The left-wing favored class struggle, land reform, autonomy to the regions and reduction in church and monarchist power. The right-wing groups, the largest of which was CEDA, a right wing Roman Catholic coalition, held opposing views on most issues. In 1936, the left united in the Popular Front and was elected to power. However, this coalition, dominated by the centre-left, was undermined both by the revolutionary groups such as the anarchist CNT and FAI and by anti-democratic far-right groups such as the Falange and the Carlists. The political violence of previous years began to start again. There were gunfights over strikes, landless labourers began to seize land, church officials were killed and churches burnt. On the other side, right wing militias (such as the Falange) and gunmen hired by employers assassinated left wing activists. The Republican democracy never generated the consensus or mutual trust between the various political groups that it needed to function peacefully. As a result, the country slid into civil war. The right wing of the country and high ranking figures in the army began to plan a coup, and when Falangist politician José Calvo-Sotelo was shot by Republican police, they used it as a signal to act.

On 17 July 1936, General Francisco Franco led the colonial army from Morocco to attack the mainland, while another force from the north under General Sanjurjo moved south from Navarre. Military units were also mobilised elsewhere to take over government institutions. Franco's move was intended to seize power immediately, but successful resistance by Republicans in places such as Madrid, Barcelona, Valencia, the Basque country and elsewhere meant that Spain faced a prolonged civil war. Before long, much of the south and west was under the control of the Nationalists, whose regular Army of Africa was the most professional force available to either side. Both sides received foreign military aid, the Nationalists, from Nazi Germany, Fascist Italy and Portugal, the Republic from the USSR and organised volunteers in the International Brigades.

The Siege of the Alcázar at Toledo early in the war was a turning point, with the Nationalists winning after a long siege. The Republicans managed to hold out in Madrid, despite a Nationalist assault in November 1936, and frustrated subsequent offensives against the capital at Jarama and Guadalajara in 1937. Soon, though, the Nationalists began to erode their territory, starving Madrid and making inroads into the east. The north, including the Basque country fell in late 1937 and the Aragon front collapsed shortly afterwards. The bombing of Guernica was probably the most infamous event of the war and inspired Picasso's painting. It was used as a testing ground for the German Luftwaffe's Condor Legion. The Battle of the Ebro in July-November 1938 was the final desperate attempt by the Republicans to turn the tide. When this failed and Barcelona fell to the Nationalists in early 1939, it was clear the war was over. The remaining Republican fronts collapsed and Madrid fell in March 1939.

The war, which cost between 300,000 to 1,000,000 lives, ended with the destruction of the Republic and the accession of Francisco Franco as dictator of Spain. Franco amalgamated all the right wing parties into a reconstituted Falange and banned the left-wing and Republican parties and trade unions.

The conduct of the war was brutal on both sides, with massacres of civilians and prisoners being widespread. After the war, many thousands of Republicans were imprisoned and up to 151,000 were executed between 1939 and 1943. Many other Republicans remained in exile for the entire Franco period.

The dictatorship of Francisco Franco (1936–1975)

Main article: Spanish State

Spain remained officially neutral in World Wars I and II, but suffered through a devastating Civil War (1936–1939). During Franco's rule, Spain remained largely economically and culturally isolated from the outside world, but began to catch up economically with its European neighbors.

Under Franco, Spain actively sought the return of Gibraltar by the UK, and gained some support for its cause at the United Nations. During the 1960s, Spain began imposing restrictions on Gibraltar, culminating in the closure of the border in 1969. It was not fully reopened until 1985.

Spanish rule in Morocco ended in 1967. Though militarily victorious in the 1957–1958 Moroccan invasion of Spanish West Africa, Spain gradually relinquished its remaining African colonies. Spanish Guinea was granted independence as Equatorial Guinea in 1968, while the Moroccan enclave of Ifni had been ceded to Morocco in 1969.

The latter years of Franco's rule saw some economic and political liberalization, the Spanish Miracle, including the birth of a tourism industry. Francisco Franco ruled until his death on 20 November 1975, when control was given to King Juan Carlos.

In the last few months before Franco's death, the Spanish state went into a paralysis. This was capitalized upon by King Hassan II of Morocco, who ordered the 'Green March' into Western Sahara, Spain's last colonial possession.

Spain since 1975

Main article: History of Spain (1975–present)

Transition to democracy

Main article: Spanish transition to democracy

The Spanish transition to democracy or new Bourbon restoration was the era when Spain moved from the dictatorship of Francisco Franco to a liberal democratic state. The transition is usually said to have begun with Franco's death on 20 November 1975, while its completion is marked by the electoral victory of the socialist PSOE on 28 October 1982.

Between 1978 and 1982, Spain was led by the *Unión del Centro Democrático* governments.

in 1981 the 23-F coup d'état attempt took place. On 23 February Antonio Tejero, with members of the Guardia Civil entered the Congress of Deputies, and stopped the session, where Leopoldo Calvo Sotelo was about to be named prime minister of the government. Officially, the coup d'état failed thanks to the intervention of King Juan Carlos. Spain joined NATO before Calvo-Sotelo left office.

Along with political change came radical change in Spanish society. Spanish society had been extremely conservative under Franco, but the transition to democracy also began a liberalization of values and societal mores.

Modern Spain

Main article: Modern Spain

From 1982 until 1996, the social democratic PSOE governed the country, with Felipe González as prime minister. In 1986, Spain joined the European Economic Community (EEC, now European Union), and the country hosted the 1992 Barcelona Olympics and Seville Expo '92.

In 1996, the centre-right *Partido Popular* government came to power, led by José María Aznar. On 1 January 1999, Spain exchanged the *peseta* for the new Euro currency. The peseta continued to be used for cash transactions until January 1, 2002. On 11 March 2004 a number of terrorist bombs exploded on busy commuter trains in Madrid during the morning rush-hour days before the general election, killing 191 persons and injuring thousands. Although José María Aznar and his ministers were quick to accuse ETA of the atrocity, soon afterwards it became apparent that the bombing was the work of an extremist Islamic group linked to Al-Qaeda. Many people believe that the fact that qualified commentators abroad were beginning to doubt the official Spanish version the very same day of the attacks while the government insisted on ETA's implication directly influenced the results of the election. Opinion polls at the time show that the difference between the two main contenders had been too close to make any accurate prediction as to the outcome of the elections. The election, held three days after the attacks, was won by the PSOE, and José Luis Rodríguez Zapatero replaced Aznar as prime minister.

On 3 July 2005, the country became the first country in the world to give full marriage and adoption rights to homosexual couples (Belgium has allowed same-sex marriage since 2003 and co-parenting since April 2006, and the Netherlands has allowed same-sex marriage since 2001 and now has a law in preparation to provide full adoption rights in equal conditions to opposite-sex marriages).

At present, Spain is a constitutional monarchy, and comprises 17 autonomous communities (Andalucía, Aragón, Asturias, Islas Baleares, Islas Canarias, Cantabria, Castile and León, Castile-La Mancha, Cataluña, Extremadura, Galicia, La Rioja, Community of Madrid, Region of Murcia, País Vasco, Comunidad Valenciana, Navarra) and two autonomous cities (Ceuta and Melilla).

Bibliography

- Barton, Simon. *A History of Spain* (2009) excerpt and text search [1]
- Carr, Raymond, ed. *Spain: A History* (2001) excerpt and text search [2]
- Casey, James. *Early Modern Spain: A Social History* (1999) excerpt and text search [3]
- Edwards, John. *The Spain of the Catholic Monarchs 1474-1520* (2001) excerpt and text search [4]
- Esdaile, Charles J. *Spain in the Liberal Age: From Constitution to Civil War, 1808-1939* (2000) excerpt and text search [5]
- Gerli, E. Michael, ed. *Medieval Iberia: an encyclopedia.* New York 2005. ISBN 0-415-93918-6
- Kamen, Henry. *Spain. A Society of Conflict* (3rd ed.) London and New York: Pearson Longman 2005. ISBN
- Lynch, John. *The Hispanic World in Crisis and Change: 1598-1700* (1994) excerpt and text search [6]
- O'Callaghan, Joseph F. *A History of Medieval Spain* (1983) excerpt and text search [7]
- Philips, William D., Jr., and Carla Rahn Phillips. *A Concise History of Spain* (2010)
- Pierson, Peter. *The History of Spain* (2nd ed. 2008) excerpt and text search [8]
- Shubert, Adrian. *A Social History of Modern Spain* (1990) excerpt and text search [9]
- Tusell, Javier. *Spain: From Dictatorship to Democracy, 1939 to the Present* (2007) excerpt and text search [10]

External links

- History of Spain - World History Database [11]
- History of Spain: Primary Documents [12]
- Spanish History Sources & Documents [13]
- Stanley G. Payne The Seventeenth-Century Decline [14]
- Henry Kamen, "The Decline of Spain: A Historical Myth?", Past and Present,) (Explains the complexities of this subject) [15]
- WWW-VL "Spanish History Index [16]
- Carmen Pereira-Muro. *Culturas de España.* Boston and New York: Houghton Mifflin Company 2003. ISBN

See also

- Spanish architecture
- Black Legend
- Economic history of Spain
- Global Empire
- Spanish Empire
- List of Spanish wars
- Spanish Armada in Ireland
- Ottoman-Habsburg wars
- Timeline of the Muslim presence in the Iberian peninsula

Geography of Spain

Geography of Spain	
Continent	Europe
Region	Southern Europe Iberian Peninsula
Coordinates	40°00'N 4°00' W
Area	Ranked 50th 504782 km^2 (194897.4 sq mi) 98.96% land 1.04 % water
Borders	Total land borders: 1917.8 km (1191.7 mi) Portugal: 1214 km (754 mi) France: 623 km (387 mi) Andorra: 63.7 km (39.6 mi) Morocco (Melilla): 9.6 km (5.97 mi) Morocco (Ceuta): 6.3 km (3.91 mi) Gibraltar: 1.2 km (0.75 mi)
Highest point	Teide (Canary Islands) 3718 m (12198 ft) Mulhacén (Iberian Peninsula) 3477 m (11407 ft)
Lowest point	Atlantic Ocean, Mediterranean Sea 0 m (0 ft) (Sea level)
Longest river	Tagus
Largest lake	Lago de Sanabria

Spain is located in southwestern Europe and comprises about 84 percent of the Iberian Peninsula. Its total area is 504782 km^2 (194897 sq mi) of which 499542 km^2 (192874 sq mi) is land and 5240 km^2 (2023 sq mi) is water. , and the Atlantic coast is 710 km (441 mi) long. The Pyrenees mountain range, extends 435 km (270 mi) from the Mediterranean to the Bay of Biscay. In the extreme south of Spain lie the Straits of Gibraltar, which separate Spain and the rest of Europe from Morocco in north Africa; at its narrowest extent, Spain and Morocco are separated by only 13 km (8.1 mi).

Off the Iberian Peninsula there are several other Spanish areas: the Balearic Islands in the Mediterranean, the Canary Islands to the southwest, 108 km (67 mi) off northwest Africa, and five places of sovereignty (*plazas de soberanía*) on and off the coast of Morocco: Ceuta, Melilla, Islas Chafarinas, Peñón de Alhucemas, and Peñón de Vélez de la Gomera.

External boundaries and landform regions

Most of Spain's boundaries are water: the Mediterranean Sea on the south and east from Gibraltar to the French border and the Atlantic Ocean on the northwest and southwest (in the south as the Golfo de Cádiz and in the north as the Bay of Biscay). Spain also shares land boundaries with France and Andorra along the Pyrenees in the northeast, with Portugal on the west, and with the small British Overseas Territory of Gibraltar near the southernmost tip. The affiliation of Gibraltar has continued to be a contentious issue between Spain and Britain and so is the sovereignty of the plazas de soberanía, claimed by Morocco.

Spain also has a small exclave inside France called Llívia.

The majority of Spain's peninsular region consists of the Meseta Central, a highland plateau rimmed and dissected by mountain ranges. Other landforms include narrow coastal plains and some lowland river valleys, the most prominent of which is the Andalusian Plain in the southwest. The country can be divided into ten natural regions or subregions: the dominant Meseta Central, the Cantabrian Mountains (Cordillera Cantabrica) and the northwest region, the *Ibérico* region, the Pyrenees, the *Penibético* region in the southeast, the Andalusian Plain, the Ebro Basin, the coastal plains, the Balearic Islands, and the Canary Islands. These are commonly grouped into four types: the Meseta Central and associated mountains, other mountainous regions, lowland regions, and islands.

The Inner Plateau and associated mountains

The *Meseta Central* ("Inner Plateau") is a vast plateau in the heart of peninsular Spain, has elevations that range from 610 to 760 m. Rimmed by mountains, the Meseta Central slopes gently to the west and to the series of rivers that form some of the border with Portugal. The Sistema Central, described as the "dorsal spine" of the Meseta Central, divides the Meseta into northern and southern subregions, the former higher in elevation and smaller in area than the latter. The Sistema Central rims the capital city of Madrid with peaks that rise to 2,400 m north of the city and to lower elevations south of it. West of Madrid, the Sistema Central shows its highest peak, Pico Almanzor, of 2,592 m. The mountains of the Sistema Central, which continue westward into Portugal, display some glacial features; the highest of the peaks are snow-capped for most of the year. Despite their height, however, the mountain system does not create a major barrier between the northern and the southern portions of the Meseta Central because several passes permit road and railroad transportation to the northwest and the northeast.

The southern portion of the Meseta is further divided by twin mountain ranges, the Montes de Toledo running to the east and the Sierra de Guadalupe, to the west. Their peaks do not rise much higher than 1,500 m. With many easy passes, including those that connect the Meseta with the Andalusian Plain, the Montes de Toledo and the Sierra de Guadalupe do not present an obstacle to transportation and communication. The two mountain ranges are separated from the Sistema Central to the north by the longest river in the Iberian Peninsula: the Tagus River.

The mountain regions that rim the Meseta Central and are associated with it are the Sierra Morena, the Cordillera Cantábrica, and the Sistema Ibérico. Forming the southern edge of the Meseta Central, the Sierra Morena merges in the east with the southern extension of the Sistema Iberico and reaches westward along the northern edge of the Rio Guadalquivir valley to join the mountains in southern Portugal. The massif of the Sierra Morena extends northward to the Río Guadiana, which separates it from the Sistema Central. Despite their relatively low elevations, seldom surpassing 1,300 m, the mountains of the Sierra Morena are rugged.

The Cordillera Cantábrica, a limestone formation, runs parallel to, and close to, the northern coast near the Bay of Biscay. Its highest points are the Picos de Europa, surpassing 2,600 m. The Cordillera Cantábrica extends 182 km and abruptly drops 1,500 m some 30 km from the coast. To the west lie the hills of the northwest region and to the east the Basque mountains that link them to the Pyrenees.

The Sistema Ibérico extends from the Cordillera Cantábrica southeastward and, close to the Mediterranean, spreads out from the Río Ebro to the Río Júcar. The barren, rugged slopes of this mountain range cover an area of close to 21,000 square kilometers. The mountains exceed 2,000 m in their northern region and reach a maximum height of over 2,300 m east of the headwaters of the Rio Duero. The extremely steep mountain slopes in this range are often cut by deep, narrow gorges.

Other mountainous regions

External to the Meseta Central lie the Pyrenees in the northeast and the Sistema Penibético in the southeast. The Pyrenees, extending from the eastern edge of the Cordillera Cantábrica to the Mediterranean Sea, form a solid barrier and a natural border between Spain and both France and Andorra that, throughout history, has effectively isolated the countries from each other. Passage is easy in the relatively low terrain at the eastern and western extremes of the mountain range; it is here that international railroads and roadways cross the border. In the central section of the Pyrenees, however, passage is difficult. In several places, peaks rise above 3,000 m; the highest, Pico de Aneto, surpasses 3,400 m.

The Sistema Penibético extends northeast from the southern tip of Spain, running parallel to the coast until it merges with the southern extension of the Sistema Ibérico near the Rio Júcar and with the eastern extension of the Sierra Morena. The Sierra Nevada, part of the Sistema Penibético south of Granada, includes the highest mountain on the peninsula and continental Spain, Mulhacén, which rises to 3,479 m. Other peaks in the range also surpass 3,000 m.

Lowland regions

The major lowland regions are the Andalusian Plain in the southwest, the Ebro Basin in the northeast, and the coastal plains. The Andalusian Plain is essentially a wide river valley through which the Río Guadalquivir flows. The river broadens out along its course, reaching its widest point at the Golfo de Cadiz. The Andalusian Plain is bounded on the north by the Sierra Morena and on the south by the Sistema Penibético; it narrows to an apex in the east where these two mountain chains meet. The Ebro Basin is formed by the Río Ebro valley, contained by mountains on three sides—the Sistema Ibérico to the south and west, the Pyrenees to the north and east, and their coastal extensions paralleling the shore to the east. Minor low-lying river valleys close to the Portuguese border are located on the Tagus and the Río Guadiana.

The Coastal Plains regions are narrow strips between the coastal mountains and the seas. They are broadest along the Golfo de Cádiz, where the coastal plain adjoins the Andalusian Plain, and along the southern and central eastern coasts. The narrowest coastal plain runs along the Bay of Biscay, where the Cordillera Cantábrica ends close to shore.

The islands

Teide, the highest mountain in Spain (Tenerife, Canary Islands)

The remaining regions of Spain are the Balearic and the Canary Islands, the former located in the Mediterranean Sea and the latter in the Atlantic Ocean. The Balearic Islands, encompassing a total area of 5,000 square kilometers, lie 80 kilometers off Spain's central eastern coast. The mountains that rise up above the Mediterranean Sea to form these islands are an extension of the Sistema Penibetico. The archipelago's highest points, which reach 1,400 meters, are in northwestern Mallorca, close to the coast. The central portion of Majorca is a plain, bounded on the east and the southeast by broken hills.

The Canary Islands, ninety kilometers off the west coast of Africa, are of volcanic origin. The large central islands, Tenerife and Gran Canaria, have the highest peaks. Pico de Las Nieves, on Gran Canaria, rises to 1,949 meters, and the Teide, on Tenerife, to 3,718 meters. Teide, a dormant volcano, is the highest peak of Spain and the third largest volcano in the world from its base.

Drainage

See also: List of rivers of Spain

Of the roughly 1,800 rivers and streams in Spain, only the Tagus is more than 960 kilometers long; all but 90 extend less than 96 kilometers. These shorter rivers carry small volumes of water on an irregular basis, and they have seasonally dry river beds; however, when they do flow, they often are swift and torrential. Most major rivers rise in the mountains rimming or dissecting the Meseta Central and flow westward across the plateau through Portugal to empty into the Atlantic Ocean. One significant exception is the river with the most abundant flow in Spain, the Ebro, which flows eastward to the Mediterranean. Rivers in the extreme northwest and in the narrow northern coastal plain drain directly into the Atlantic Ocean. The northwestern coastline is also truncated by rias, waterbodies similar to fjords.

The major rivers flowing westward through the Meseta Central include the Duero, the Tagus, the Guadiana, and the Guadalquivir. The Rio Guadalquivir is one of the most significant rivers in Spain because it irrigates a fertile valley, thus creating a rich agricultural area, and because it is navigable inland, making Seville the only inland river port for ocean-going traffic in Spain. The major river in the northwest region is the Miño.

El Atazar Dam is a major dam built near Madrid to provide a water supply.

Climate

Due to both its geographical situation which exposes only its northern part to the Jet Stream's typical path and its orographic conditions, the climate in Spain is extremely diverse.

Peninsular Spain experiences three major climatic types: Continental, Oceanic, and Mediterranean.

Continental climate

The locally generated tempered continental climate covers the majority of peninsular Spain, influencing the Meseta Central, the

Spanish climate areas

adjoining mountains to the east and the south, and the Ebro Basin. A continental climate is characterized by wide diurnal and seasonal variations in temperature and by low, irregular rainfall with high rates of evaporation that leave the land arid. Annual rainfall generally is 300 to 640 mm (11.8 to 25.2 in); most of the Meseta region receives about 500 mm (19.7 in). The northern Meseta, the Sistema Central, and the Ebro Basin have two rainy seasons, one in spring (April-June) and the other in autumn (October-November), with late spring being the wettest time of the year. In the southern Meseta also, the wet seasons are spring and autumn, but the spring one is earlier (March), and autumn is the wetter season. Even during the wet seasons, rain is irregular and unreliable. Continental winters are cold at −1 °C (30.2 °F), with strong winds and high humidity, despite the low precipitation. Except for mountain areas, the northern foothills of the Sistema Iberico are the coldest area, and frost is common. Summers are warm and cloudless, producing average daytime temperatures that reach 21 °C (69.8 °F) in the northern Meseta and 24 °C (75.2 °F) to 27 °C (80.6 °F) in the southern Meseta; nighttime temperatures range from 7 °C (44.6 °F) to 10 °C (50 °F). The Ebro Basin, at a lower altitude, is extremely hot during the summer, and temperatures can exceed 40 °C (104 °F). Summer humidities are low in the Meseta Central and in the Ebro Basin, except right along the shores of the Río Ebro, where humidity is high.

Oceanic climate

An oceanic climate prevails in the northern part of the country, often called "Green Spain", from the Pyrenees to the northwest region, characterized by relatively mild winters, warm but not hot summers, and generally abundant rainfall at 1000 mm (39.4 in) spread out over the year, with the driest month above 30 mm (1.2 in). Temperatures vary only slightly, both on a diurnal and a seasonal basis, averages range from 9 °C (48.2 °F) in January to 21 °C (69.8 °F) in July. The moderating effects of the sea, however, abate in the inland areas, where temperatures are more extreme than temperatures on the

"Green Spain"

coast. Distance from the Atlantic Ocean also affects precipitation, and there is less rainfall in the east than in the west. Autumn (October through December) is the wettest season, while July is the driest month. The high humidity and the prevailing off-shore winds make fog and mist common along the northwest coast, this phenomenon is less frequent a short distance inland, however, because the mountains form a barrier keeping out the sea moisture.

Mediterranean climate

The Mediterranean climate region roughly extends from the Andalusian Plain along the southern and eastern coasts up to the Pyrenees, on the seaward side of the mountain ranges that parallel the coast. Total rainfall in this region is concentrated mostly in late autumn-winter and spring periods. The rain pattern is often irregular which make drought periods likely. Temperatures in the Mediterranean region are higher in winter, and diurnal temperature changes more limited, than those of the continental inland region. Temperatures in January normally average 10 °C (50 °F) to 13 °C (55.4 °F) in most of the Mediterranean region, getting cooler in the northeastern coastal area north of Barcelona. In winter, temperatures inland in the Andalusian Plain are slightly lower than those on the coasts. Temperatures in July and August average 22 °C (71.6 °F) to 27 °C (80.6 °F) on the coast and 29 °C (84.2 °F) to 31 °C (87.8 °F) farther inland, with high humidity. The Mediterranean region is marked by Leveche winds: hot, dry, easterly or southeasterly air currents that originate over North Africa. Episodes of these winds, which sometimes carry fine Saharan dust are more likely in spring, associated to a sudden, usually short-lived, rise of the temperatures. A cooler easterly wind, the Levante, funnels between the Sistema Penibetico and the Atlas Mountains of North Africa. These easterly winds are the ones which most influence the Mediterranean climate, for they are mild in temperature and humid.

Other climate types

Besides the above three major types, there are important exceptions, as follows:

- A Semiarid climate in the Southeasternmost part of Spain (covering most of Alicante, Murcia and Almería provinces). Summers here are hot to very hot and winters mild to cool. Very dry, virtually sub-desertic, rainfall as low as 150 mm (5.9 in) a year in the Cabo de Gata which is reported to be the driest place in Europe.
- The highest section of the Pyrenees and Sierra Nevada qualify as Alpine climate.
- The Canary Islands are a Subtropical climate in terms of temperature, being these mild and stable (18 °C/64.4 °F to
  24 °C/75.2 °F) throughout the year. In terms of precipitation, the Eastern islands are semiarid and moister the westernmost ones, with some very wet areas in the mountains of Gomera and La Palma, the cloud forest known as laurisilva. Then, the southern Mediterranean coast (Malaga and Granada's coastal strip) shares traits with both Mediterranean and Subtropical.

Extreme temperature records in selected cities

The record of temperatures in Spain have been, -32°C in Lago Estangento in the Pyrenees (Lleida) for the coldest, for the hottest 47°C in Seville and Murcia.

Location	Record highs		Record lows	
	(°C)	(°F)	(°C)	(°F)
Mediterranean				
Murcia	47.2 °C	117.0 °F	−6.0 °C	21.2 °F
Malaga	44.2 °C	111.6 °F	−3.8 °C	25.1 °F
Valencia	42.5 °C	108.5 °F	−7.2 °C	19 °F
Alicante	41.4 °C	106.5 °F	−4.6 °C	23.7 °F
Palma	40.6 °C	105.1 °F	—	—
Barcelona	39.8 °C	103.6 °F	−10.0 °C	14 °F
Girona	41.7	107 °F	−13.0 °C	8.6 °F
Interior				
Seville	47.0 °C	117 °F	−5.5 °C	22.1 °F
Cordoba	46.6 °C	115.9 °F	—	—
Badajoz	45.0 °C	113 °F	—	—
Albacete	42.6 °C	108.7 °F	−24.0 °C	−11.2 °F
Zaragoza	43.1 °C	108.7 °F	-16.0° °C	3.1° °C
Madrid	42.2 °C	108.0 °F	−14.8 °C	5.4 °F

	(°C)	(°F)	(°C)	(°F)
Burgos	41.8 °C	107.2 °F	−22.0 °C	−7.6 °F
Valladolid	40.2 °C	104.4 °F	—	—
Salamanca	—	—	−20.0 °C	−4.0 °F
Teruel	—	—	−27.0 °C	−22.2 °F
Northern Atlantic coast	(°C)	(°F)	(°C)	(°F)
Orense	42.6 °C	108.7 °F	−9.0 °C	15.8 °F
Bilbao	42.0 °C	107.6 °F	−8.6 °C	16.5 °F
La Coruña	37.6 °C	99.7 °F	−4.8 °C	23.4 °F
Gijón	36.4 °C	97.5 °F	−4.8 °C	23.4 °F
The Canary Islands				
Las Palmas de Gran Canaria	38.6 °C	102 °F	11.4 °	48.6 °F
Santa Cruz de Tenerife	39.6 °C	103 °F	14.4 °	49.7 °F

Population geography

Main article: demographics of Spain

Largest cities by population

- Madrid 3,228,359
- Barcelona 1,582,738
- Valencia 797,654 [1]
- Seville 709,975
- Zaragoza 626,081
- Málaga 547,105
- Murcia 391,146

- Las Palmas de Gran Canaria 377,600
- Palma 367,277
- Bilbao 353,567
- Valladolid 321,143
- Córdoba 318,628
- Alicante 305,911
- Vigo 292,566
- Gijón 270,875
- Hospitalet de Llobregat 246,415
- A Coruña (Corunna) 243,902
- Granada 237,663
- Vitoria-Gasteiz 223,257
- Santa Cruz de Tenerife 220,022
- Badalona 214,440
- Oviedo 207,699
- Elche 207,163
- Móstoles 201,789
- Terrassa 200,000
- Pamplona 198,750

Biggest metropolitan areas

The most important metropolitan areas and their 2007 populations are:

1. Madrid 5,603,285
2. Barcelona 4,667,136
3. Valencia 1,671,189
4. Sevilla 1,294,081
5. Bilbao 950,829
6. Málaga 897,563
7. Asturias (Gijón-Oviedo) 857,079
8. Alicante-Elche 748,565
9. Zaragoza 731,803
10. Vigo 662,412
11. Las Palmas de Gran Canaria 616,903
12. Bahía de Cádiz (Cádiz-Jerez de la Frontera) 615,494
13. Santa Cruz de Tenerife 573,825
14. Murcia 563,272
15. Palma de Mallorca 474,035
16. Granada 472,638

17. San Sebastián 402,168
18. Tarragona 406,042
19. A Coruña 403,007
20. Valladolid 400,400
21. Santander - Torrelavega 391,480
22. Cordoba 323,600
23. Pamplona 309,631

Further information: List of metropolitan areas in Spain by population

Islands

Islander population:

- 1. Tenerife 886.033
- 2. Mallorca 846.210
- 3. Gran Canaria 829.597
- 4. Lanzarote 132.366
- 5. Ibiza 113.908
- 6. Fuerteventura 94.386
- 7. Menorca 86.697
- 8. La Palma 85.933
- 9. La Gomera 22.259
- 10. El Hierro 10.558
- 11. Formentera 7.957
- 12. Arosa 4.889
- 13. La Graciosa 658
- 14. Tabarca 105
- 15. Ons 61

Resources and land use

Natural resources: coal, lignite, iron ore, uranium, mercury, pyrites, fluorspar, gypsum, zinc, lead, tungsten, copper, kaolin, potash, hydropower, arable land

Land use:

- *Arable land:* 30%
- *Permanent crops:* 9%
- *Permanent pastures:* 21%
- *Forests and woodland:* 32%
- *Other:* 8% (1993 est.)

Irrigated land: 34,530 km² (1993 est.)

Environmental concerns

Natural hazards: periodic droughts, wildfires

Environment - Current Issues:

- pollution of the Mediterranean Sea from raw sewage and effluents from the offshore production of oil and gas
- water quality and quantity nationwide
- air pollution
- deforestation
- desertification

Environment - International Agreements:

- *Party to:* Air Pollution, Air Pollution-Nitrogen Oxides, Air Pollution-Sulphur 94, Air Pollution-Volatile Organic Compounds, Antarctic-Environmental Protocol, Antarctic Treaty, Biodiversity, Climate Change, Endangered Species, Environmental Modification, Hazardous Wastes, Law of the Sea, Marine Dumping, Marine Life Conservation, Nuclear Test Ban, Ozone Layer Protection, Ship Pollution, Tropical Timber 83, Tropical Timber 94, Wetlands, Whaling
- *Signed, but not ratified:* Air Pollution-Persistent Organic Pollutants, Climate Change-Kyoto Protocol, Desertification

Maritime claims

- *contiguous zone:* 24 nmi (44.4 km; 27.6 mi)
- *exclusive economic zone:* 200 nmi (370.4 km; 230.2 mi) (applies only to the Atlantic Ocean)
- *territorial sea:* 12 nmi (22.2 km; 13.8 mi)

See also

- Autonomous communities of Spain
- Comarcas of Spain
- Extreme points of Spain
- Provinces of Spain

References

- ⓐ *This article incorporates public domain material from websites or documents* [2] *of the Library of Congress Country Studies.*
- ⓐ *This article incorporates public domain material from websites or documents* [3] *of the CIA World Factbook.*

External links

- Loyd, Nick (2007). "IberiaNature: A guide to the environment, climate, wildlife, geography and nature of Spain" [4]. Retrieved 2008-12-04.
- Data Spain [5]: Satellite relief maps, aerial photography, outline maps, travel maps and useful themed maps of Spain
- Virtual Cadastral [6]: Lookup official Spanish property (catastro) deeds and other Spanish property information: exact map location, altitude, land area, and distances.

Geographical coordinates: 40°00′N 4°00′W

Politics of Spain

Spain
This article is part of the series: **Politics and government of Spain**
Other countries · Atlas **Politics portal**

The **Politics of Spain** take place in the framework of a parliamentary representative democratic constitutional monarchy, whereby the Monarch is the Head of State and the President of the Government is the head of government in a multi-party system. Executive power is vested in the government. Central legislative power is vested in the two chambers of parliament. The Judiciary is independent of the executive and the legislature.

Political developments

Parliamentary democracy was restored following the death of General Franco in 1975, who had ruled since the end of the civil war in 1939. The 1978 constitution established Spain as a parliamentary monarchy, with the President of the Government (equivalent to Prime Minister) responsible to the bicameral Cortes Generales (*Cortes*) elected every 4 years. On 23 February 1981, in an event known as "23-F", rebel elements among the security forces seized the Cortes and tried to impose a military-backed government. However, the great majority of the military forces remained loyal to King Juan Carlos, who used his personal and constitutional authority as Commander-in-Chief of the Armed Forces, to put down the bloodless coup attempt.

In October 1982, the Spanish Socialist Workers Party (PSOE), led by Felipe González Márquez, swept both the Congress of Deputies and Senate, winning an absolute majority. González and the PSOE ruled for the next 13 years. During that period, Spain joined NATO and the European Community. Spain also created new social laws and large scale infrastructural building, as well as programmes in Education, Health and Work. Liberalization policies were heavily contested by trade unions but largely implemented. The country was massively modernized in this period, becoming an economically developed, culturally shifted, contemporary open society.

In March 1996, José María Aznar's People's Party (PP) received more votes than any other party, winning almost half the seats in the Congress. Aznar moved to further liberalize the economy, with a program of privatizations, labor market reform, and measures designed to increase competition in selected markets, principally telecommunications. During Aznar's first term, Spain qualified for the Economic and Monetary Union of the European Union. During this period, Spain participated, along with the United States and other NATO allies, in military operations in the former Yugoslavia. Spanish planes took part in the air war against Serbia in 1999 and Spanish armed forces and police personnel are included in the international peacekeeping forces in Bosnia (IFOR, SFOR) and Kosovo (KFOR).

Prime Minister Aznar and the PP won reelection in March 2000, obtaining absolute majorities in both houses of parliament. This mandate allowed Aznar to form a government unencumbered by the coalition building that had characterized his earlier administration. As Prime Minister, Aznar was a staunch supporter of transatlantic relations and the War on Terrorism. For the March 2004 elections the PP named First Vice President Mariano Rajoy to replace him as the People's Party candidate.

However, in the aftermath of the March 11 terrorist bomb attacks in Madrid, the PP lost the 2004 elections to the Spanish Socialist Workers' Party (PSOE) and its leader José Luis Rodríguez Zapatero. Rodríguez Zapatero was appointed Prime Minister after having secured the support of a few minor parties. He nominated the first Spanish government ever to have the same number of male and female ministers. In this period the Spanish economy continued expanding, while new social and cultural laws were passed, and a more pan-European way was adopted in foreign politics.

In the 2008 general elections, Prime Minister Zapatero and the PSOE got reelected by a plurality, short of a majority. He was elected Prime Minister April 11 by 169 votes to 158, with 23 abstaining. The

Economic crisis of 2008 took a heavy toll on economy in the following months.

The Crown

Article 1.3. of the Spanish Constitution of 1978 lays down that *"the political form of the Spanish State is that of a Parliamentary Monarchy"*.

Art. 56 of the Spanish Constitution of 1978 lays down that:

- 1. The King is the Head of State and Supreme Commander in Chief of the armed forces, the symbol of its unity and permanence. He arbitrates and moderates the regular working of the institutions, assumes the highest representation of the Spanish State in international relations, especially with those nations belonging to the same historic community, and performs the functions expressly conferred on him by the Constitution and the law.

- 2. His title is King of Spain, and he may use the other titles appertaining to the Crown.

- 3. The person of the King is inviolable and shall not be held accountable. His acts shall always be countersigned in the manner established in Article 64. Without such countersignature they shall not be valid, except as provided under Article 65,2.

Art. 57 of the Spanish Constitution of 1978 lays down that:

- 1. The Crown of Spain shall be inherited by the successors of H.M. Juan Carlos I de Borbon, the legitimate heir of the historic dynasty. Succession to the throne shall follow the regular order of primogeniture and representation, in the following order of precedence: the earlier shall precede the more distant; within the same degree, the male shall precede the female; and for the same sex, the older shall precede the younger.

Art. 62 of the Spanish Constitution of 1978 lays down that it is incumbent upon the King:

- a) to sanction the laws and promulgate them;
- b) to summon and dissolve the Cortes Generales and to call elections;
- c) to call a referendum;
- d) to propose a candidate for President of the Government and, as the case may be, appoint him or remove him from office;
- e) to appoint and dismiss members of the Government;
- f) to issue the decrees agreed upon by the Council of Ministers, to confer civil and military employments and award honours and distinctions;
- g) to keep himself informed regarding affairs of State and, for this purpose, to preside over the meetings of the Council of Ministers whenever he deems opportune;
- h) to exercise supreme command of the Armed Forces;
- i) to exercise the right to grant pardons;

- j) to exercise the High Patronage of the Royal Academies.

Art. 63 of the Spanish Constitution of 1978 lays down that:

- 1. The King accredits ambassadors and other diplomatic representatives. Foreign representatives in Spain are accredited to him.

- 2. It is incumbent on the King to express the State's assent to the entering into of international commitments through treaties.

- 3. It is incumbent on the King, after authorization by the Cortes Generales, to declare war and to make peace.

Executive power

Executive power in Spain lies with the Council of Ministers (Spanish *Consejo de Ministros*). It is headed by the President of the Government (Prime Minister) who is nominated by the King, confirmed by a vote of the lower house of parliament and then appointed by the king. After a candidate has been nominated he must win a majority of the votes of the lower house, failing which, a second vote will be held where he only needs a plurality of votes. The Prime Minister designates the rest of the members of the Council who are then appointed by the king. He directs the activities of the government as a whole. The President of the Government can also designate various vice presidents (although it is not mandatory). There is also a Council of State that is the supreme consultative organ of the government.

Legislative branch

On the national level, Spain directly elects a legislature, the **Cortes Generales** (*literally*: General Courts), which consists of two chambers, the **Congress of Deputies** (*Congreso de los Diputados*) and the **Senate** (*Senado*). The Congress and Senate serve concurrent terms that run for a maximum of four years.

There are two essential differences between the two houses. The first is by way of electoral practice. Both are elected on a provincial basis. The number of seats in Congress is allocated in proportion to population. However, this is only done after each province (with the exception of Ceuta and Melilla) has been given two members. The result of this is a slight over-representation for the smaller provinces. For example the smallest province, Soria, with an electorate of 78,531, elected 2 members of congress (or 1 for every 39,265 voters) while Madrid, the largest, with 4,458,540 voters, elected 35 members of congress (or 1 for every 127,387 voters). In the Senate the members are elected on a provincial basis . The electoral system used is different with proportional party closed lists being used for Congress and the Senate elected by partial bloc voting. Additionally some senators are designated by the Autonomous legislatures. The second difference is in legislative power. With few exceptions, every law is approved with the votes of Congress. The Senate can make changes or refuse laws but the Congress can ignore these amendments.

Political parties and elections

Main article: Spanish legislative election, 2008

Summary of the 9 March 2008 Congress of Deputies election results

Parties and alliances	Contested Provinces (out of 50)	Votes	%	Change	Seats	Change
Spanish Socialist Workers' Party (*Partido Socialista Obrero Español*)	50	11,288,698	43.87	+1.28	169	+5
People's Party (*Partido Popular*)	50	10,277,809	39.94	+2.22	154	+6
United Left (*Izquierda Unida*)	42	969,871	3.77	-1.19	2	-3
Convergence and Union (*Convergència i Unió*) • Democratic Convergence of Catalonia (*Convergència Democràtica de Catalunya*) • Democratic Union of Catalonia (*Unió Democràtica de Catalunya*)	4	779,425	3.03	−0.20	10	±0
Basque Nationalist Party (*Partido Nacionalista Vasco/Euzko Alderdi Jeltzalea*)	3	306,128	1.19	−0.44	6	−1
Union, Progress and Democracy (*Unión, Progreso y Democracia*)	48	306,078	1.19	—	1	+1
Republican Left of Catalonia (*Esquerra Republicana de Catalunya*)	4	298,139	1.16	−1.36	3	−5
Galician Nationalist Bloc (*Bloque Nacionalista Galego*) • Union of the Galician People (*Unión do Povo Galego*) • Nationalist Left (*Esquerda Nacionalista*) • Galician Unity (*Unidade Galega*) • Socialist Collective (*Colectivo Socialista*) • Inzar • Galician Nationalist Party–Galeguista Party (*Partido Nacionalista Galego–Partido Galeguista*)	4	212,543	0.83	+0.02	2	±0

Canarian Coalition (*Coalición Canaria*)	2	174,629	0.68	−0.23	2	−1
Navarre Yes (*Nafarroa Bai*) • Basque Solidarity (*Eusko Alkartasuna*) • Aralar • Batzarre • Basque Nationalist Party (*Partido Nacionalista Vasco/Euzko Alderdi Jeltzalea*)	1	62,398	0.24	±0.0	1	±0
Basque Solidarity (*Eusko Alkartasuna*)	3	50,371	0.20	−0.12	0	−1
Aragonese Union (*Chunta Aragonesista*)	3	38,202	0.15	−0.22	0	
Communist Party of the Peoples of Spain (*Partido Comunista de los Pueblos de España*)	16	20,030	0.08	+0.03	0	+0
Ciudadanos en Blanco	29	14,193	0.06	-0.10	0	+0
Falange Española de las JONS	10	14,023	0.06	+0.01	0	+0
Democracia Nacional	15	12,836	0.05	-0.01	0	+0
Els Verds-L'Alternativa Ecologista	31	12,561	0.05	-0.07	0	+0
Family and Life (*Familia y Vida*)	7	9,882	0.04	-0.03	0	+0
Humanist Party (*Partido Humanista*)	24	9,056	0.04	-0.05	0	+0
Partido de Almeria	1	8,451	0.03	-	0	+0
Els Verdes-Los Verdes	38	7,824	0.03	-	0	+0
Representacion Cannabica Navarra	1	7,769	0.03	-	0	+0
Partido Obrero Socialista Internacionalista	8	7,386	0.03	-0.00	0	+0
Alternativa Española	20	7,300	0.03	-	0	+0
España 2000	11	6,906	0.03	+0.01	0	+0
Partit Republica Catala	3	6,746	0.03	-	0	+0
Coalicio Valenciana	3	5,424	0.02	-	0	+0
Escons Insubmisos-Alternativa dels Democrates Descontents	10	5,035	0.02	-	0	+0
Tierra Comunera	5	4,796	0.02	-	0	+0
Authentic Falange (*Falange Auténtica*)	8	4,607	0.02	+0.00	0	+0
Leonese People's Union (*Unión del Pueblo Leonés*)	3	4,509	0.02	-0.04	0	+0
Solidaridad y Autogestión Internacionalista	14	3,885	0.02	-	0	+0
Alternativa Motor y Deportes	17	3,829	0.01	-	0	+0

Partido de los Pensionistas en Acción	9	3,050	0.01	-	0	+0
Izquierda Republicana (*Republican Left*)	4	2,899	0.01	-0.06	0	+0
Partido Riojano	1	2,837	0.01	-	0	+0
Alianza Nacional	7	2,737	0.01	-	0	+0
Alternativa en Blanco	12	2,460	0.01	-	0	+0
Extremadura Unida	2	2,346	0.01	-0.01	0	+0
Els Verds-Alternativa Verda	22	2,028	0.01	+0.00	0	+0
Partido Carlista	4	1,956	0.01	+0.00	0	+0
Partit per Catalunya	4	1,919	0.01	-	0	+0
Partido de los No-Fumadores	7	1,616	0.01	-	0	+0
Union por Leganes	1	1,566	0.01	-	0	+0
Frente Español	6	1,539	0.01	-	0	+0
Centro Democratico Liberal	21	1,503	0.01	-	0	+0
Opcio Nacionalista Valenciana	3	1,490	0.01	-	0	+0
Centro Democratico Social	17	1,362	0.01	-	0	+0
Andecha Astur	1	1,299	0.01	-0.0	0	+0
Partido Regionalista del País Leonés	1	1,278	0.0	-	0	+0
Centro Democratico Español	4	1,047	0.0	-	0	+0
Alternativa Nacionalista Canaria	2	1,017	0.0	-	0	+0
Partido de las Libertades Civiles	2	888	0.0	-	0	+0
Unida	1	848	0.0	-	0	+0
Partido Liberal del Empleo y la Vivienda Estatal	7	786	0.0	-	0	+0
Lucha Internacionalista	10	722	0.0	+0.0	0	+0
Unidad del Pueblo	3	699	0.0	-	0	+0
Per la Republica Valenciana	3	645	0.0	-	0	+0
Partido Centristas	1	509	0.0	-	0	+0
Movimiento por la Unidad del Pueblo Canario	2	497	0.0	-	0	+0
Partido Ciudadanos Unidos de Aragon	3	475	0.0	-	0	+0
Union Ciudadana Progresistas Independientes de Can	2	464	0.0	-	0	+0
Identitat Regne de Valencia	3	449	0.0	-	0	+0

Unidad Regionalista de Castilla y Leon	9	423	0.0	-	0	+0
Partido Unionista Estado de España	6	414	0.0	-	0	+0
Gentes de El Bierzo	1	385	0.0	-	0	+0
Partit Illenc de Ses Illes Balears	1	360	0.0	-	0	+0
Partido Positivista Cristiano	8	300	0.0	-0.0	0	+0
Comunion Tradicionalista Carlista	1	218	0.0	-	0	+0
Convergencia Democratica Asturiana	1	216	0.0	-	0	+0
Iniciativa Merindades de Castilla	14	202	0.0	-	0	+0
Unidad Castellana	15	198	0.0	-0.0	0	+0
Partido de Alianza Iberoamericana Europea	3	174	0.0	-	0	+0
Coalicio Treballadors per la Democracia	2	159	0.0	-0.0	0	+0
Partido Regionalista de Guadalajara	1	152	0.0	-0.0	0	+0
Aliança Balear	1	145	0.0	-	0	+0
Asamblea de Votacion Electronica	4	144	0.0	-	0	+0
Union Centrista Liberal	7	124	0.0	-0.0	0	+0
Alianza por Burgos	1	123	0.0	-	0	+0
Iniciativa Ciudadana Burgalesa	1	109	0.0	-	0	+0
Nosaltres Som	6	105	0.0	-	0	+0
Independentes por Cuenca	1	100	0.0	-	0	+0
Agrupacion Ciudadana	2	79	0.0	-	0	+0
Movimiento Falangista de España	1	69	0.0	-	0	+0
Total (turnout 64.6%)					350	0
Source: Spanish Interior Ministry election results database [1]						

Summary of the 9 March 2008 Senate of Spain election results

Parties and alliances	Seats	Change
People's Party (*Partido Popular*)	101	−1
Spanish Socialist Workers' Party (*Partido Socialista Obrero Español*)	88	+7

Entesa Catalana de Progrés • Republican Left of Catalonia (*Esquerra Republicana de Catalunya*) • Socialists' Party of Catalonia (*Partit dels Socialistes de Catalunya*) • Initiative for Catalonia Greens (*Iniciativa per Catalunya Verds*) • United and Alternative Left (*Esquerra Unida i Alternativa*)	12	±0
Basque Nationalist Party (*Partido Nacionalista Vasco/Euzko Alderdi Jeltzalea*)	2	−4
Convergence and Union (*Convergència i Unió*) • Democratic Convergence of Catalonia (*Convergència Democràtica de Catalunya*) • Democratic Union of Catalonia (*Unió Democràtica de Catalunya*)	4	±0
Canarian Coalition (*Coalición Canaria*)	1	−2
Members appointed by the regional legislatures	56	+5
Total (turnout %)	**264**	**+5**
Source: Spanish Interior Ministry election results database [1]		

Spaniards started voting in the Spanish general election, 2008 on March 9, 2008, after a divisive campaign dominated by a cooling economy and concerns over immigration but jolted by a last-minute killing by suspected Basque separatists (ETA).[2]

Judiciary

The Spanish Judiciary is exercised by professional judges and magistrates and composed of different courts depending on The Jurisdictional Order and what is to be judged, the highest ranking court of the judicial structure in Spain is the Supreme Court. The role of the judiciary is governed by the General Council Of the Judiciary Power of Spain whose Chairperson is also the Chairperson of the Supreme Court. See also *Audiencia Nacional*.

Administrative divisions

Spain is divided into 17 autonomous communities (*comunidades autónomas*, singular - *comunidad autónoma*); Andalucía (Andalusia), Aragón, Asturias, Illes Balears (Balearic Islands), Canarias (Canary Islands), Cantabria, Castilla-La Mancha, Castilla y León, Catalunya (Catalonia), Comunidad Valenciana (Valencian Community), Extremadura, Galicia, La Rioja, Madrid, Murcia, Navarra (Navarre) and País Vasco (Basque Country).

Note: There are five places of sovereignty near Morocco: Ceuta and Melilla are administered as autonomous cities, with more powers than cities but fewer than autonomous communities; Islas Chafarinas, Peñón de Alhucemas, and Peñón de Vélez de la Gomera are under direct Spanish administrations.

Regional

The 1978 constitution authorised the creation of regional autonomous governments. By 1985, 17 regions covering all of peninsular Spain, the Canaries and the Balearic Islands had passed a Charter of Autonomy. In 1979, the first autonomous elections were held in the Basque and Catalan regions, which have the strongest nationalist movements. Since then, autonomous governments have been created in the remainder of the 17 regions.

The central government continues to devolve powers to the regional governments, which might eventually have full responsibility for health care and education, as well as other social programs. This process is limited by the exclusive powers of the state in article 149 of the Spanish Constitution.

All autonomous communities are ruled by a government elected by a unicameral legislature.

Spain is, at present, what is called a *State of Autonomies*, formally unitary but, in fact, functioning almost as a Federation of Autonomous Communities, each one with different powers (for instance, some have their own educational and health systems co-ordinated by the Central government, co-official language and particular cultural identity) and laws. There are some irregularities within this system, since power has been devolved from the centre to the periphery asymmetrically, with some autonomous governments (especially those dominated by nationalist parties) seeking a more federalist kind of relationship with Spain. This system of asymmetrical devolution has been described as coconstitutionalism and has similarities to the devolution process adopted by the United Kingdom since 1997. At the same time, Spain's further integration into the European Union causes it to cede powers from the State to the Union's institutions.

Provincial

In the communities with more than one province the government is held by the *diputación provincial* (literally Provincial Deputation). With the creation of Autonomous Communities, deputations have lost much of their power except for those single-province communities, where deputations have been absorbed by the Autonomous power, and in the Basque Autonomous Community where the power of deputations remains very strong. The members of provincial deputations are indirectly elected by citizens according to the results of municipal elections, and all of their members must be councillors of a town or city in the province, except in the Basque Provinces where direct elections take place. Some Spanish politicians have called for the abolition of provincial deputations.

Provincial Deputations are considered by law as Local Administrations and are regulated by the Regulating Act of the Bases of the Local regime of 1985.

Municipal

Spanish municipal administration is highly homogeneous, most of the municipalities having the same powers, such as municipal police, traffic enforcement, urban planning and development, social services, municipal taxes and civil defence, and the same rules of membership and leadership.

Most Spanish municipalities are ruled in a parliamentary style, where citizens elect the municipal council, that acts as a sort of legislative body, that is responsible for electing the mayor who can appoint a board of governors out of councillors of his party or coalition as an executive. The only exception for this rule is in municipalities of under 50 inhabitants, which act as an open council, with a directly elected mayor and an assembly of neighbours as control and legislative body.

Membership of Municipal councils in Spain is chosen in municipal elections held every four years at the same time over Spain, and councillors are allotted using the D'Hondt method for proportional representation, with the exception of municipalities of under 100 inhabitants where bloc voting is used. The number of Councillors is determined by the population of the municipality, the smallest municipalities having 5 and Madrid (the biggest) 55.

The nationality debate

Main article: Nationalities in Spain

In order to understand the political forces and debates in Spain two dimensions have to be considered: the Right vs. Left dimension and the Nation State vs. Plurinational State dimension. The political parties' agendas and the individual citizens' opinions can only be understood when looked at on both dimensions. The Constitution of the Kingdom of Spain states that 1) it is a Nation and 2) that it is formed by Nationalities and Regions. This statement is a contradiction (since Nationality and Nation essentially mean the same thing in political theory), but it was an agreement that struck a balance between the political parties advocating the nation state and those advocating the plurinational state. The territorial organization of Spain into Autonomous Communities of Spain is the administrative realization of this constitutional balancing act.

Historically, parties advocating the Nation State claim that there is only one nation and favour a state with a highly-powered government (with some degree of regional decentralization). Nationalist Catalan, Basque and Galician political parties claim to represent their respective 'nations', different from the 'Spanish nation'. These political parties share the belief that the Kingdom of Spain is a state formed by four 'nations', namely the Catalan nation, the Basque nation, the Galician nation and what might be called the Castilian-Spanish nation (for lack of better word, since they would simply call it Spain). Some of these parties often mention Switzerland as a model of Plurinational State shared by German, French, and Italian nationalities, while others advocate independence. Notice that these nations/nationalities are related to, but different from the current administrative borders of the Autonomous Communities of Spain.

The current situation can be understood as the sum of two historical failures: 1) the Nation State parties were unable to build a unified Nation State such as France, the model that the political and territorial organization of Spain has followed, while 2) the "national resistance" movements (especially Catalans and Basques) were also unable to break free from the Spanish state.

ETA & GRAPO

The Government of Spain has been involved in a long-running campaign against Basque Fatherland and Liberty (ETA), an armed secessionist organization founded in 1959 in opposition to Franco and dedicated to promoting Basque independence through violent means, though originally violence was not a part of their method. They consider themselves a guerrilla organization and are considered internationally as a terrorist organisation. Although the Basque Autonomous government does not condone any kind of violence, their different approaches to the separatist movement are a source of tension between the Central and Basque governments.

Initially ETA targeted primarily Spanish security forces, military personnel and Spanish Government officials. As the security forces and prominent politicians improved their own security, ETA increasingly focused its attacks on the tourist seasons (scaring tourists was seen as a way of putting pressure on the government, given the sector's importance to the economy) and local government officials in the Basque Country. The group carried out numerous bombings against Spanish Government facilities and economic targets, including a car bomb assassination attempt on then-opposition leader Aznar in 1995, in which his armored car was destroyed but he was unhurt. The Spanish Government attributes over 800 deaths to ETA during its campaign of terrorism.

On 17 May 2005, all the parties in the Congress of Deputies, except the PP, passed the Central Government's motion giving approval to the beginning of peace talks with ETA, without making political concessions and with the requirement that it give up its weapons. PSOE, CiU, ERC, PNV, IU-ICV, CC and the mixed group —BNG, CHA, EA and NB— supported it with a total of 192 votes, while the 147 PP parliamentarians objected. ETA declared a "permanent cease-fire" that came into force on March 24, 2006 and was broken by Barajas T4 International Airport Bombings on December 30, 2006. In the years leading up to the permanent cease-fire, the government had had more success in controlling ETA, due in part to increased security cooperation with French authorities.

Spain has also contended with a Marxist resistance group, commonly known as GRAPO. GRAPO (Revolutionary group of May the 1st) is an urban guerrilla group, founded in Vigo, Galicia; that seeks to overthrow the Spanish Government and establish a Marxist-Leninist state. It opposes Spanish participation in NATO and U.S. presence in Spain and has a long history of assassinations, bombings, bank robberies and kidnappings mostly against Spanish interests during the 1970s and 1980s.

In a June 2000 communiqué following the explosions of two small devices in Barcelona, GRAPO claimed responsibility for several attacks throughout Spain during the past year. These attacks included two failed armored car robberies, one in which two security officers died, and four bombings of political party offices during the 1999-2000 election campaign. In 2002, Spanish authorities were successful in hampering the organization's activities through sweeping arrests, including some of the group's leadership. GRAPO is not capable of maintaining the degree of operational capability that they once enjoyed. Most members of the groups are either in jail or abroad.

Armed Islamic fundamentalism in Spain

Al Qaeda has been known to operate cells in Spain, both logistically to support operations in other countries and with the potential to mount attacks within Spain itself. Spanish investigative services and the judicial system have aggressively sought to arrest and prosecute their members, with the most notable raid occurring in Barcelona in January 2003. In that effort, Spanish authorities arrested 16 suspected terrorists and seized explosives and other chemicals. Spain also actively cooperates with foreign governments to diminish the transnational terrorist threat.

Spain suffered a shocking terrorist attack, the March 11, 2004 Madrid attacks on its capital's commuter train network, killing 191 persons. Al-Qaeda has been blamed for this attack. Some have attributed the fall of the Aznar government to this attack, which took place just four days before the 2004 elections. At first the Government and media accused ETA for the bombing. As the facts about its organisation by Islamic fundamentalism were appearing many voters lashed out at the public media and Aznar's government, believing the two had colluded to deceive the public since the Spanish government's support of the war in Iraq might be blamed as the trigger for the attack, a war which a considerable number of Spaniards had opposed, and therefore, many Spaniards believed Aznar's government had tried to deceive the public because of the elections.

One of the first moves of Prime Minister Zapatero was to pull all Spanish troops out of Iraq, but at the same time he increased the amount of soldiers in Afghanistan, believing that the nation represented a clear terrorist threat.

Political pressure groups

- Business and landowning interests (CEOE, CEPYME);
- Free labour unions (authorised in April 1977, which meant the legalisation of previous clandestine unions and the creation of new ones). The most powerful unions are the Workers' Commissions or *CC.OO.* and the Socialist General Union of Workers or UGT. There are many others, in which workers unionise according to their trade or their ideology: Workers Syndical Union or USO, Solidarity of Basque Workers (ELA, Basque), Galician Inter-Unions Confederation (CIG, Galician).
- Catholic Church and other religious organisations (such as Opus Dei)) campaign to influence governments' policies.
- Armed rebellion: Basque Country and Liberty or ETA and the First of October Anti-Fascist Resistance Group or GRAPO use violence to oppose the government. They are considered terrorists by the state and most of the population.

International organization participation

Spain is member of AfDh, AsDB, Australia Group, BIS, CCC, CE, CERN, EAPC, EBRD, ECE, ECLAC, EIB, EMU, ESA, EU, FAO, IADB, IAEA, IBRD, ICAO, ICC, ICC, ICFTU, ICRM, IDA, IEA, IFAD, IFC, IFRCS, IHO, ILO, IMF, IMO, Inmarsat, Intelsat, Interpol, IOC, IOM (observer), ISO, ITU, LAIA (observer), NATO, NEA, NSG, OAS (observer), OECD, OPCW, OSCE, PCA, UN, UNCTAD, UNESCO, UNHCR, UNIDO, UNMIBH, UNMIK, UNTAET, UNU, UPU, WCL, WEU, WHO, WIPO, WMO, WToO, WTrO, Zangger Committee

Economy of Spain

Economy of Spain	
Rank	9th (nominal) / 13th (PPP)
Currency	1 Euro = 100 eurocent
Fiscal year	Calendar year
Trade organizations	EU, WTO and OECD
Statistics	
GDP	€1.051 trillion ($1.443 trillion) (4th term 2009)
GDP growth	0,1% (1T/2010)
GDP per capita	€22,486 ($30,862) (2009)
GDP by sector	agriculture (2.3%), energy (2.3%), industry (11.7%), construction (10.0%), services (66.6%) (Dec. 2009)
Inflation (CPI)	1.4% (Mar. 2010)
Population below poverty line	19.8% (2005)
Gini index	32% (2005)
Labour force	23.0 million (Apr. 2010)
Labour force by occupation	services (70.7%), industry (14.1%), construction (9.9%), agriculture, farming and fishing (4.5%), energy (0.7%) (Sep. 2009)
Unemployment	20.05% (Apr. 2010)
Main industries	metals and metal manufactures, chemicals, shipbuilding, automobiles, machine tools, Tourism, textiles and apparel (including footwear), food and beverages.
Ease of Doing Business Rank	62nd
External	
Exports	€248.9 billion ($341.6 billion) F.O.B. (2009)
Export goods	Machinery, motor vehicles, chemicals, shipbuilding, foodstuffs, pharmaceuticals and medicines, other consumer goods
Main export partners	France 18.3%, Germany 10.6%, Portugal 8.7%, Italy 8%, U.K. 6.7%, U.S. 4.2% (2008)

Imports	€270.4 billion ($371.1 billion) (Oct. 2009)
Import goods	Fuels, chemicals, semifinished goods, Machinery and equipment, foodstuffs, consumer goods, measuring and medical control instruments
Main import partners	Germany 14.5%, France 11.1%, Italy 7.4%, China 6.2%, U.K. 4.5%, Netherlands 4.4% (2008)
FDI stock	$649.9 billion (31 December 2009 est.)
Gross external debt	$2.41 trillion (30 June 2009)
Public finances	
Public debt	€455.95 billion 43.1% GDP (Nov. 2009) or $653.10 billion
Revenues	$420.4 billion (2009 est.)
Expenses	$536.3 billion (2009 est.)
Economic aid	$1.33 billion (donor) (1999)
Foreign reserves	$20.25 billion (31 December 2008 est.)
Main data source: CIA World Fact Book [1] *All values, unless otherwise stated, are in US dollars*	

The **economy of Spain** is the ninth-largest economy in the world, based on nominal GDP comparisons, and the fifth-largest in Europe . It is regarded as the world's 15th most developed country. Until 2008 the economy of Spain had been regarded as one of the most dynamic within the EU, attracting significant amounts of foreign investment. Spain's economy had been credited with having avoided the virtual zero growth rate of some of its largest partners in the EU. In fact, the country's economy had created more than half of all the new jobs in the European Union over the five years ending 2005, a process that is rapidly being reversed.

More recently, the Spanish economy had benefited greatly from the global real estate boom, with construction representing an astonishing 16% of GDP and 12% of employment in its final year. According to calculations by the German newspaper *Die Welt*, Spain had been on course to overtake countries like Germany in per capita income by 2011. However, the downside of the now defunct real estate boom was a corresponding rise in the levels of personal debt; as prospective homeowners had struggled to meet asking prices, the average level of household debt tripled in less than a decade. This placed especially great pressure upon lower to middle income groups; by 2005 the median ratio of indebtedness to income had grown to 125%, due primarily to expensive boom time mortgages that now often exceed the value of the property.. A European Commission forecast had predicted Spain would enter a recession by the end of 2008. According to Spain's Finance Minister, "Spain faces its deepest recession in half a century". Spain's government forecast the unemployment rate would rise to 16% in 2009. The ESADE business school predicted 20%. After a steep plunge in late 2008 and throughout 2009, in which the unemployment rate met ESADE's forecast, the economy stabilised in the first quarter of 2010. Due to its own economic development and the recent EU enlargements up to 27 members (2007), Spain as a whole exceeded (105%) the average of the EU GDP in 2006 placing it ahead of Italy (103% for 2006). As for the extremes within Spain, three regions in 2005 were included in the leading EU group exceeding 125% of the GDP average level (Madrid, Navarre and the Basque Autonomous Community) and one was at the 85% level (Extremadura). According to the growth rates post 2006, noticeable progress from these figures happened until early 2008, when the Spanish economy was heavily affected by the puncturing of its property bubble by the global financial crisis.

The centre-right government of former prime minister José María Aznar had worked successfully to gain admission to the group of countries launching the euro in 1999. Unemployment stood at 7.6% in October 2006, a rate that compared favorably to many other European countries, and especially with the early 1990s when it stood at over 20%. Perennial weak points of Spain's economy include high inflation, a large underground economy, and an education system which OECD reports place among the poorest for developed countries. However, the property bubble that had begun building from 1997, fed by historically low interest rates and an immense surge in immigration, imploded in 2008, leading to a rapidly weakening economy and soaring unemployment. By the end of May 2009 unemployment had already reached 18.7% (37% for youths).

2008–2009 financial crisis

Main article: 2008–2009 Spanish financial crisis

Spain continued on the path of economic growth when the ruling party changed in 2004, maintaining robust GDP growth during the first term of prime minister José Luis Rodríguez Zapatero, even though some fundamental problems in the Spanish economy were now becoming clearly evident. Among these, according to the *Financial Times*, was Spain's rapidly growing trade deficit, which had reached a staggering 10% of the country's GDP by the summer of 2008, the "loss of competitiveness against its main trading partners" and, also, as a part of the latter, an inflation rate which had been traditionally higher than the one of its European partners, back then especially affected by house price increases of 150% from 1998 and a growing family indebtedness (115%) chiefly related to the Spanish Real Estate boom and rocketing oil prices.

The Spanish government official GDP growth forecast for 2008 in April was 2,3%. This figure was successively revised down by the Spanish Ministry of Economy to 1.6. This figure looked better than those of most other developed countries. In reality, this rate effectively represented stagnant GDP per person due to Spain's high population growth, itself the result of a high rate of immigration. Retrospective studies by most independent forecasters estimate that the rate had actually dropped to 0.8% instead, far below the strong 3% plus GDP annual growth rates during the 1997-2007 decade. Then, during the third quarter of 2008 the national GDP contracted for the first time in 15 years and, in February 2009, it was confirmed that Spain, along other European economies, had officially entered recession.

In July 2009, the IMF worsened the estimates for Spain's 2009 contraction, to minus 4% of GDP for the year (close to the European average of minus 4.6%), besides, it estimated a further 0.8% contraction of the Spanish economy for 2010, the worst prospect amid advanced economies. The estimation of the IMF was proven to be somewhat too pessimistic, as Spain's GDP sank less than that of most advanced economies in 2009 and by the first quarter of 2010 had already emerged from the recession.

In 2008 the total Spanish public debt (government debt) relative to the total GDP was well below the European Union average, and in fact the government budget was in surplus, but the financial situation rapidly deteriorated with the onset of the recession.

Spanish banking system

The Spanish banking system has been credited as one of the most solid of all western banking systems in coping with the ongoing worldwide liquidity crisis, thanks to the country's conservative banking rules and practices. Banks are required to have high capital provisions and to demand various guarantees and securities from intending borrowers. This has allowed the banks, particularly the geographically and industrially diversified large banks like BBVA and Santander, to weather the real estate deflation better than expected. Indeed, these banks have been able to capitalise on their strong position to buy up distressed banking assets elsewhere in Europe and in the United States.

Nevertheless, with the unprecedented deepening of the country's housing crisis, smaller local savings banks are known to have delayed the registering of bad loans, especially those backed by houses and land, to avoid declaring losses. This has occurred despite the fact that these credits are backed by the borrower's present and future assets.[citation needed]

CCM (Caja Castilla la Mancha), is still the only local savings bank to have suffered a run by depositors. The Banco Central de España (equivalent of the US Federal Reserve) forcibly took over CCM to prevent its financial collapse. Price Waterhouse estimated an imbalance between CCM's assets and debts of €3,500 million, not counting the industrial corporation. One of the investment mistakes this bank had indulged in during the height of the property boom was the funding of an airport at Ciudad Real. It turned out that no airline wanted to operate from there, resulting in a financial fiasco (as well as wasting a lot of land and ruining vistas). There were still further errors leading to the present situation. In May 22, 2010, the Banco Central took over another "caja", CajaSur, as part of a national program to put the country's smaller banks on a firm financial basis.

The 2010 Euro debt crisis

Main article: 2010 European sovereign debt crisis

In the first weeks of 2010, renewed anxiety about the excessive levels of debt in some EU countries and, more generally, about the health of the euro has spread from Ireland and Greece to Portugal, Spain and Italy. In somewhat of a very similar way as in the U.S. and U.K., or many others countries without using the Euro.

Some European think-tanks such as the CEE Council have argued that the predicament some mainland EU countries find themselves in today is the result of a decade of debt-fueled Keynesian economic policies pursued by local policy makers and complacent EU central banker. CEE's claim is contradicted in Spain's case; where the budget prior to the crisis was in surplus, the public debt as a percentage of GDP was relatively low, and had, in fact, been substantially reduced over the previous five years.

Many economists have recommended the imposition of a battery of corrective policies to control public debt- such as drastic austerity measures and substantially higher taxes. Some senior German policy makers went as far as to say that emergency bailouts should bring harsh penalties to EU aid recipients such as Greece.

Although rising rapidly with the onset of the crisis, Spain's public debt at the beginning of 2010, as a percentage of GDP, was still not high by European standards. Indeed, it was still less than the public debt levels of Britain, France and Germany. However, commentators became concerned that the central government has little control over the spending of the regional governments. Under the shared structure of governmental responsibilities that have evolved since 1975, much responsibility for spending had been given back to the regions without also handing over the responsibility of raising the required taxes. The central government now finds itself unable to gain support for unpopular spending cuts from the recalcitrant regional governments.

On May 23, 2010, the government announced further austerity measures, consolidating the ambitious plans announced in January.

Employment crisis

As for the employment, after having completed substantial improvements over the second half of the 1990s and during the 2000s which put a few regions on the brink of full employment, Spain suffered a severe setback in October 2008 when it saw its unemployment rate surging to 1996 levels. During the period October 2007-October 2008 Spain had its unemployment rate climbing 37%, exceeding by far the unemployment surge of past economic crises like 1993. In particular, during the month of October 2008, Spain suffered its worst unemployment rise ever recorded and, so far, the country is suffering Europe's biggest unemployment crisis. By July 2009, it had shed 1.2 million jobs in one year and was to have the same number of jobless as France and Italy combined. Spain's unemployment rate hit 17.4% at the end of March, with the jobless total having doubled over the previous 12 months, when two million people lost their jobs; with the oversized building and housing related industries contributing greatly to the rising unemployment numbers. In this same month, Spain for the first time in its history had over 4,000,000 people unemployed, an especially shocking figure even for a country which had become used to grim unemployment data. Although rapidly slowing, immigration continued throughout 2008 despite the escalating unemployment crisis, worsening the situation. In 2009 some established immigrants began to leave, although many that did continued to maintain homes in Spain due to poor conditions in their country of origin.

Some critics say the Spanish labor market is too rigid, preventing employers from removing unproductive employees and putting upward pressure on unemployment as employers are wary of taking risks on new hires.

Prices

Due to the lack of own resources, Spain has to import all of its fossil fuels. In a scenario of record prices this means adding much pressure to the inflation rate. As a matter of fact, in June 2008 the inflation rate reached a 13-year high at 5.00%. Then, with the dramatic decrease of oil prices that took place in the second half of 2008 plus the manifest bursting of the real estate bubble, concerns quickly shifted over to the risk of deflation, as Spain recorded in January 2009 its lowest inflation rate in 40 years, followed shortly afterwards, in March 2009 by a negative inflation rate for the first time since the gathering of these statistics started.

Energy

See also: Renewable energy in Spain

The Comisión Nacional de la Energía (National Energy Commission) is the regulatory body for energy systems, created by Law 34/1998, of 7 October of the Hydrocarbons Sector, and developed by Royal Decree 1339/1999, of 31 July, which approved its regulations. The National Energy Commission has been assigned to the Ministry of Industry, Tourism And Trade.

Economic ties

Since the 1990s some Spanish companies have gained multinational status, often expanding their activities in culturally close Latin America. Spain is the second biggest foreign investor there, after the United States. Others have expanded into Asia, especially China.

Spanish companies lead fields like renewable energy (Iberdrola is the world's largest renewable energy operator) and infrastructure, with six of the ten biggest international construction firms specialising in transport being Spanish, like Ferrovial, Acciona, ACS, OHL and FCC.

Sectors of the economy

Tourism

See also: Tourism in Spain

During the last four decades the Spanish tourism industry has grown to become the second biggest in the world, worth approximately 40 billion Euros, about 5% of GDP, in 2006. Being the second tourism destination in the world, Spain has a tourism industry sector which contributes nearly 11% to the country's GDP, employing about 2 million of the total labor force.

Automobile industry

See also: Automotive industry in Spain

The automobile industry in Spain is a large employer in the country, employing 9% of the total workforce in 2009 and contributing to 3.3% of the Spanish GDP, despite the decline due to the economic recession of the past couple of years. In 2009, Spain was in the top ten of the largest automobile producer countries in the world.

Apart from its domestic brand SEAT which is the major contributor to the automotive sector of the country and Santana Motor, many suppliers and foreign car and truck makers - like Volkswagen, Nissan, Daimler Mercedes-Benz, Ford, Renault, GM/Opel, PSA Peugeot/Citroën, Iveco etc - have facilities and plants in Spain today developing and producing vehicles and components, not only for the needs of the internal market but also for exportation purposes, with the contribution of the automobile industry in 2008 rising up to the second place with 17,6% out of the country's total exports.

External links

Statistical resources

- Banco de España (Spanish Central Bank); features the latest and in depth statistics [2]
- Statistical Institute of Andalusia [3]
- National Institute of Statistics [4]
- Statistical Institute of Catalonia [5]
- Statistical Institute of Galicia [6]
- OECD's Spain country Web site [7] and OECD Economic Survey of Spain [8]

Further reading

- Article: Investing in Spain [9] by Nicholas Vardy - September, 2006. A global investor's discussion of Spain's economic boom.
- The Pain in Spain: On May Day, Nearly 1 in 5 are Jobless [10] by Andrés Cala, *The Christian Science Monitor*, May 1, 2009
- Alternatives to Fiscal Austerity in Spain [11] from the Center for Economic and Policy Research, July 2010
- O'Neill, Michael F.; McGettigan, Gerard (2005), "Spanish biotechnology: anyone for PYMEs?", *Drug Discovery Today*, News and Comment (London: Elsevier) **10** (16): 1078–1081, 15 August 2005, doi:10.1016/S1359-6446(05)03549-X [12], ISSN 1359-6446 [13]

Foreign relations of Spain

Spain
This article is part of the series: **Politics and government of Spain**
Other countries · Atlas **Politics portal**

After the return of democracy following the death of General Franco in 1975, Spain's foreign policy priorities were to break out of the diplomatic isolation of the Franco years and expand diplomatic relations, enter the European Community, and define security relations with NATO, later joining the organisation in 1982.

Spain has established itself as a major participant in multilateral international security activities. Spain's EU membership represents an important part of its foreign policy. Even on many international issues beyond western Europe, Spain prefers to coordinate its efforts with its EU partners through the European political cooperation mechanisms.

Regional relations

Spain has maintained its special identification with its fellow Spanish-speaking countries. Its policy emphasizes the concept of an Ibero-American community, essentially the renewal of the historically liberal concept of "Hispano-Americanismo" (or hispanism as it is often referred to in English), which has sought to link the Iberian peninsula to the Spanish-speaking countries in Central and South America through language, commerce, history and culture. Spain has been an effective example of transition from dictatorship to democracy, as shown in the many trips that Spain's King and Prime Ministers have made to the region. Spain maintains economic and technical cooperation programs and cultural exchanges with Latin America, both bilaterally and within the EU.

Meanwhile, Spain has gradually begun to broaden its contacts with Sub-Saharan Africa. It has a particular interest in its former colony of Equatorial Guinea, where it maintains a large aid program. More recently Madrid has sought closer relation with Senegal, Mauritania, Mali and others to find solutions for the issue of illegal immigration to the Canary Islands.

Spain is also known as a broker in the Middle East. In its relations with the Arab world, Spain frequently supports Arab positions on Middle East issues. The Arab countries are a priority interest for

Spain because of oil and gas imports and because several Arab nations have substantial investments in Spain.

Spain has been successful in managing its relations with its two European neighbours, France and Portugal. The accession of Spain and Portugal to the EU has helped ease some of their periodic trade frictions by putting these into an EU context. Franco-Spanish bilateral cooperation is enhanced by joint action against Basque ETA terrorism. Ties with the United Kingdom are generally good, although the question of Gibraltar remains a sensitive issue.

Today, Spain is trying to expand its still narrow relations with east Asian nations. The People's Republic of China and Japan are the main points of interest for Spain in the region. Thailand and Indonesia are Spain's main allies in the ASEAN region, having a considerable number of agreements and a very good relationship. In the recent years Spain has also been boosting its contacts, relations and investment in other Asian countries, most notably Vietnam, South Korea and Malaysia. Relations with the Philippines are, despite of the colonial past, considerably weaker than the ones Spain has with other countries in the area, dealing mostly with cultural aspects and humanitary assistance programs.

Disputes - international

Disputed status of Gibraltar with the United Kingdom; Spain controls five places of sovereignty (*plazas de soberanía*) on and off the coast of Morocco - the coastal enclaves of Ceuta and Melilla, which Morocco contests, as well as the islands of Peñon de Alhucemas, Peñon de Vélez de la Gomera, and Islas Chafarinas; by the Vienna Treaty of 1815, Spain recognized the Portuguese claims over Olivenza as "legitimate", but didn't agree to return the place to Portugal. The historic disputes with this country about the government of the Savage Islands in the Atlantic Ocean disappeared in recent times.

Illicit drugs

Spain is a key European gateway country for Latin American cocaine and North African hashish entering the European market. It is also a consumer of south-west Asian heroin.

Bilateral relations

Europe

Country	Formal Relations Began	Notes
Belarus	1992-02-13	• Belarus is represented in Spain through it embassy in Paris (France). • Spain is represented in Belarus through it embassy in Moscow (Russia). • Both countries are full members of the Organization for Security and Co-operation in Europe. • Spanish Ministry of Foreign Affairs and Cooperation about relations with Belarus (in Spanish only) [1] • Spanish Ministry of Foreign Affairs and Cooperation: Spanish representations in Belarus [2]
Bulgaria	1910-05-08	• Relations were severed in 1946 and were restored in 1970 at the level of Consular Office and Trade Mission. • Since January 27, 1970, the diplomatic relations were elevated to embassy level. • Bulgaria has an embassy in Madrid and an honorary consulate in Barcelona. • Spain has an embassy in Sofia. • Both countries are full members of the NATO and of the European Union. • Spanish Ministry of Foreign Affairs about relations with Bulgaria (in Spanish only) [3]
Croatia	1992-03-09	See Croatia–Spain relations • Croatia has an embassy in Madrid and 4 honorary consulates (in Barcelona, Palma de Mallorca, Pamplona and Seville). • Spain has an embassy in Zagreb and 2 honorary consulates (in Dubrovnik and Split). • Croatian Ministry of Foreign Affairs and European Integration: list of bilateral treaties with Spain [4] • Spanish Ministry of Foreign Affairs about relations with Croatia (in Spanish only) [5]
Cyprus		See Foreign relations of Cyprus
Denmark		See Denmark-Spain relations
Estonia		See Foreign relations of Estonia
Finland		See Foreign relations of Finland
France		Spain has very good relations with France, especially since May 16, 2007, when Nicolas Sarkozy was elected President of France. The police of Spain and France are now cooperating to suppress the terrorist group ETA.
Germany		Spain had very good relations with Germany, until since March 14, 2004, when Zapatero was elected Spanish Prime Minister. The Prime Minister's relationship with the present Chancellor, Angela Merkel, is less close but remains civil.
Greece		See Foreign relations of Greece
Holy See	1530	See Holy See – Spain relations • The Holy See has a nunciature in Madrid. • Spain has an embassy in Rome.
Hungary		See Foreign relations of Hungary
Ireland		See Foreign relations of the Republic of Ireland

Italy		See Italy–Spain relations
		Both countries established diplomatic relations after the unification of Italy. Relations between Italy and Spain have remained strong and affable for centuries owing to various political, cultural, and historical connections between the two nations. In the Early modern period, southern and insular Italy came under Spanish control, having been previously a domain of the Crown of Aragon. This extended period of foreign domination left marked influences in the modern southern Italian dialects. During the Spanish civil war, the Corps of Volunteer Troops, a fascist expeditionary force from Italy, supported the Nationalist forces led by Francisco Franco. It's estimated that around 75,000 Italians fought in the war.
Malta	1977	• Malta has an embassy in Madrid and 5 honorary consulates (in Barcelona, Palma de Mallorca, Santander, Seville and Valencia). • Spain has an embassy in Valletta. • Both countries are full members of the European Union and of the Union for the Mediterranean.
▮◈▮ Moldova	1992-01-30	See Moldova–Spain relations
		As of 2009 Spain does not have an Embassy in Chișinău. Spain is represented in Moldova through Ambassador D. Juan Pablo García-Berdoy Cerezo in Bucharest in Romania.
		In 2008, the Spanish government indicated that 12,582 Moldovan citizens were legally working there. Spain is a significant investor in Moldova through Unión Fenosa which owns three of Moldova's five energy distribution companies.
Portugal		See Portugal–Spain relations
		Relations between Portugal and Spain are also good. They cooperate in the fight against drug trafficking and tackling forest fires (common in the Iberian Peninsula in summers), for example. These close relations are facilitated by similar governments: the government of conservative Spanish PM José María Aznar coincided with the government of also conservative José Manuel Durão Barroso in Portugal; today, both José Luis Rodríguez Zapatero of Spain and José Sócrates of Portugal are socialists.
		Portugal also holds claim to the disputed territory of Olivença in the Portuguese-Spanish border.
▮▮ Romania	1967-01-05	• Both countries re-established diplomatic relations on January 5, 1967, 21 years after they were broken. • Romania has an embassy in Madrid, 3 general consulates (in Barcelona, Castellon de la Plana and Sevilla) and 2 honorary consulates (in Murcia and Valencia). • Spain has an embassy in Bucharest. • Both countries are full members of the Latin Union, of NATO and of the European Union. • There are around 730,000 people of Romanian descent living in Spain.

Russia	1520	See Russia–Spain relations
		• Russia has an embassy in Madrid and a consulate-general in Barcelona.
		• Spain has an embassy in Moscow.
		Spain and the Grand Duchy of Moscow first exchanged envoys in 1520s; regular embassies were established in 1722. Soviet-Spanish relations, once terminated after the Spanish Civil War, were gradually reestablished since 1963 and fully established in 1977. Trade between two countries amounts to two billion Euros (2008); in March 2009 two countries signed an energy agreement providing national energy companies access to other party's domestic markets.
Serbia	1916-10-14	• Serbia has an embassy in Madrid.
		• Spain has an embassy in Belgrade.
		• In light of the February 2008 unilateral declaration of independence by the Kosovo authorities, Spain has become a staunch supporter of Serbia's sovereignty and territorial integrity, and relations have thrived in recent years as a result.
		• Serbian Ministry of Foreign Affairs about relations with Spain [6]
		• Spanish Ministry of Foreign Relations about relations with Serbia (in Spanish only) [7]
Turkey		See Spanish–Turkish relations
		• Spain has an embassy in Ankara.
		• Turkey has an embassy in Madrid.
		• Both countries are full members of NATO and the Union for the Mediterranean. Also, Spain is an EU member and Turkey is a candidate.
		• Turkish Ministry of Foreign Affairs about relations with Spain [8]
Ukraine	1992-01-30	• Spain recognized Ukraine's independence in 1991.
		• Spain has an embassy in Kiev.
		• Ukraine has an embassy in Madrid, a general consulate in Barcelona and a consulate in Málaga.
		• Both countries are full members of the Council of Europe. Since 1991, many Ukrainians have emigrated to Spain to work.
		• Spanish Ministry of Foreign Affairs about relations with Ukraine (in Spanish only) [9]
United Kingdom		See Spain–United Kingdom relations
		In 2001 60,000 Spanish born people were living in the UK, and 160,000 British people were of Spanish descent, in total estimates state 960,000 UK citizens as having full or partial Spanish blood (with the remaining 800,000 being South Americans of Spanish descent). In comparison it is estimated that 990,000 British born people live in Spain, the ancestral numbers are likely to be much, much lower, as British people have only recently begun to migrate to Spain (the coastal areas in particular) post retirement and/ or for work. See also Spanish Briton, Latin American Briton.

Latin America

Main article: Spanish-American relations

With Latin American countries: During Aznar's government, Spanish relations with some Latin-American countries like Mexico, Venezuela and Cuba got worse, but were exceptionally good with others like Colombia, Dominican Republic and several Central America small republics. Zapatero's victory in the 2004 general elections changed this setting. Today, relations with Venezuela are quite good, which has caused an upset with the United States, who have been in recent conflicts with Venezuela via both countries presidents and Venezuela's growing relations with "Anti-American Nations", such as Cuba, China, and several other nations including Russia and Islamic Middle Eastern countries.

Besides Venezuela, the Spanish government has strongly increased its relations in recent years with Brazil, Argentina and Chile.

Country	Formal Relations Began	Notes
Bolivia		A diplomatic crisis with Bolivia in 2005 due to a misunderstanding was quickly resolved by Zapatero and Spain became the first European country visited by Evo Morales on January 4, 2006. However, there remain problems surrounding the exploitation of oil and gas fields in the country by Spanish corporations like Repsol. Bolivian President Evo Morales met King Juan Carlos and held talks with Prime Minister Jose Luis Rodriguez Zapatero during a visit to Spain in September 2009 with the intention of resolving issues concerning the nationalisation of the Bolivian energy sector. The move has the potential to hurt some Spanish companies however relations were said to be "positive" between the Bolivian state and Spanish private sector energy companies. Evo Morales said that Bolivia is ready to accept outside investment in its energy and natural resource industries as long as foreign firms do not act as owners and that Bolivia is "looking for investment, be it from private or state sector. We want partners, not owners of our natural resources." It was suggested that Bolivia would also negotiate with Spanish companies to produce car parts and lithium batteries in the future.
▥ Cuba		Relations with Cuba have historically been better. The relations with Cuba were always good, even during the strongly anti-communist dictatorship of Francisco Franco. This is a historic cause of little frictions with the United States.
Mexico		See Mexico–Spain relations • Mexico currently has an embassy in Madrid and a consulate-general in Barcelona. • Spain has an embassy in Mexico City and two consulates-general in the country; in Guadalajara and in Monterrey. • During the Spanish Civil War, Mexican volunteers joined the Republican side to fight Francisco Franco. Though the Republicans had lost the war, this helped improve the relationship between the two countries. Also, many Spanish immigrants immigrated to Mexico to escape the Spanish Civil War.

Paraguay	1880-09-10	See Paraguay–Spain relations • Paraguay has an embassy in Madrid, a general consulate in Barcelona and a consulate in Málaga. • Spain has an embassy in Asuncion. • Both countries are full members of the Latin Union, of the Association of Spanish Language Academies, and of the Organization of Ibero-American States. • Spanish Ministry of Foreign about the relation with Paraguay (in Spanish only) [10]
Uruguay		See Spain–Uruguay relations • Spain has an embassy in Montevideo. • Uruguay has an embassy in Madrid and 3 consulate general (in Barcelona, Santiago de Compostela and Valencia) and 7 honorary consulates (in Bilbao, Palma de Majorca, Pamplona, Salamanca, Santa Cruz de Tenerife, Seville and Vigo). • Both countries are full members of the Latin Union, of the Association of Spanish Language Academies, and of the Organization of Ibero-American States. • Spanish Ministry of Foreign about relations with Uruguay (in Spanish only) [11]

Elsewhere

Country	Formal relations began	Notes
Armenia	1992-01-27	• Armenia is represented in Spain through its embassy in Rome and there is an honorary consulate in Valencia. • Spain is represented in Armenia through its embassy in Moscow (Russia) and an honorary consulate in Yerevan. • There are around 42,000 people of Armenian descent living in Spain, specially in Valencia and Barcelona (See also Armenians in Spain) • Spanish Ministry of Foreign Affairs and Cooperations about the relation with Armenia (in Spanish only) [12]
Canada		See Foreign relations of Canada
Israel	1975	• Israel has an embassy in Madrid. • Spain has an embassy in Tel Aviv and an honorary consulate in Haifa. • Both countries are full members of the Union for the Mediterranean. • Spanish Ministry of Foreign Affairs about relations with Israel (in Spanish only) [13]
Morocco		Spain continues to focus attention Morocco. This concern is dictated by geographic proximity and long historical contacts, as well as by the two Spanish exclave cities of Ceuta and Melilla on the northern coast of Africa. While Spain's departure from its former colony of Western Sahara ended direct Spanish participation in Morocco, it maintains an interest in the peaceful resolution of the conflict brought about there by decolonization. These issues were highlighted by a crisis in 2002, when Spanish forces evicted a small contingent of Moroccans from a tiny islet off Morocco's coast following that nation's attempt to assert sovereignty over the Spanish island.

North Korea	2001	With the normalization of diplomatic relations with North Korea in 2001, Spain completed the process of universalizing its diplomatic relations.
United States		See Spain – United States relations Under the government of José María Aznar, Spain developed exceptionally good relations with the USA, in great part due to the personal empathy between Aznar and George W. Bush. Following Zapatero's decision to withdraw Spanish troops from Iraq immediately after the 2004 general elections, relations predictably soured, although important commercial links remained intact. When elected, President Barack Obama expressed his wish to enhance cooperation between both countries, specially in policies like the Green Energy plan from Zapatero , introducing the AVE (the Spanish High Speed Train) in United States and aiding US by receiving in Spanish prisons Guantanamo Prison detainees

See also

- List of diplomatic missions in Spain
- List of diplomatic missions of Spain
- Spanish Institute for Foreign Trade

Further reading

- Gillespie, Richard (April 2007). "Spanish foreign policy: party alternatives or the pursuit of consensus?". *Journal of Southern Europe and the Balkans* **9** (1): 29–45. doi:10.1080/14613190701216995 [14].

- Iglesias-Cavicchioli, Manuel (Summer/Fall 2007). "A Period of Turbulent Change: Spanish-US Relations Since 2002" [15]. *Whitehead Journal of Diplomacy and International Relations* **8** (2): 113–129.

Culture of Spain

The culture of Spain is a European culture based on a variety of influences. These include the pre-Roman cultures, mainly the celts and the Iberians cultures; but mainly in the period of Roman influences. In the areas of language and religion, the Ancient Romans left a lasting legacy. The subsequent course of Spanish history also added elements to the country's cultural development. The Visigothic Kingdom left a sense of a united Christian Hispania that was going to be welded in the Reconquista. Muslim influences were strong during the period of 711 A.D. to the 15th century, especially with loan words. The Spanish language, derives directly from Vulgar Latin, and has minor influences from pre-roman languages like *barro* -mud-, gothic *guerra* -war-, Arabic and basque Other minorities includes the Jewish population in some cities, but after the defeat of the Muslims during the Christian "Reconquista" (Reconquest) period between 1000 and 1492, Spain became an almost entirely Roman Catholic country. In addition, the history of the nation and its Mediterranean and Atlantic environment have played a significant role in shaping its culture. By the end of the 19th and 20th , the Spaniards made expressions of cultural diversity easier than it had been for the last seven centuries. This occurred at the same period that Spain became increasingly drawn into a diverse international culture. Spain has the second highest number of UNESCO World Heritage Sites in the world, with a total of 42.

Literature

Main article: Spanish literature

Literature of Spain
• Medieval literature
• Renaissance
• Miguel de Cervantes
• Baroque
• Enlightenment
• Romanticism
• Realism
• *Modernismo*
• Generation of '98
• *Novecentismo*
• Generation of '27

> • Literature subsequent to the Civil War

The term "Spanish literature" refers to literature written in the Spanish language, including literature composed by Spanish, other European,and Latin American writers. It may include Spanish poetry, prose, and novels.

Spanish literature is the name given to the literary works written in Spain throughout time, and those by Spanish authors worldwide. Due to historic, geographic and generational diversity, Spanish literature has known a great number of influences and it is very diverse. Some major movements can be identified within it.

Highlights include the Cantar de Mio Cid, the oldest preserved Spanish cantar de gesta. It is written in medieval Spanish, the ancestor of modern Spanish.

The Celestina is a book published anonymously by Fernando de Rojas, about whom we know little, in 1499. This book is considered to be one of the greatest in Spanish literature, and traditionally marks the end of medieval literature and the beginning of the literary renaissance in Spain.

Besides its importance in the Spanish literature of the Golden Centuries, Lazarillo de Tormes is credited with founding a literary genre, the picaresque novel, so called from Spanish pícaro meaning "rogue" or "rascal". In these novels, the adventures of the pícaro expose injustice while amusing the reader.

Published by Miguel de Cervantes in two volumes a decade apart, Don Quixote is the most influential work of literature to emerge from the Spanish Golden Age and perhaps the entire Spanish literary canon. As a founding work of modern Western literature, it regularly appears at or near the top of lists of the greatest works of fiction ever published.

Painting and sculpture

Main article: Spanish art

Spain's greatest painters during the Golden age period included El Greco, Bartolomé Esteban Murillo, Diego Velázquez, and Francisco Goya, who became world-renowned artist between the period of the 16th century to 19th century. However, Spain's best known artist since the 20th century has been Pablo Picasso, who is known for abstract sculptures, drawings, graphics, and ceramics in addition to his paintings. Other leading artist include Salvador Dalí, Juan Gris, Joan Miró, and Antoni Tàpies.

Architecture

Main article: Spanish architecture

During the Prehistoric period, the Megalithic and the Iberian and Celtic architectures are developed. Through the Roman period, both the urban development (Emerita Augusta) and constructions (Aqueduct of Segovia) flourish. After the Pre-Romanesque period, in the architecture of Al-Andalus, important contributions are made by the Caliphate of Cordoba (the Great Mosque of Córdoba), the Taifas (Aljafería, in Zaragoza), the Almoravids and Almohads (La Giralda, Seville), and the Nasrid of the Kingdom of Granada (Alhambra, Generalife).

During the Islamic period. Spanish architecture encompasses a wide range of both secular and religious styles from the foundation of Islam to the present day, influencing the design and construction of buildings and structures in Islamic culture. The principal Islamic architectural types are: the Mosque, the Tomb, the Palace and the Fort. From these four types, the vocabulary of Islamic architecture is derived and used for buildings of lesser importance such as public baths, fountains and domestic architecture.[1][2]

Islamic art prohibited the painting of people or figures, so beautiful designs and floral patterns covered every wall of important buildings. When they tried to involve the presence of God they made beautiful pillars to make you feel lost and in awe. Art was very important in Spain at that time. The three main religions in Spain then were: Islam, Christianity, and Judaism. These three religions bonded very well and worked alongside each other. The places of worship involved all three different aspects.

After them, several currents appear: the Mudéjar Style (Alcázar of Seville), the Romanesque period (Cathedral of Santiago de Compostela), the The Gothic period (the Cathedrals of Burgos, León and Toledo), the Renaissance (Palace of Charles V in Granada), the Baroque period (Granada Cathedral), the Spanish Colonial architecture, and Neoclassical Style (El Prado Museum) are the most important ones. In the 19th century the Eclecticism and Regionalism, the Neo-Mudéjar Style, and the Glass architecture bloom. In the 20th century the Catalan Modernisme (La Sagrada Família by Gaudí), the Modernist architecture, and the Contemporary architecture germinate.

Cinema

Main article: Cinema of Spain

The art of motion-picture making within the nation of Spain or by Spanish filmmakers abroad is collectively known as "Spanish Cinema".

In recent years, Spanish cinema has achieved high marks of recognition as a result of its creative and technical excellence. In the long history of Spanish cinema, the great filmmaker Luis Buñuel was the first to achieve universal recognition, followed by Pedro Almodóvar in the 1980s. Spanish cinema has also seen international success over the years with films by directors like Segundo de Chomón, Florián Rey, Luis García Berlanga, Carlos Saura, Julio Medem and Alejandro Amenábar. Woody Allen, upon receiving the prestigious Prince of Asturias Award in 2002 in Oviedo remarked: "when I left New York, the most exciting film in the city at the time was Spanish, Pedro Almodovar's one. I hope that Europeans will continue to lead the way in film making because at the moment not much is coming from the United States."

Non-directors have obtained less international notability. Only the cinematographer Néstor Almendros, the actress Penélope Cruz and the actors Fernando Rey, Antonio Banderas, Javier Bardem and Fernando Fernán Gómez have obtained some recognition outside of Spain. Mexican actor Gael García Bernal has also recently received international notoriety in films by Spanish directors.

Today, only 10 to 20% of box office receipts in Spain are generated by domestic films, a situation that repeats itself in many nations of Europe and the Americas. The Spanish government has therefore implemented various measures aimed at supporting local film production and movie theaters, which include the assurance of funding from the main national television stations. The trend is being reversed with the recent screening of mega productions such as the €30 million film Alatriste (starring Viggo Mortensen), the Academy Award winning Spanish/Mexican film Pan's Labyrinth (El Laberinto del Fauno), Volver (starring Penélope Cruz), and Los Borgia (€10 million), all of them sold-out blockbusters in Spain.

Another aspect of Spanish cinema mostly unknown to the general public is the appearance of English-language Spanish films such as The Machinist (starring Christian Bale) The Others (starring Nicole Kidman), Basic Instinct 2 (starring Sharon Stone), and Milos Forman's Goya's Ghosts (starring Javier Bardem and Natalie Portman). All of these films were produced by Spanish firms. This attests to the dynamism and creativity of Spanish directors and producers.

- The following category is a list of percentages of attendance and gross revenues.

Year	Total number of spectators (millions)	Spectators of Spanish cinema (millions)	Percentage	Film	Spectators (millions)	Percentage over the total of Spanish cinema
1996	96.2	10.4	10.8%	*Two Much* (Fernando Trueba)	2.1	20.2%
1997	107.1	13.9	14.9%	*Airbag* (Juanma Bajo Ulloa)	2.1	14.1%
1998	119.8	14.1	13.3%	*Torrente, the stupid arm of the law* (Santiago Segura)	3	21.3%

1999	131.3	18.1	16%	*All About My Mother* (Pedro Almodóvar)	2.5	13.8%
2000	135.3	13.4	11%	*Commonwealth* (Álex de la Iglesia)	1.6	11.9%
2001	146.8	26.2	17.9%	*The Others* (Alejandro Amenábar)	6.2	23.8%
2002	140.7	19.0	13.5%	*The Other Side of the Bed* (Emilio Martínez Lázaro)	2.7	14.3%
2003	137.5	21.7	15.8%	*Mortadelo & Filemón: The Big Adventure* (Javier Fesser)	5.0	22.9%
2004	143.9	19.3	13.4%	*The Sea Inside* (Alejandro Amenábar)	4.0	20.7%
2005	126.0	21.0	16.7%	*Torrente 3: The Protector* (Santiago Segura)	3.6	16.9%
2006 (provisional)	67.8	6.3	9.3%	*Volver* (Pedro Almodóvar)	1.8	28.6%

Language

Main article: Languages of Spain

Castilian

"Spanish" (*españa*) or "Castilian" (Castellano) is a Romance language originally from the northern area of Spain. From there, its use gradually spread inside the Kingdom of Castile, where it evolved and eventually became the principal language of the government and trade. It was later taken to Africa, the Americas and the Philippines when they were brought under Spanish colonial rule between the 15th and 19th centuries.

Today, it is one of the official languages of Spain, most Latin American countries and Equatorial Guinea. In total, 21 nations use Spanish as their primary language. Spanish is also one of six official languages of the United Nations.

Catalan or Valencian

"Catalan", with its "Valencian" dialect is a Romance language, the national language of Andorra, and a co-official language in the Spanish autonomous communities of The Balearic Islands, Catalonia and Valencian Community, and in the city of Alghero in the Italian island of Sardinia. It is also spoken, although with no official recognition, in the autonomous communities of Aragon (in La Franja) and Murcia (in Carche) in Spain, and in the Roussillon region of southern France, which is more or less equivalent to the *département* of the Pyrénées-Orientales.

Basque

Basque language (Euskera or Euskara) is a non indo-European language. Until the 1970s it was in recession, but with the democracy it is taught in the schools and it is more common to hear Basque in the cities and in the areas where it was lost.

Euskera is the only non-indoeuropean language in all western Europe. The origins of this language are a complete mystery. Anyway it is thought that the language was spoken before the Romans came to the Iberian peninsula.

Galician

"Galician" (Galician: *Galego* [ɡaˈleɡo]) is a language of the Western Ibero-Romance branch, spoken in Galicia, an autonomous community with the constitutional status of "historic nationality," located in northwestern Spain and small bordering zones in neighbouring autonomous communities of Asturias and Castilla y León.

Galician and Portuguese were, in medieval times, a single language which linguists call Galician-Portuguese, Medieval Galician, or Old Portuguese, spoken in the territories initially ruled by the medieval Kingdom of Galicia. Both languages are even today united by a dialect continuum[citation needed] located mainly in the northern regions of Portugal.

Aranese

Aranese (Occitan: *Aranés*) is a standardized form of the Pyrenean Gascon variety of the Occitan language spoken in the Val d'Aran, in north western Catalonia on the border between Spain and France, where it is one of the three official languages besides Catalan and Spanish.

Other languages

The following category is a list of languages, dialects and varieties.

- Asturian
- Aragonese
- Cantabrian or *montañés*.
- Leonese
- Extremaduran
- Andalusian Spanish
- Canarian Spanish
- Murcian Spanish

Religion

Main article: Religion in Spain

About 79% of Spaniards identify as belonging to the Roman Catholic religion; 2% identify with another religious faith, and about 19% as non-religious.

Holidays

Main article: Public holidays in Spain

The most important Spanish holiday is "Semana Santa" (Holy Week), celebrated the week before Easter with large parades and other religious events. Spaniards also hold celebrations to honour their local patron saints in churches, cities, towns and villages. The people decorate the streets, build bonfires, set off fireworks and hold large parades, bullfights and beauty contest. One of the best known Spanish celebration is the festival of "San Fermin", which is celebrated every year in July in Pamplona. Bulls are released into the streets, while people run ahead of the animals to the bullring.

Sport

Main article: Sport in Spain

Association Football (Spanish: *Fútbol*) is the most popular Sport of Spain. Notable teams include Atlético de Madrid, FC Barcelona, C.D. Tenerife, Valencia CF and Real Madrid C. F..

A game of Football (Fútbol)

Cuisine

Main article: Spanish cuisine

A significant portion of Spanish cuisine derives from the Roman, Jewish, and Arab traditions. The Moorish people were a strong influence in Spain for many centuries. However, pork is popular and for centuries eating pork was also a statement of Christian ethnicity or "cleanliness of blood", because it was not eaten by Jews or Muslims. Several native foods of the Americas were introduced to Europe through Spain, and a modern Spanish cook could not do without potatoes, tomatoes, peppers, and beans. These are some of the primary influences that have differentiated Spanish cuisine from Mediterranean cuisine, of which Spanish cuisine shares many techniques and food items.

The essential ingredient for real Spanish cooking is olive oil, as Spain produces 44% of the world's olives. However, butter or lard are also important, especially in the north.

Daily meals eaten by Spaniards in many areas of the country are still very often made traditionally by hand, from fresh ingredients bought daily from the local market. This practice is more common in the rural areas and less common in the large urban areas like Barcelona or Madrid, where supermarkets are beginning to displace the open air markets. However, even in Madrid food can be bought from the local shops; bread from the "panadería" and meat from the "carnicería".

One popular custom when going out is to be served tapas with a drink, including sherry, wine and beer. In some areas, like Almería, Granada or Jaén in Andalusia and Madrid or Salamanca in the centre tapas are given for free with a drink and have become very famous for that reason. It should be noted that almost every bar serves something edible when a drink is ordered, without charge. However many bars exist primarily to serve a purchased "tapa".

Another traditional favorite is the churro with a mug of thick hot chocolate to dip churros in. "Churrerías", or stores that serve churros, are quite common. The Chocolatería San Ginés in Madrid is especially famous as a place to stop and have some chocolate with churros, often late into the night (even dawn) after being out on the town. Often traditional Spanish singers and musicians will entertain the guests. [1]

As is true in many countries, the cuisines of Spain differ widely from one region to another, even though they all share certain common characteristics, which include:

- The use of olive oil as a cooking ingredient in items such as fritters. It is also used raw.
- The use of sofrito to start the preparation of many dishes.
- The use of garlic and onions as major seasonings.
- The custom of drinking wine during meals.
- Serving bread with the vast majority of meals.
- Consumption of salads, especially in the summer.
- The consumption of a piece of fruit or a dairy product as dessert. Desserts such as tarts and cakes are typically reserved for special occasions.

A type of Spanish food known as "Tapas" from a bar in Seville.

Education

Main article: Education in Spain

Obligatory Education

	Age	Name
Educacion Primaria (Primary Education)	5-6	Primero (1st grade)
	6-7	Segundo (2nd Grade)
	8-9	Tercero (3rd Grade)
	9-10	Cuarto (4th Grade)
	10-11	Quinto (5th Grade)
	11-12	Sexto (6th Grade)
ESO (Secondary School)	12-13	Primero (first grade)
	13-14	Segundo (second grade)
	14-15	Tercero (third grade)
	15-16	Cuarto (fourth grade)

Optional Education: Bachillerato

- Common subjects are in red;
- Optional Subjects are in pink ;
- Modality Subjects are in blue;
- Technology Via are in yellow
- Natural Sciences Via are in green
- Humanities Via are in olive
- Social Sciences Via are in brown
- Arts Via are in beige

Natural Sciences/Technology	Humanities and Social Sciences	Arts
Physics	History/Geography	
Chemistry	Economy	Technical drawing
Biology	Maths	Painting
Maths	Latin	Sculpture
Technology	Ancient Greek	Audiovisual
Technical drawing	Art History	
2nd Foreign Language French, German, Italian		
Communication and Information Technologies		
Psychology		
Spanish Language		
Philosophy		
1st Foreign Language		
Physical Education only the first year		
Autonomical Languages (only in the autonomies where is spoken) Catalan, Basque, Galician		
Religion only the first year		

Politics

Main article: Politics of Spain

Spain is a democratic parliamentary constitutional monarchy. The Monarch is the head of state, and the President of the Government is the head of government. There are multiple parties and free elections. Executive power is vested in the government. Central legislative power is vested in the two chambers of parliament. The Judiciary is independent of the executive and the legislative.

Regionalism

Main article: Nationalisms and regionalisms of Spain

A strong sense of regional identity exists in many regions of Spain. These regions or nationalities—even those that least identify themselves as Spanish—have contributed greatly to many aspects of mainstream Spanish culture. Spaniards are very proud of their heritage and culture.

Most notably, the Basque Country and Catalonia have widespread nationalist sentiment. Many Basque and Catalan nationalists back statehood for their respective territories. Basque aspirations to statehood have been a cause of violence (notably by ETA), although most Basque nationalists (like virtually all Catalan nationalists) currently seek to fulfill their aspirations peacefully.

There are also several communities where there is a great sense of regional identity: Galicia, Andalusia, Asturias, Navarre, Balearic Islands and Valencia (the last two feeling attached to Catalan culture in different ways) each have their own version of nationalism, but generally with a smaller percentage of nationalists than in the Basque Country and Catalonia.

There are other regions which, despite a broad Spanish nationalist feeling, have strong regional identities: Cantabria, Rioja, Aragon, and Extremadura.

There are also the cases of Madrid, an administrative autonomous community inside the two Castilles; the two north African autonomous cities of Ceuta and Melilla, and the autonomous community of Murcia. Castile was the core kingdom under which Spain eventually unified after centuries of evolution and incorporations. Yet there are also strong movements in the provinces of the extinct region of Leon, pushing to separate from Castile and León.

Spain has a long history of tension between centralism and regionalism. The current organisation of the state into autonomous communities (similar to a federal organisation) under the Spanish Constitution of 1978 is intended as a way to incorporate these communities into the state.

While everyone in Spain can speak Spanish, other languages figure prominently in many regions: Basque "Euskara" in the Basque Country and Navarre; Catalan in Catalonia, Balearic Islands and Valencia (where it is usually referred to as Valencian), and Galician in Galicia. Spanish is official throughout the country; the rest of these have co-official status in their respective regions and all are major enough that there are numerous daily newspapers in these languages and (especially in Catalan) a significant book publishing industry. Many citizens in these regions consider their regional language as their primary language and Spanish as secondary; these languages cover broad enough regions to have multiple distinct dialects. Spanish itself also has distinct dialects around the country, with the Andalusian ('Andaluz') dialect being closer to the Spanish of the Americas, which is heavily influenced.

See also

- Culture
- Iberians
- History of Spain
- Spanish Dance
- Music of Spain

Burgos Cathedral

Burgos Cathedral*	
UNESCO World Heritage Site	
State Party	Spain
Type	Cultural
Criteria	ii, iv, vi
Reference	316 [1]
Region**	Europe and North America
Inscription history	
Inscription	1984 (8th Session)
* Name as inscribed on World Heritage List. [2] ** Region as classified by UNESCO. [3]	

The **Burgos Cathedral** (Spanish: *Catedral de Burgos*) is a Gothic-style Roman Catholic cathedral in Burgos, Spain. It is dedicated to the Virgin Mary and is famous for its vast size and unique architecture. Its construction began in 1221, following French Gothic parameters.

It had very important modifications in the 15th and 16th centuries (spires of the principal façade, Chapel of the Constable, cimborio of the transept: these elements of advanced Gothic give the cathedral its distinguished profile). The last works of importance (the sacristy or the Chapel of Saint Thecla) occurred during the 18th century, the century in which the Gothic statuary of the doors of the principal façade was also transformed.

At the beginning of the 20th century, some semidetached construction to the cathedral was eliminated, such as the Archepiscopal Palace and the upper floor of the cloister. The style of the cathedral is Gothic, although it has inside some Renaissance and Baroque decorations.

In the cathedral, works of extraordinary artists are kept, such as the architects and sculptors of the Colonia family (Juan, Simón and Francisco), the sculptors Gil de Siloé, Felipe Vigarny or Juan de Anchieta, the sculptor and architect Diego de Siloé, the grillworker Cristóbal de Andino or the painter Sebastiano del Piombo ("Holy Family On A Voyage"), among many others.

The cathedral was declared a World Heritage Site by UNESCO on October 31, 1984. It is the only Spanish cathedral that has this distinction independently, without being joined to the historic center of a city (as in Salamanca, Santiago de Compostela, Ávila, Córdoba, Toledo, Alcalá de Henares or Cuenca) or in union with others buildings, as in Seville.

The principal façade was inspired in the purest French Gothic style of the cathedrals of Paris and of Reims. It consists of three bays topped by two lateral, square towers. The steep spires of German influence were added in the 15th century and are the work of Juan de Colonia.

Some elements of great interest of within of the cathedral are the 'Papamoscas (Flycatcher), *an articulated statue which opens its mouth upon the sounding of the bells at each hour, the Romanesque sepulchre of Mudarra, the vengeful stepbrother of the death of the seven princes de Lara (brought to the cathedral from its original location in the Monastery of San Pedro de Arlanza due to its abandonment by alienation), the carved chairs of the choir, the sepulchre of the Bishop Mauricio, the tomb of El Cid and his wife Doña Jimena, the letter of security of El Cid and his chest.*

History

Mayor chapel

The construction of the cathedral was ordered by King Ferdinand III of Castile and Mauricio, the English-born Bishop of Burgos. Construction started on the site of the former Romanesque cathedral on July 20, 1221, beginning at the chevet, which was completed in nine years. The high altar was first consecrated in 1260, then there was a lengthy hiatus of almost 200 years before construction was recommenced. The cathedral was completed in 1567, with the completion of the lantern spire over the main crossing (which rises above a delicate openwork star vault).

The architects principally responsible for its construction were a Frenchman in the 13th century and a German in the 15th century. In 1417, the bishop of Burgos attended the Council of Constance and returned with the master builder John of Cologne (*Juan de Colonia*), who completed the towers with spires of open stonework tracery.

Among the most famous of the bishops of Burgos was the 15th-century scholar and historian Alphonsus a Sancta Maria.

In 1919 the cathedral became the burial place of Rodrigo Díaz de Vivar ("El Cid"), and his wife Doña Jimena. On October 31, 1984, it was designated a World Heritage Site by UNESCO.

Architecture

The 15th-century west front of northern French gothic style is flanked by towers on square plans terminating in octagonal spires covered with open stonework traceries. The façade, in three stories, has triple entrances in ogival arched framing, with a gallery enclosed by a pinnacled balustrade and a delicately-pierced rose window. In the uppermost story, there are two ogival double-arched windows and statues on pedestals, crowned with a balustrade of letters carved in stone: PULC[H]RA ES ET DECORA ("Beautiful art Thou, and graceful"), in the center of which is a statue of the Virgin Mary. There are more balustrades and balconies in the towers, with further open-carved inscriptions: needle-pointed octagonal pinnacles finish the four corners. The main spires are 88 meters tall.

Condestable chapel.

Its cruciform floorplan, with a 106 meter long nave and wide aisles is almost hidden, in exterior views,by the fifteen chapels added at all angles to the aisles and transepts, by the beautiful 14th-century cloister on the northwest and the archiepiscopal palace on the southwest. Over the three central doorways of the main or western façade rise the two lofty and graceful towers, crowned by their spires. Many of the altars, chapels and monuments within the cathedral are of artistic and historical interest.

The north transept portal, known as the *Portada de la Coronería*, has statues of the Twelve Apostles. Above, ogival windows and two spires crown the portal. On the south portal, the portada depicts the evangelists at their writing desks.

The magnificent octagonal Chapel of the Condestable is of Flamboyant Gothic style, filled with traceries, knights and angels and heraldry. It was destined for the graves of Pedro Fernández de Velasco, 2nd Count of Haro, Condestable of Castile and his family.

See also

- Roman Catholic Archdiocese of Burgos

External links

- World Heritage Site profile [4]
- Virtual visit of the cathedral on high resolution [5]

Geographical coordinates: 42°20′26.9″N 3°42′16.1″W

El Escorial

"El Real Monasterio de El Escorial"	
A distant view of "El Real Monasterio de El Escorial"	
Location:	San Lorenzo de El Escorial, Spain
Coordinates:	40°34′54.3″N 4°07′35.1″W
Architect:	Juan Bautista de Toledo
Governing body:	Ministry of the Presidency
UNESCO World Heritage Site	
Official name: Monastery and Site of the Escorial, Madrid	
Type:	Cultural
Criteria:	i, ii, iv
Designated:	1984 (8th session)
Reference #:	318 [1]
State Party:	Spain
Region:	Europe and North America
Spanish Property of Cultural Interest	
Official name: Monasterio de San Lorenzo	
Type:	Real property
Criteria:	Monument
Designated:	3 June 1931
Reference #:	(R.I.) - 51 - 0001064 - 00000
Location of El Escorial within Madrid	

El Escorial is a historical residence of the king of Spain, in the town of San Lorenzo de El Escorial, about 45 kilometres (28 miles) northwest of the Spanish capital, Madrid. It is one of the Spanish royal sites and functions as a monastery, royal palace, museum, and school.

El Escorial comprises two architectural complexes of great historical and cultural significance: *El Real Monasterio de El Escorial* itself and *La Granjilla de La Fresneda*, a royal hunting lodge and monastic retreat about five kilometres away. These sites have a dual nature; that is to say, during the 16th and 17th centuries, they were places in which the temporal power of the Spanish monarchy *and* the ecclesiastical predominance of the Roman Catholic religion in Spain found a common architectural manifestation. El Escorial was, at once, a monastery and a Spanish royal palace. Originally a property of the Hieronymite monks, it is now a monastery of the Order of Saint Augustine.

Façade of the Monastery of El Escorial

Philip II of Spain, reacting to the Protestant Reformation sweeping through Europe during the 16th century, devoted much of his lengthy reign (1556-1598) and much of his seemingly inexhaustible supply of New World gold to stemming the Protestant tide. His protracted efforts were, in the long run, partly successful; however, the same counter-reformational impulse had a much more benign expression thirty years earlier in Philip's decision to build the complex at El Escorial.

Philip engaged the Spanish architect, Juan Bautista de Toledo, to be his collaborator in the design of El Escorial. Juan Bautista had spent the greater part of his career in Rome, where he had worked on the basilica of St. Peter's, and in Naples, where he had served the king's viceroy, whose recommendation brought him to the king's attention. Philip appointed him architect-royal in 1559, and together they designed El Escorial as a monument to Spain's role as a center of the Christian world.

On November 2, 1984, UNESCO declared The Royal Site of San Lorenzo of El Escorial a World Heritage Site. It is an extremely popular tourist attraction, often visited by day-trippers from Madrid - more than 500,000 visitors come to El Escorial every year.

Design and conception

El Escorial is situated at the foot of Mt. Abantos in the Sierra de Guadarrama. It is a bleak, semi-forested, wind-swept place that owes its name to nearby piles of slag or tailings, called *scoria*, the detritus of long-played-out iron mines in the Guadarrama.

This austere location, hardly an obvious choice for the site of a royal palace, was chosen by King Philip II of Spain, and it was he who ordained the building of a grand edifice here to commemorate the 1557 Spanish victory at the Battle of St. Quentin in Picardy against Henry II, king of France. He also intended the complex to serve as a necropolis for the interment of the remains of his parents, Charles I and Isabella of Portugal, himself, and his descendants. In addition, Philip envisioned El Escorial as a center for studies in aid of the Counter-Reformation cause.

The building's cornerstone was laid on April 23, 1563. The design and construction were overseen by Juan Bautista de Toledo, who did not live to see the completion of the project. With Toledo's death in 1567, direction passed to his apprentice, Juan de Herrera, under whom the building was completed in 1584, in less than 21 years.

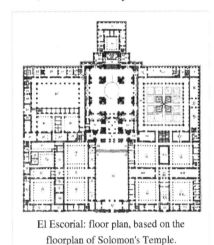

El Escorial: floor plan, based on the floorplan of Solomon's Temple.

Since then, El Escorial has been the burial site for most of the Spanish kings of the last five centuries, Bourbons as well as Habsburgs. The Royal Pantheon contains the tombs of the Holy Roman Emperor, Charles V (who ruled Spain as King Charles I), Philip II, Philip III, Philip IV, Charles II, Louis I, Charles III, Charles IV, Ferdinand VII, Isabella II, Alfonso XII, and Alfonso XIII. Two Bourbon kings, Philip V (who reigned from 1700 to 1746) and Ferdinand VI (1746-1759), as well as King Amadeus (1870-1873), are not buried in the monastery.

The floor plan of the building is in the form of a gridiron. The traditional belief is that this design was chosen in honor of St. Lawrence, who, in the third century AD, was martyred by being roasted to death on a grill. St. Lawrence's feast day is August 10, the same date as the 1557 Battle of St. Quentin.

In fact, however, the origin of the building's layout is quite controversial. The grill-like shape, which did not fully emerge until Herrera eliminated from the original conception the six interior towers of the facade, was, by no means, unique to El Escorial. Other buildings had been constructed with interior courtyards fronting on churches or chapels; King's College, Cambridge, dating from 1441, is one such example; the old Ospedale Maggiore, Milan's first hospital, begun in 1456 by Antonio Filarete, is another grid-like building with interior courtyards. In fact, palaces of this approximate design were commonplace in the Byzantine and Arab world. Strikingly similar to El Escorial is the layout of the

Alcázar of Seville and the design of the Alhambra at Granada where, as at El Escorial, two courtyards in succession separate the main portal of the complex from a fully-enclosed place of worship.

Nonetheless, the most persuasive theory for the origin of the floor plan is that it is based on descriptions of the Temple of Solomon by the Judeo-Roman historian, Flavius Josephus: a portico followed by a courtyard open to the sky, followed by a second portico and a second courtyard, all flanked by arcades

El Escorial was constructed from a plan based on the descriptions of Solomon's temple.

and enclosed passageways, leading to the "holy of holies". Statues of David and Solomon on either side of the entrance to the basilica of El Escorial lend further weight to the theory that this is the true origin of the design. A more personal connection can be drawn between the David-warrior figure, representing Charles V, and his son, the stolid and solomonically prudent Philip II. Echoing the same theme, a fresco in the center of El Escorial's library, a reminder of Solomon's legendary wisdom, affirms Philip's preoccupation with the great Jewish king, his thoughtful and logical character, and his extraordinary monumental temple.

The Temple-of-Solomon design, if indeed it was the basis for El Escorial, was extensively modified to accommodate the additional functions and purposes Philip II intended the building to serve. Beyond being a monastery, El Escorial is also a pantheon, a basilica, a convent, a school, a library, and a royal palace. All these functional demands resulted in a doubling of the building's size from the time of its original conception.

Built primarily from locally-quarried gray granite, square and sparsely-ornamented, El Escorial is austere, even forbidding, in its outward appearance, seemingly more like a fortress than a monastery or palace. It takes the form of a gigantic quadrangle, approximately 224 m by 153 m, which encloses a series of intersecting passageways and courtyards and chambers. At each of the four corners is a square tower surmounted by a spire, and, near the center of the complex (and taller than the rest) rise the pointed belfries and round dome of the basilica. Philip's instructions to Toledo were simple and clear, directing that the architects should produce "simplicity in the construction, severity in the whole, nobility without arrogance, majesty without ostentation."

Aside from its explicit purposes, the complex is also an enormous storehouse of art. It displays masterworks by Titian, Tintoretto, El Greco, Velázquez, Roger van der Weyden, Paolo Veronese, Alonso Cano, José de Ribera, Claudio Coello and others. The library contains thousands of priceless manuscripts; for example, the collection of the sultan, Zidan Abu Maali, who ruled Morocco from 1603 to 1627, is housed at El Escorial. Giambattista Castello designed the magnificent main staircase.

Sections of the building

In order to describe the parts of the great building in a coherent fashion, it may be useful to undertake an imaginary walking tour, beginning with the main entrance at the center of the western facade:

The patio of the kings

Patio of the Kings and the Basilica.

The first thing you find upon arriving to El Escorial is the main Façade. This has three doors: the middle one leads to the Patio de los Reyes and the side ones lead to a school and the other to a monastery. On the façade there is a niche where the image of a saint has been placed. The Patio de los Reyes is an enclosure that owes its name to the statues of the Kings of Judah that adorn the façade of the Basílica, located at the back, from which you can access from the patio. This spectacular basilica has a floor in the shape of a Greek cross and an enormous cupola inspired by St. Peter's Basilica in Rome. The naves are covered with canyon vaults decorated with frescoes by Lucas Jordán. The large chapel is one of the highlights in the basilica, presided by steps of red marble. Its main altarpiece is 30 meters high and divided in compartments of different sizes where are find bronze sculptures and canvas authored by Tibaldi, Zuccari or Leoni. In the Capitulary and the Sacristy Rooms, painting such as *Joseph's Coat* by Velázquez, *The Last Supper* by Titian, or *The Adoration of the Sacred Host by Charles II* by Claudio Coello are on exhibit.

Under the royal chapel of the Basilica is the Royal Pantheon. This is the place of burial for the kings of Spain. It is an octagonal Baroque mausoleum made of marble where all of the Spanish monarchs since Charles I have been buried, with the exception of Philip V, Ferdinand of Savoy, and Amadeus of Savoy. The remains of Juan de Borbon, father of Juan Carlos I (Spain's current king), also rest in this pantheon despite the fact that he never became king himself. The enclosure is presided over by an altar of veined marble, and the sarcaphogi are bronze and marble. also find the Pantheon of the Princes, where the bodies of the queens who did not have a crowned succession and the princes and princesses were laid to rest. This part was built in the nineteenth century.

After the Basilica is the Patio of the Evangelists. This is a gardened patio in whose center rises a magnificent pavilion by Juan de Herrera in which you can find sculptures of the Evangelists. Around the patio are the galleries of the main cloister, decorated with frescoes in which scenes from the history of the Redemption are represented. In the East gallery, you find the splendid main stair case with a fresco-decorated vaulted ceiling depicting *The glory of the Spanish monarchy.*

Next is the Palacio de los Austrias, also known as the Casa del Rey (House of the King), which is found behind the presbytery of the basilica. The outbuildings of this palace are distributed around the patio of the Mascarones, of Italian style. Inside the House of the King are the *Sala de las Batallas* (Hall of Battles), which contains frescoes of the battles of San Quintín and Higueruela, among others. The next building contains the rooms of Philip II and of the Infanta Isabel Clara Eugenia. Another outbuilding is that of Alcoba del Rey, housing the bed in which Philip II died.

The basilica

The basilica of San Lorenzo el Real, the central building in the El Escorial complex, was originally designed, like most of the late Gothic cathedrals of western Europe, to take the form of a Latin cross. As such, it has a long nave on the west-east axis intersected by a pair of shorter transepts, one to the north and one directly opposite, to the south, about three-quarters of the way between the west entrance and the high altar. This plan was modified by Juan de Herrera to that of a Greek cross, a form with all four arms of equal length. Coincident with this shift in approach, the bell towers at the western end of the church were somewhat reduced in size and the small

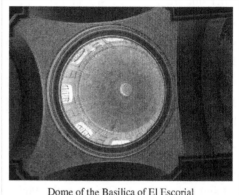

Dome of the Basilica of El Escorial

half-dome intended to stand over the altar was replaced with a full circular dome over the center of the church, where the four arms of the Greek cross meet.

Clearly Juan Bautista de Toledo's experience with the dome of St. Peter's basilica in Rome influenced the design of the dome of San Lorenzo el Real at El Escorial. However, the Roman dome is supported by ranks of tapered Corinthian columns, with their extravagant capitals of acanthus leaves and their elaborately fluted shafts, while the dome at El Escorial, soaring nearly one hundred metres into the air, is supported by four heavy granite piers connected by simple Romanesque arches and decorated by simple Doric pilasters, plain, solid, and largely unprepossessing. It would not be a flight of fancy to interpret St. Peter's as the quintessential expression of Baroque sensuality and the basilica at El Escorial as a statement of the stark rigidity and grim purposefulness of the Inquisition, the two sides of the Counter-Reformation.

The most highly-decorated part of the church is the area surrounding the high altar. Behind the altar is a three-tiered reredos, made of red granite and jasper, nearly twenty-eight metres tall, adorned with gilded bronze statuary by Leone Leoni, and three sets of religious paintings commissioned by Philip II. To either side are gilded life-size bronzes of the kneeling family groups of Charles and Philip, also by Leoni with help from his son Pompeo. In a shallow niche at the center of the lowest level is a repository for the physical elements of the communion ceremony, a so-called "House of the Sacrament", designed by Juan de Herrera in jasper and bronze.

Pantheon of the Evangelists.

To decorate the *reredos*, or altar screens, the king's preferences were Michelangelo or Titian, but both of these giants were already more than eighty years old and in frail health. Consequently, Philip consulted his foreign ambassadors for recommendations, and the result was a lengthy parade of the lesser European artists of that time, all swanning through the construction site at El Escorial seeking the king's favor.

Palace of Philip II

Situated next to the main altar of the Basilica, the residence of King Philip II is made up of a series of austerely decorated rooms. It features a window from which the king could observe mass from his bed when incapacitated by the gout that afflicted him.

Hall of Battles

Fresco paintings here depict the most important Spanish military victories. These include a medieval victory over the Moors, as well as several of Philip's campaigns against the French.

Pantheon of the Kings

This consists of twenty-six marble sepulchers containing the remains of the kings and queens regnant (the only queen regnant since Philip II being Isabella II), of the Habsburg and Bourbon dynasties from Charles I to the present, except for Philip V and Ferdinand VI.

The sepulchers also contain the remains of royal consorts who were parents of monarchs. The only king consort is Francis of Asis de Bourbon, husband of queen Isabella II. The most recent remains in the sepulcher are those of King Alfonso XIII. Those of his wife, as well as his son Juan, Count of Barcelona, and daughter-in-law Maria de las Mercedes (the parents of the current king, Juan Carlos I), lie at a prepared place called a *pudridero*, or decaying chamber.

There are two *pudrideros* at El Escorial, one for the Pantheon of the Kings and the other for that of the Princes, which can only be visited by monks from the Monastery. In these rooms, the remains of the deceased are placed in a small leaden urn, which in turn will be placed in the marble sepulchers of the pantheon after the passage of fifty years, the estimated time necessary for the complete decomposition of the bodies.

When the remains of Juan and Maria Mercedes are deposited in the Royal Pantheon, they will, in a sense, constitute exceptions to tradition. First, the Count Barcelona was never able to reign, due to the institution of the Second Republic and the exile of Alfonso XIII and his entire family, though they are the parents of a King, and their remains are in the Pantheon. Second, the Pantheon also contains the remains of Victoria Eugenie of Battenberg, who, although the wife of a King, was never the mother of a king in the strict sense. Some, however, do consider Juan to have been *de jure* King of Spain, which in turn would make Queen Victoria Eugenia the mother of a king. With the interment of Juan and Maria's remains, all the sepulchers in the Royal Pantheon will be filled; no decision has yet been announced as to the final resting place of the currently-living members of the Royal Family.

There has already been one exception to this old tradition: Elisabeth of Bourbon is for the moment the only queen in the pantheon who has not been mother to a King. That is because her only son, the presumed Heir to the Throne, died after her.

The walls of polished Toledo marble are ornamented in gold-plated bronze.

All of the wood used in El Escorial comes from the ancient forests of Sagua La Grande, on the so-called Golden Coast of Cuba.

Pantheon of the Princes

Completed in 1888, this is the final resting place of princes, princesses and queens who were not mothers of kings. With floors and ceiling of white marble, the tomb of Prince John of Austria is especially notable. Currently, thirty-seven of the sixty available niches are filled.

Art Gallery

Consists of works of the German, Flemish, Venetian, Lombard, Ligurian and more Italian and Spanish schools from the fifteenth, sixteenth and seventeenth centuries.

Architectural Museum

Its eleven rooms showcase the tools, cranes and other materials used in the construction of the edifice, as well as reproductions of blueprints and documents related to the project, containing some very interesting facts.

Gardens of the Friars

Constructed at the order of Philip II, a great lover of nature, these constitute an ideal place for repose and meditation. Manuel Azaña, who studied in the monastery's Augustinian-run school, mentions them in his *Memorias* (Memoirs) and his play *El jardín de los frailes* (The Garden of the Friars). Students at the school still use it today to study and pass the time.

Library

Philip II donated his personal collection of documents to the building, and also undertook the acquisition of the finest libraries and works of Spain and foreign countries. It was planned by Juan de Herrera, who also designed the library's shelves; the frescoes on the vaulted ceilings were painted by Pellegrino Tibaldi. The library's collection consists of more than 40,000 volumes, located in a great hall fifty-four meters in length, nine meters wide and ten meters tall with marble floors and beautifully carved wood shelves.

Benito Arias Montano produced the initial catalog for the library, selecting many of the most important volumes. In 1616 he was granted the privilege of receiving a copy of every published work, though there is no evidence that he ever took advantage of this right.

The vault of the library's ceiling is decorated with frescoes depicting the seven liberal arts: Rhetoric, Dialectic, Music, Grammar, Arithmetic, Geometry and Astronomy.

The reliquaries

Following a rule approved by the Council of Trent dealing with the veneration of saints, Philip II donated to the monastery one of the largest reliquaries in all of Catholicism. The collection consists of some 7500 relics, which are stored in 570 sculpted reliquaries designed by Juan de Herrera. Most of them were constructed by the artisan, Juan de Arfe Villafañe. These reliquaries are found in highly varied forms (heads, arms, pyramidal cases, coffers, etc.) and are distributed throughout the monastery, with the most important being concentrated in the basilica.

Adjacent buildings

Juan de Herrera also designed the Casas de Oficios or Official Buildings opposite the monastery's north façade, and his successor, Francisco de Mora, designed the Casa de la Compaña (Company Quarters).

See also

- La Granjilla de La Fresneda de El Escorial
- Juan Bautista de Toledo
- Juan de Herrera
- Philip II of Spain
- Charles V, Holy Roman Emperor
- Town of El Escorial
- San Lorenzo de El Escorial, Madrid
- List of World Heritage Sites in Spain
- Valle de los Caídos
- Golden Age
- Renaissance
- Replicas of the Jewish Temple

References

- *This article draws heavily on the 31 December 2006 version of the corresponding article in the Spanish-language Wikipedia.*

External links

- Practical Information for Public Visits [1]
- Patrimonio Nacional | Royal Seat of San Lorenzo de El Escorial [2]
- Jardin del Monasterio de El Escorial - a Gardens Guide review [3]
- El Escorial Monastery - History and Photos [4]
- 74 Photos of El Escorial [5]
- Maps showing areas of outstanding natural beauty, educational, scientific or cultural importance in Spain [6]
- El Escorial tourist and travel connexions guide (Eng) [7]
- COPYRIGHT IN THE RENAISSANCE [8]
- HISTORIA DEL REAL MONASTERIO DE SAN LORENZO [9]

Poblet Monastery

Poblet Monastery*	
UNESCO World Heritage Site	
Type	Cultural
Criteria	i, iv
Reference	518 [1]
Region**	Europe and North America
Inscription history	
Inscription	1991 (15th Session)
* Name as inscribed on World Heritage List. [2] ** Region as classified by UNESCO. [3]	

The **Monastery of Santa Maria de Poblet** (Catalan: *Reial Monestir de Santa Maria de Poblet*, Spanish: *Real Monasterio de Santa María de Poblet*) is a Cistercian monastery, founded in 1151, located in the comarca of Conca de Barberà, in Catalonia (Spain). It was founded by Cistercian monks from France. The main architect was Arnau Bargués.

It was the royal pantheon of the kings of the Crown of Aragon since James I of Aragon.

Closed down due to the State's laws in 1835, the monastery was refounded in 1940 by Italian monks of the same order. Poblet belongs to the Cistercian Congregation of the Crown of Aragon, along with Santa Maria de Solius and nunneries such as Santa Maria de Vallbona and Santa Maria de Valldonzella. The Abbot of Poblet is the ex officio chairman of the Congregation. Today the monastic community of Poblet is composed of 29 professed monks, 1 regular oblate, 1 novice and 2 familiars.

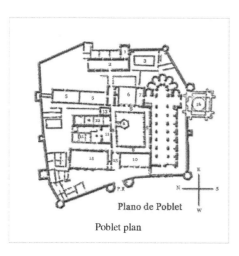

Plano de Poblet

Poblet plan

This monastery was the first of three sister monasteries, known as the Cistercian triangle, that helped consolidate power in Catalonia in the 12th century. (The other two are Vallbona de les Monges and Santes Creus)

It is a UNESCO World Heritage Site, since 1991. The altar (1527) was sculpted by Damián Forment.

Patrons

• Pedro Antonio de Aragón

External links

• Monestir de Poblet Official website [2] (Catalan) (Spanish) (English)
• Adrian Fletcher's Paradoxplace Poblet Pages (photos) [3]
• Monestirs de Catalunya. Poblet [4] (Catalan only)

Geographical coordinates: 41°22′51″N 1°04′57″E

Palmeral of Elche

Geographical coordinates: 38°16′10″N 0°41′54″W

<table>
<tr><td colspan="2" align="center">Palmeral of Elche*
UNESCO World Heritage Site</td></tr>
<tr><td colspan="2" align="center"></td></tr>
<tr><td>State Party</td><td>▨ Spain</td></tr>
<tr><td>Type</td><td>Cultural</td></tr>
<tr><td>Criteria</td><td>ii, v</td></tr>
<tr><td>Reference</td><td>930 [1]</td></tr>
<tr><td>Region**</td><td>Europe and North America</td></tr>
<tr><td colspan="2" align="center">Inscription history</td></tr>
<tr><td>Inscription</td><td>2000 (24th Session)</td></tr>
<tr><td colspan="2">* Name as inscribed on World Heritage List. [2]
** Region as classified by UNESCO. [3]</td></tr>
</table>

The **Palmeral of Elche** (Spanish: *Palmeral de Elche*, Valencian: *Palmerar d'Elx*) is a plantation of palm trees in the Spanish province of Alicante. It is the largest palm grove (Spanish: *palmeral*) in Europe and one of the largest in the world, surpassed in size only by some in Arab countries.

The Palmeral includes the *Parque Municipal* and many other orchards (*huertos*), covering over 3.5 km^2 (1.4 sq mi), including 1.5 km^2 (0.58 sq mi) within the city of Elche (Elx). It contains more than 11,000 palm trees, mostly date palms (*Phoenix dactylifera*), with individual specimens up to 300 years old. At its peak, in the 18th century, it may have covered an area twice as large, with up to 200,000 trees. The dates are harvested in December. A famous date palm is the "Imperial Palm" (*Palmera Imperial*), with 7 stems in the shape of a candelabra, named after Elisabeth, known as Sissi, the Empress consort of Franz Joseph, who visited the plantation in 1894.

It is thought that palms were originally planted in this location as early as the 5th century BC by Carthaginians who settled in south-east Spain. The plantation survived under the Romans and the

Moors. The irrigation system was extended in the times of Abd ar-Rahman I and remains in use. The formal landscape of the palmeral that still exists today was created when the city was under Moorish control in the 10th century. Although the area has an annual rainfall of only 300 mm (12 in), the palm trees planted along a network of irrigation canals from the salty River Vinalopó creates a patchwork of agricultural plots (*huertos*), each demarcated and shaded by the palm trees to create a protected microclimate. Laws were passed to protect the plantation after the *Reconquista*.

In 2005, it was discovered that the larvae of the red palm weevil (*Rhynchophorus ferrugineus*) had infested some trees, laying its eggs inside the stems.

References

- *This article is based on a translation of the equivalent article of the Spanish Wikipedia, dated 4 July 2006*
- Palmeral of Elche [1] from UNESCO
- El Palmeral de Elche - A Cultural Landscape Inherited from Al-Andalus [2]

External links

- Elche Spain [3] City overview with detailed map. From a local citizen.
- Information on the *picudo rojo* (red palm weevil) [4] (Spanish)

View of the palm trees in the *Parque Municipal*.

Overview of Valencia

Valencia, Spain

Valencia València	
Aerial view of Central Valencia	
 Flag	 **Coat of arms**
Location of Valencia in the Valencian Community	
Valencia  Location of Valencia in Spain	
Coordinates: 39°28′13″N 0°22′36″W	
Country	Spain
Autonomous Community	Valencian Community
Province	Valencia
Comarca	Valencia
Founded	137 BC
Districts	Ciutat Vella, Eixample, Extramurs, Campanar, Saïdia, Pla del Real, Olivereta, Patraix, Jesús, Quatre Carreres, Poblados Marítimos, Caminos al Grao, Algirós, Benimaclet, Poblados del Norte, Poblados del Oeste, Poblados del Sur

Government	
- Type	Mayor-council government
- Body	Ajuntament de València
- Mayor	Rita Barberá Nolla (PP)
Area	
- City	134.65 km^2 (52 sq mi)
Elevation	15 m (49 ft)
Population (2009)INE	
- City	814208
- Density	6046.8/km^2 (15661.3/sq mi)
- Urban	1,175,000 to 1,564,145
- Metro	1,705,742 to 2,300,000
Demonym	valencià (m), valenciana (f) valenciano (m), valenciana (f)
Time zone	CET (GMT +1)
- Summer (DST)	CEST (GMT +2) (UTC)
Postcode	46000-46080
ISO 3166-2	ES-V
Website	http://www.valencia.es

Valencia (Spanish IPA: [baˈlenθja]) or **València** (Valencian IPA: [vaˈlensja]) is the capital and most populous city of the Autonomous Community of Valencia and the third largest city in Spain, with a population of 814,208 in 2009. It is the 15th-most populous municipality in the European Union. About 1,175,000 or 1,564,145. people live in the Valencia urban area and 1,705,742 or 2,300,000 in the Valencia metropolitan area.

It is integrated into an industrial area on the Costa del Azahar. Its main festival, the Falles, is known worldwide, while the traditional dish, paella, originated around Valencia.

The city contains a dense monumental heritage, including the Llotja de la Seda (World Heritage Site since 1996), but its landmark is undoubtedly the City of Arts and Sciences, an avant-garde and futuristic museum complex.

Name

The original Latin name of the city was *Valentia* (/wa'lentia/), meaning "strength", "valour", the city being named for the Roman practice of recognizing the valour of former Roman soldiers after a war. The Roman historian Titus Livius (Livy) explains that the founding of Valentia in the 2nd century BC was due to the settling of the Roman soldiers who fought against Iberian local rebel, Viriatus.

During the rule of the Muslim Empires in Spain, it was known as بلنسية (*Balansiya*) in Arabic.

By regular sound changes, this has become *Valencia* Spanish pronunciation: [ba'lenθja] in Castillian and *València* Catalan pronunciation: [va'lensja] in Standard Valencian.

History

In Roman times Valencia formed part of the then province of *Edetania*. The Roman historian Florus says that in 140 BC Junius Brutus transferred the soldiers who had fought under him to that province: the Roman city, known as *Valentia Edetanorum*, was founded in 137 BC on the site of a former Iberian town, by the river Turia.

Later it was a Roman military colony. In punishment for its adherence to Sertorius it was destroyed by Pompey, but was later rebuilt, and Pomponius Mela says that it was one of the principal cities of Tarraconensis province.

The city has been occupied by the Visigoths, the Moors and the Catalan and Aragonese.

The Moors (Berbers and Arabs) occupied the territory peacefully in 714 A.D. When Islamic culture settled in, Valencia − then Balansiya − prospered, thanks to a booming trade in paper, silk, leather, ceramics, glass and silver-work. The architectural legacy from this period is abundant in Valencia and can still be appreciated today in the remains of the old walls, the Baños del Almirante bath house, Portal de Valldigna street and even the Cathedral and the tower, El Micalet, which was the minaret of the old mosque.

After the death of Almanzor and the unrest that followed, Muslim Al-Andalus broke up into numerous small states known as taifas, one of which was the Taifa of Valencia which would exist for four distinct periods - 1010 to 1065, 1075 to 1099, 1145 to 1147 and last from 1229 to 1238.

'the Cid' conquered Valencia for the short period from 15 June 1094 − July 1099. He turned nine mosques into churches and installed the French monk Jérôme as bishop (this victory was immortalised in the Lay of the Cid). On the death of the Cid (July 1099), his wife, Doña Ximena, retained power for two years, after which Valencia was besieged by the Almoravids.

The city was returned to the Almoravids in 1102. Although the 'Emperor of Spain' Alfonso drove them from the city, he was not strong enough to hold it. The Christians set fire to it, abandoned it, and the Almoravid Masdali took possession of it on 5 May 1109. The event was commemorated in a poem by Ibn Khafaja in which he thanked Yusuf ibn Tashfin for the liberation of the city. The Almoravid and the Almohad dynasty would rule Valencia for more than a century.

In 1238, King James I of Aragon the Conqueror, with an army composed of French, English, Germans and Italians, laid siege to Valencia and on September 28 in that same year forced a surrender. 50,000 Moors were forced to leave. Poets like Ibn al-Abbar and Ibn Amira mourned their exile from their beloved Valencia.

On October 9, King James, followed by his retinue and army, took possession. The principal mosque was - a Christians regarded it - purified and turned into a Church where Mass was celebrated and the "Te Deum" sung. James incorporated city and territory into the newly formed Kingdom of Valencia, one of the kingdoms forming the Crown of Aragon, and populated the new Kingdom with Catalan people on the coast and Aragonese people on the interior.

Catholic sources state that Saint Vincent Ferrer preached so successfully (sometime between 1390 and 1411), converting thousands of Jews, that he was permitted to employ the synagogue for his newly-founded hospital of San Salvador.

In the 15th and 16th centuries, Valencia was one of the major cities in the Mediterranean. The writer Joanot Martorell, author of *Tirant lo Blanch*, and the poet Ausiàs March are famous Valencians of that era.

The first printing press in the Iberian Peninsula was located in Valencia. The first printed Bible in a Romance language, Valencian Bible, was printed in Valencia circa 1478, attributed to Bonifaci Ferrer.

Valencian bankers lent funds to Queen Isabella for Columbus' trip in 1492.

In 1519–1522 the *Guilds revolts* took place. In 1609, the *Moriscos* were expelled from the city.

During the War of the Spanish Succession, Valencia sided with Charles of Austria. On 24 January 1706, Charles Mordaunt, 3rd Earl of Peterborough, 1st Earl of Monmouth, led a handful of English cavalrymen into the city after riding south from Barcelona, capturing the nearby fortress at Sagunt, and bluffing the Spanish Bourbon army into withdrawal.

The English held the city for 16 months and defeated several attempts to expel them. English soldiers advanced as far as Requena on the road to Madrid. After the victory of the Bourbons at the Battle of Almansa (25 April 1707), the English army evacuated Valencia and the city subsequently lost its privileges, including important civil rights called *furs* by the way the Bourbons decided to burn important cities like Xativa, where actually is still the picture of the Spanish Bourbon turned back as protest.

During the Peninsular War Valencia was besieged by the French under Marshal Suchet from Christmas Day 1811, until it fell on January 8 the next year.

The last victim of the Spanish Inquisition, a local schoolteacher called Cayetano Ripoll, was executed in Valencia in July 1826 accused of being a deist and freemason.

During the Spanish Civil War, the capital of the Republic was moved to Valencia. The city suffered from the blockade and siege by Franco's forces. The postwar period was hard for Valencians. During the Franco years, speaking or teaching Valencian was prohibited; in a significant reversal it is now compulsory for every child studying in Valencia.

Modern history

In 1957 the city suffered a severe flood by the Turia River, with 5 metres (16 ft) of water in some streets. One consequence of this was that a decision was made to drain and reroute the river and it now passes around the Western and southern suburbs of the city. A plan to turn the drained area into a motorway was dropped in favour of a picturesque 7 km (4 mi) park which bisects the city.

Valencia was granted Autonomous Statutes in 1982.

On 9 July 2006, during Mass at Valencia's Cathedral, Our Lady of the Forsaken Basilica, Pope Benedict XVI used, at the World Day of Families, the *Santo Caliz*, a 1st-century Middle-Eastern artifact believed by many to be the Holy Grail. It was supposedly brought to that church by Emperor Valerian in the 3rd century, after having been brought by St. Peter to Rome from Jerusalem. The *Santo Caliz* ("Holy Chalice") is a simple, small stone cup. Its base was added in medieval times and consists of fine gold, alabaster and gem stones.

Valencia was selected in 2003 to host the historic America's Cup yacht race, the first European city ever to do so. The America's Cup matches took place in summer 2007. On 3 July 2007, *Alinghi* defeated *Team New Zealand* and successfully defended the America's Cup. 22 days later, on 25 July 2007, the leaders of the Alinghi syndicate, holder of the America's Cup, officially announced that Valencia would be the host city for the 33rd America's Cup, held in June 2009.

Architecture

The ancient winding streets of the Barrio del Carmen contain buildings dating to Roman and Arabic times. The Cathedral, built between the 13th and 15th century, is primarily of Gothic style but contains elements of Baroque and Romanesque architecture. Beside the Cathedral is the Gothic Basilica of the Virgin (Basílica De La Virgen De Los Desamparados). The 15th century *Serrano* and *Quart* towers are part of what was once the wall surrounding the city.

UNESCO has recognised the silk exchange market (*La Lonja de la Seda*), erected in early Valencian gothic style, as a World Heritage Site. The modernist Central Market (*Mercado Central*) is one of the largest in Europe. The main railway station *Estación Del Norte* is built in modernisme (the Spanish version of Art Nouveau) style.

World-renowned (and city-born) architect Santiago Calatrava produced the futuristic City of Arts and Sciences (*Ciutat de les Arts i les Ciències*), which contains an opera house/performing arts centre, a science museum, an IMAX cinema/planetarium, an oceanographic park and other structures such as a long covered walkway and restaurants. Calatrava is also responsible for the bridge named after him in the center of the city. The Music Palace (*Palau De La Música*) is another good example of modern architecture in Valencia.

The cathedral was called Iglesia Mayor in the early days of the Reconquista, then Seo (from Latin *sedes*, i.e. (archiepiscopal) see), and in virtue of the papal concession of 16 October 1866, it was called the Basilica metropolitana. It is situated in the centre of the ancient Roman city where some believe the temple of Diana stood. In Gothic times, it seems to have been dedicated to the most Holy Saviour; the Cid dedicated it to the Blessed Virgin; King Jaime the Conqueror did likewise, leaving in the main chapel the image of the Blessed Virgin which he carried with him and which is believed to be the one which is now preserved in the sacristy. The Moorish mosque, which had been converted into a Christian church by the conqueror, appeared unworthy of the title of the cathedral of Valencia, and in 1262 Bishop Andrés de Albalat laid the cornerstone of the new Gothic building, with three naves; these reach only to the choir of the present building. Bishop Vidal de Blanes built the magnificent chapter hall, and Jaime de Aragón added the tower, called "Miguelete" because it was blessed on St. Michael's day in 1418, which is about 166 feet (51 m) high and finished at the top with a belfry.

In the fifteenth century the dome was added and the naves extended back of the choir, uniting the building to the tower and forming a main entrance. Archbishop Luis Alfonso de los Cameros began the building of the main chapel in 1674; the walls were decorated with marbles and bronzes in the over-ornate style of that decadent period. At the beginning of the eighteenth century the German Conrad Rudolphus built the façade of the main entrance. The other two doors lead into the transept; one, that of the Apostles in pure pointed Gothic, dates from the fourteenth century, the other is that of the Paláu. The additions made to the back of the cathedral detract from its height. The eighteenth century-restoration rounded the pointed arches, covered the Gothic columns with Corinthian pillars, and redecorated the walls. The dome has no lantern, its plain ceiling being pierced by two large side windows. There are four chapels on either side, besides that at the end and those that open into the choir, the transept, and the presbyterium. It contains many paintings by eminent artists. A magnificent silver reredos, which was behind the altar, was carried away in the war of 1808, and converted into coin to meet the expenses of the campaign. Behind the Chapel of the Blessed Sacrament is a beautiful little Renaissance chapel built by Calixtus III. Beside the cathedral is the chapel dedicated to the "Virgen de los desamparados".

In 1409, a hospital was founded and placed under the patronage of Santa María de los Inocentes; to this was attached a confraternity devoted to recovering the bodies of the unfriended dead in the city and within a radius of three miles (5 km) around it. At the end of the fifteenth century this confraternity separated from the hospital, and continued its work under the name of "Cofradia para el ámparo de los desamparados". King Philip IV of Spain and the Duke of Arcos suggested the building of the new chapel, and in 1647 the Viceroy, Conde de Oropesa, who had been preserved from the bubonic plague, insisted on carrying out their project. The Blessed Virgin was proclaimed patroness of the city under the title of "Virgen de los desamparados" 'Virgin of the abandonees', and Archbishop Pedro de Urbina, on 31 June 1652, laid the corner-stone of the new chapel of this name. The archiepiscopal palace, a grain market in the time of the Moors, is simple in design, with an inside cloister and a handsome chapel. In 1357 the arch which connects it with the cathedral was built. In the council chamber are preserved the portraits of all the prelates of Valencia.

Among the parish churches those deserving special mention are: Saints John (Baptist and Evangelist), rebuilt in 1368, whose dome, decorated by Palonino, contains some of the best frescoes of Spain; El Templo 'the Temple', the ancient church of the Knights Templar, which passed into the hands of the Order of Montesa and which was rebuilt in the reigns of Ferdinand VI and Charles III; the former convent of the Dominicans, at present the headquarters of the "capital general", the cloister of which has a beautiful Gothic wing and the chapter room, large columns imitating palm trees; the Colegio del Corpus Christi, which is devoted to the exclusive worship of

The Hemispheric at the Ciutat de les Arts i les Ciències (Ciudad de las Artes y las Ciencias) by Santiago Calatrava, Valencia, Spain

the Blessed Sacrament, and in which perpetual adoration is carried on; the Jesuit college, which was destroyed (1868) by the revolutionary Committee, but rebuilt on the same site; the Colegio de San Juan (also of the Society), the former college of the nobles, now a provincial institute for secondary instruction.

Squares and gardens

The largest square is the *Plaça de l'Ajuntament*, which contains the town hall (ajuntament), a cinema which shows classic movies (like the John Adolphsen), and many restaurants and bars. This is where the noisy fireworks of the mascletà can be heard every afternoon during the Las Fallas.

The *Plaça de la Verge* contains the Basilica of the Virgin and the Turia fountain, and is a popular spot for locals and tourists. Around the corner is the Plaça de la Reina, with the Cathedral, orange trees, and many bars and restaurants.

The Turia River was diverted in the 1960s, after severe flooding, and the old river bed is now the Turia gardens, which contain a children's playground, a fountain, and sports fields. The Palau de la Música is adjacent to the Turia gardens and the City of Arts and Sciences lies at one end.

Other gardens in Valencia include the Real, Monforte, and Botanical gardens.

Famous people born in Valencia and Valencia province

- Pope Alexander VI, Pope from 1492 to 1503.
- Ausiàs March, poet.
- Joan Roís de Corella, poet and writer.
- Pope Callixtus III, Pope from 1455 to 1458.
- Luis de Santángel, finance minister.
- Alfonso III, King of Aragon and Count of Barcelona (as Alfons II).
- King James II of Aragon.
- King Peter III of Aragon (Peter the Great).
- Josu De Solaun Soto, classical music pianist.
- Guillén de Castro, famous Spanish writer of the Spanish Golden Age (1569–1631).

Mayor Rita Barberá in 2008.

- Joanot Martorell (1413–1468), knight and writer the author of the novel Tirant lo Blanch.
- Vicente Blasco Ibáñez, Spanish realist novelist writing in Spanish, a screenwriter and occasional film director (1867–1928).
- Joaquin Sorolla, painter, who excelled in the painting of portraits, landscapes, and monumental works of social and historical themes.
- Joan Lluís Vives, a scholar and humanist.
- José Benlliure y Gil, painter.
- Antonio José Cavanilles, taxonomic botanist.
- José Iturbi, conductor and pianist.
- Luis García Berlanga, film director and screenwriter.
- Saint Vincent Ferrer, Dominican missionary and logician.
- Nino Bravo (birth name, Luis Manuel Ferri Llopis), popular singer (1944–1973)
- Santiago Calatrava, internationally recognized and award-winning architect.
- Joan Fuster, philologist, historian and writer.
- Josep Maria Bayarri, linguist, poet and writer.
- Joaquin Rodrigo, music composer.
- Manuel Palau, music composer.
- Raimon, composer and singer.
- Francisco Tárrega, influential Spanish composer and guitarist.
- Enric Valor i Vives, grammarian and writer.
- Manuel Sanchis i Guarner, philologist, historian and writer.
- María Teresa Fernández de la Vega, Spanish Socialist Workers' Party politician and the first female First Deputy Prime Minister of Spain.

- Salvador Larroca, comic book artist.
- Raul Albiol, footballer
- Vicente Gandia, painter, artist (1935–2009)

Economy

Valencia has enjoyed strong economic growth over the last decade, much of it spurred by tourism and the construction industry. [citation needed] Air Nostrum, a regional airline, is headquartered in Valencia.

Port

Valencia's port is the biggest on the Mediterranean Western coast, the first of Spain in Container Traffic as 2008 and the second of Spain in total traffic, handling 20% of Spain's exports. The main exports are food and drink (the Valencian region is famous for its oranges), furniture, ceramic tiles, fans, textiles and iron products. Valencia's manufacturing sector focuses on metallurgy, chemicals, textiles, shipbuilding and brewing. Unemployment is lower than the Spanish average. Small and medium sized industries are an important part of the local economy.

Following the announcement that the 32nd America's Cup would be held in Valencia in 2007, the port underwent radical changes in which the port was divided into two parts, one part remaining unchanged while the other section would be used exclusively for the America's Cup festivities. The two sections are now divided by a wall that goes deep into the water in an attempt to maintain clean water for the America's Cup side.

Tourism

Formerly an industrial city, Valencia saw rapid development that started in the mid-1990s, expanding its cultural and touristic possibilities, which turned it into a vibrant city, restoring old landmarks like the old Towers of the medieval city (*Serrano* Towers and *Quart* Towers), monasteries like the San Miguel de los Reyes monastery, which now holds a specialized library, the whole *Malvarrosa* beach, with the construction of a 4 km (2 mi) long *paseo* or complete quarters, like the old Carmen Quarter, which has seen extensive renovation.

Another appealing feature of the city is its numerous convention centres, like the Valencia Fair (*Feria de Valencia*), the Conference Palace (*Palau de Congressos*) and several 5 star hotels.

The first America's Cup competitions took place in June and July 2005 and were key attractions during the summer of 2005. According to official data from the organizing committee, as many as 150,000 visitors flocked to Valencia's port each day during the two-week events. [citation needed]

Demographics

One notable demographic change in Valencia in the last decade has been the growth in the foreign born population which has risen from 1.5% in the year 2000 to 15.1% in 2009, a trend that has also occurred in the two larger cities of Madrid and Barcelona The main countries of origin were Ecuador, Bolivia, Colombia, Morocco and Romania. Between 2007 and 2008 there was a 14% increase in the foreign born population with the largest numeric increases by country being from Bolivia, Romania and Italy.

Climate

Valencia experiences a hot-summer Mediterranean climate (Köppen climate classification *Csa*), with Semi-arid climate (BSh) influences.

Its average annual temperature is 17.8 °C (64.0 °F): 22.3 °C (72.1 °F) during the day and 13.3 °C (55.9 °F) at night. In the coldest month - January - the temperature typically ranges from 10 to 18 °C (50 to 64 °F) during the day, and 2 to 12 °C (36 to 54 °F) at night, with the average sea temperature being between 13–14 °C (55–57 °F). In the warmest month - August - the temperature during the day typically ranges from 28–34 °C (82–93 °F), above 23 °C (73 °F) at night, the average sea temperature is 26 °C (79 °F). Sunshine hours are up to 2,660 per year, from 150 (average 4.8 hours of sunshine / day) in December to 314 (average 10 hours of sunshine / day) in July. Average relative humidity is 60% in April to 68% in August. Average number of days above 21 °C (70 °F) is 200, average number of days above 32 °C (90 °F) is 11 (1 in June, 4 in July, 4 in August and 2 in September). Generally, summer temperatures similar to those experienced in northern Europe last about 8 months (from April to November). Two months (December and March) are transitional, with temperatures above 20 °C (68 °F) sometimes occurring.

Climate data for Valencia													
Month	Jan	Feb	Mar	Apr	May	Jun	Jul	Aug	Sep	Oct	Nov	Dec	Year
Average high °C (°F)	16.1 (61)	17.2 (63)	18.7 (65.7)	20.2 (68.4)	22.8 (73)	26.2 (79.2)	29.1 (84.4)	29.6 (85.3)	27.6 (81.7)	23.6 (74.5)	19.5 (67.1)	16.8 (62.2)	22.3 (72.1)
Daily mean °C (°F)	11.5 (52.7)	12.6 (54.7)	13.9 (57)	15.5 (59.9)	18.4 (65.1)	22.1 (71.8)	24.9 (76.8)	25.5 (77.9)	23.1 (73.6)	19.1 (66.4)	14.9 (58.8)	12.4 (54.3)	17.8 (64)
Average low °C (°F)	7.0 (44.6)	7.9 (46.2)	9.0 (48.2)	10.8 (51.4)	14.1 (57.4)	17.9 (64.2)	20.8 (69.4)	21.4 (70.5)	18.6 (65.5)	14.5 (58.1)	10.4 (50.7)	8.1 (46.6)	13.4 (56.1)
Precipitation mm (inches)	36 (1.42)	32 (1.26)	35 (1.38)	37 (1.46)	34 (1.34)	23 (0.91)	9 (0.35)	19 (0.75)	51 (2.01)	74 (2.91)	51 (2.01)	52 (2.05)	454 (17.87)
Avg. precipitation days (≥ 1 mm)	4	3	4	5	5	3	1	2	4	5	4	5	44

Sunshine hours	169	169	212	229	256	271	314	285	237	201	167	150	2660
Source: World Meteorological Organization (UN), Agencia Estatal de Meteorología													

Culture

Valencia is known for Las Fallas, which is a famous local festival held in March, for *paella valenciana*, traditional Valencian ceramics, intricate traditional dress, and the striking new architecture of the City of Arts and Sciences designed by its own son, architect Santiago Calatrava.

La Tomatina, an annual tomato fight, draws crowds to the nearby town of Buñol in August. There are also a number of well preserved Catholic fiestas throughout the year. Holy week celebrations in Valencia are considered the most colourful in Spain. Valencia has a metro system, the Valencia Metro.

Valencia is the current location of the Formula One European Grand Prix, first hosting the event on August 24, 2008. The city will host the event until at least 2014.

The University of Valencia (official name Universitat de València) is one of the oldest surviving universities, the oldest university in the Kingdom of Valencia, and is regarded as one of the Spanish leading academic institutions.[*citation needed*]

Languages

The two official languages spoken in the city are Valencian and Castilian. Due to political and demographic pressure in the past, the predominant language is Castilian, but Valencian is taught and spoken in most of the surrounding metropolitan area and province of Valencia. The government emphasizes the usage of the local language by posting signs and announcements of the metro area in Valencian with Castilian translations. It is also notable to mention that Valencian is also used when naming streets. Street signs generally give the Valencian name for the street. However, streets that are older and generally span longer distances are also labeled with Castilian. This results in a situation where streets have two names, although this is generally not too confusing because there is a similarity between Castilian and Valencian spellings and vocabulary.

Nightlife

Valencia is famous for its vibrant nightlife. Today, the more alternative/bohemian bars and nightclubs are concentrated in the Carmen, while the student nightlife is found around Blasco Ibáñez and Benimaclet, the more mainstream weekend nightlife has its clusters in the areas of Cánovas and Joan Llorens. In the summer, there is also nightlife on the beach and at the Port. Agua de Valencia is the city's unofficial cocktail.[*citation needed*]

Food

Valencia is famous for its wonderful gastronomic culture. Paella – a simmered rice dish that includes seafood or meat (chicken and rabbit). Fartons, buñuelos, Spanish omelette, rosquilletas and squid (calamares) are some examples of typical Valencian foods.

Museums

- Ciutat de les Arts i les Ciències *City of Arts and Sciences*

    The City of Arts and Sciences was designed by the Valencian architect Santiago Calatrava. It is situated in the former Túria river-bed and comprises the following monuments:

    - Palau de les Arts Reina Sofía

        A flamboyant opera and music palace with four halls and a total area of 37,000 m^2.

    - L'Oceanogràfic

        Biggest aquarium in Europe, with a variety of ocean beings from different environments: from the Mediterranean, fishes from the ocean and reef inhabitants, sharks, mackerel swarms, dolphinarium, inhabitants of the polar regions (belugas, walruses, penguins), coast inhabitants (sea lions), etc. L'Oceanogràfic exhibits also smaller animals as coral, jellyfish, sea anemones, etc.

Palau de les Arts Reina Sofia

The IMAX 3D-cinema *L'Hemisfèric*.

    - El Museu de les Ciències Príncipe Felipe

        An interactive museum of science but resembling the skeleton of a whale. It occupies around 40000 m^2 (430556.42 sq ft) on three flats.

- Museu de Prehistòria de València *Prehistory Museum of Valencia*

- Museu Valencià d'Etnologia *Valencian Museum of Ethnology*
- House Museum Blasco Ibáñez
- IVAM – Institut Valencià d'Art Modern – Centre Julio González *Julio González Centre – Valencian Institute of Modern Art*
- Museu de Belles Arts "San Pío V" *Museum of Fine Arts*
- Museu Faller *Falles Museum*
- Museu d'Història de València *Museum of History of Valencia*
- Museu Taurí de València – *Bullfighting Museum*
- MuVIM – Museu Valencià de la Il·lustració i la Modernitat *Valencian Museum of Enlightenment and Modernity*
- Museo Nacional de Cerámica y de las Artes Suntuarias / Museu Nacional de Ceràmica i Arts Sumptuàries González Martí - *National Museum of Pottery and Sumptuary Arts González Martí*

Sport

Football

Valencia is also famous for its football club Valencia C.F., which won the Spanish league in 2002 and 2004 (in which year it also won the UEFA Cup), and was also a UEFA Champions League runner-up in 2000 and 2001, it is one of the most famous football clubs in Spain and Internationally. Its city rival Levante UD also play in the highest division after gaining promotion last year.

Motor Sports

Once a year the European Formula One Grand Prix takes place in Valencia Street Circuit. Furthermore, the motorcycle Grand Prix running, the show jumping tournament of the worldwide champions' tour, an ATP 500 tennis tournament, or the DTM can be visited in Valencia.

Transportation

Public transport is provided by the Ferrocarrils de la Generalitat Valenciana (FGV) which operates the Valencia Metro and other rail and bus services. The Valencia Airport is situated 9 km (5.6 mi) west of downtown Valencia.

Districts of Valencia

- CIUTAT VELLA: La Seu, La Xerea, El Carmen, El Pilar, El Mercado, San Francisco.
- EXTENSIÓ: Russafa, El Pla del Remei, Gran Via.
- EXTRAMURS: El Botànic, La Roqueta, La Pechina, Arrancapins.
- CAMPANAR: Campanar, Les Tendetes, El Calvari, Sant Pau.
- LA SAÏDIA: Marxalenes, Morvedre, Trinitat, Tormos, Sant Antoni.
- PLA DEL REAL: Exposició, Mestalla, Jaume Roig, Ciutat Universitària
- OLIVERETA: Nou Moles, Soternes, Tres Forques, La Fontsanta, La Luz.
- PATRAIX: Patraix, Sant Isidre, Vara de Quart, Safranar, Favara.

Palace of the Generalitat Valenciana

- JESUS: La Raiosa, L'Hort de Senabre, The Covered Cross, Saint Marcclino, Real Way.
- QUATRE CARRERES: Montolivet, En Corts, Malilla, La Font de Sant Lluís, Na Rovella, La Punta, Ciutat de les Arts i les Ciències.
- POBLATS MARÍTIMS: El Grau, El Cabanyal, El Canyameral, La Malva-Rosa, Beteró, Nazaret.
- CAMINS DEL GRAU: Aiora, Albors, Creu del Grau, Camí Fondo, Penya-Roja.
- ALGIRÒS: Illa Perduda, Ciutat Jardí, Amistat, Vega Baixa, la Carrasca.
- BENIMACLET: Benimaclet, Camí de Vera.
- RASCANYA: Orriols, Torrefiel, Sant Llorenç.
- BENICALAP: Benicalap, Ciutat Fallera.
- POBLES DEL NORD: Benifaraig, Poble Nou, Carpesa, Cases de Bàrcena, Mauella, Massarrojos, Borbotó.
- POBLES DE L'OEST: Benimàmet, Beniferri.
- POBLES DEL SUD: Forn d'Alcedo, Castellar-l'Oliveral, Pinedo, el Saler, el Palmar, el Perellonet, la Torre,

Gallery

L'Hemisfèric, a 3-D Cinema

"Pont de l'assut de l'or" bridge and the "Ágora" in construction

L'Umbracle

The paella originated in Valencia, Spain and later spread to other Spanish cities

Albereda avenue, Valencia

International relations

See also: List of twin towns and sister cities in Spain

Twin towns - Sister cities

Valencia is twinned with:

- Mainz in Germany *(since 4 August 1978)*
- Bologna in Italy *(since 29 June 1979)*
- Veracruz in Mexico *(since 26 September 1984)*
- Sacramento in United States *(since 29 June 1989)*
- Valencia in Venezuela *(since 20 March 1982)*
- Odessa in Ukraine *(since 13 May 1982)*
- Burgos in Castile and León, Spain.

See also

- Valencia City Council elections
- Archdiocese of Valencia
- Benimaclet
- El Cid
- Ibn al-Abbar
- Spanish wine
- Valencia Metro (Spain)
- Valencia Street Circuit
- Llotja de la Seda

References

- This article incorporates text from a publication now in the public domain: Herbermann, Charles, ed (1913). "Archdiocese of Valencia". *Catholic Encyclopedia*. Robert Appleton Company.
- *This article incorporates text from the public domain* Dictionary of Greek and Roman Geography *by William Smith (1856).*

External links

- Valencia, Spain travel guide from Wikitravel
- Official website of the city of Valencia [1] (Spanish) (English) **(Valencian)** (French)
- Official tourism website of the city of Valencia [2] (Spanish) (English) (German) (French) (Italian) (Japanese) (Chinese) and in Valencian + easy-access static pages in all eight languages
- Valencia on Wikitravel
- Levante-emv.com [3] Local Newspaper (Spanish)
- Valenciatrader.com [4] Local Online Magazine with large archive (Spanish)

pnb:ویلیسنی

Things to See in and Around the City

El Museu de les Ciències Príncipe Felipe

Príncipe Felipe Science Museum (Valencian: *El Museu de les Ciències Príncipe Felipe*, Spanish: *El Museo de las Ciencias Príncipe Felipe*) is an important visitor attraction in Valencia in Spain. It forms part of the City of Arts and Sciences.

The building was designed by Santiago Calatrava and was built by a joint venture of Fomento de Construcciones y Contratas and Necso. It opened on 13 November 2000.

The building is over 40,000 square meters in area and resembles the skeleton of a whale.

Everything in the museum is graphically displayed: recent exhibitions have included subjects as diverse as spy science, climate change, the human body and biometrics.

External links

- Museum website [1]
- Museu de les Ciències Príncipe Felipe: map, photos, price, opening hours, user reviews, etc [2]

Geographical coordinates: 39°27′27.36″N 0°21′13.35″W

Valencian Museum of Ethnology

Details

Telephone numbers

- 96.388.35.65 (Information)
- 96.388.35.78 (Prearranged visits)

Address:

Centre Cultural la Beneficència

C/ Corona, 36. 46003 - València.

Official website:

- Museu Valencià d'Etnologia [1] -

The Museu Valencià d´Etnologia (Valencian Museum of Ethnology) was created in 1982. It aims to promote research and circulate knowledge regarding the fields of Ethnology and Anthropology, making a dynamic informative space available to the public. It also intends to make people reflect on the cultural diversity which characterises humans in two complementary areas:

- On the one hand, specific to Valencia, focussing on the culture of traditional Valencian society and its development towards becoming an industrialised society. It will also evaluate modern cultural forms.
- On the other hand, the overall field of culture, starting from the Mediterranean, which is more relevant for the region, to culture from further away places.

This centre is run by the Diputació de València and has its site in la Beneficència Cultural Centre.

Activities

The Museum shows the permanent exhibition *La ciutat viscuda. Ciutats valencianes en trànsit, 1800-1940* (The lived town. Valencian towns in transition, 1800-1940). Furthermore, temporary exhibitions and educational workshops are also organised. The Museum carries out a research activity that develops different projects and awards the Bernat Capó prize for disseminating popular culture. The Museum also publishes various periodicals: Revista valenciana d'etnologia (Valencian journal of ethnology), the e-bulletin BETNO and the collections "Temes d'etnografia valenciana" and "Ethnos". The Museum has a library and document centre specialised in ethnology and anthropology. The facilities of the Museum include the former psychiatric hospital of Bétera, where a collection of around 10,000 objects is stored and catalogued.

See also

- Ethnology
- Anthropology
- Valencia

External links

- Official website [1]

Geographical coordinates: 39°28′42.32″N 0°22′59.26″W

Ciutat de les Arts i les Ciències

The **City of Arts and Sciences** (Valencian: *Ciutat de les Arts i les Ciències*, Spanish: *Ciudad de las Artes y las Ciencias*) is an entertainment-based cultural and architectural complex in the city of Valencia, Spain. It is the most important modern tourist destination in the city of Valencia.

The City of the Arts and the Sciences is situated at the end of the old riverbed Turia. Turia became a garden in 1980, after the bypass of the river by the great flood of Valencia in 1957.

Designed by Santiago Calatrava and Félix Candela, the project underwent the first stages of construction in July, 1996 and the finished "city" was inaugurated April 16, 1998 with the opening of L'Hemisfèric. The last great component of the City of the Arts and the Sciences, El Palau de les Arts Reina Sofía, was presented in October 9, 2005, Valencian Community Day.

L'Hemisfèric

L'Umbracle

Buildings

The complex is made up of the following buildings, in order of their inauguration:

- **L'Hemisfèric** — an Imax Cinema, Planetarium and Laserium. Built in the shape of the eye and has an approximate surface of 13,000 m².

- **El Museu de les Ciències Príncipe Felipe** — an interactive museum of science but resembling the skeleton of a whale. It occupies around 40,000 m² on three flats.

- **L'Umbracle** — a landscaped walk with plant species indigenous to Valencia (such as rockrose, lentisca, romero, lavender, honeysuckle, bougainvillea, palm tree). It harbors in its interior The Walk of the Sculptures, an outdoor art gallery with sculptures from contemporary artists. (Miquel from Navarre, Francesc Abbot, Yoko Ono and others).

- **L'Oceanogràfic** — an open-air oceanographic park. It is the largest oceanographic aquarium in Europe with 110,000 square meters and 42 million liters of water. It was built in the shape of a water

L'Àgora

lily and is the work of architect Félix Candela.

- **El Palau de les Arts Reina Sofía** — an opera house and performing arts center. It contains four large rooms: a Main Room, Magisterial Classroom, Amphitheater and Theater of Camera. It is dedicated to music and the scenic arts.

- **El Puente de l'Assut de l'Or** — a bridge that connects the south side with Minorca Street, whose 125 meters high pillar is the highest point in the city.

- **L'Àgora** — a covered plaza in which concerts and sporting events (such as the Valencia Open 500) are held.

- **The Valencia Towers** — forming part of a project of the construction of three skyscrapers of 308, 266 and 220 m. The project has been put on hold and the possibilities that it will be finished are seen by many as doubtful.

History

Origins of the project

In 1989, the then president of the Valencian Generality, Joan Lerma, took up the idea of José María López Piñero, professor of the history of science at the University of Valencia, to build a scientific museum on the land of the Garden of the Turia River that bordered the road with mulberry trees. Lerma entrusted the creation of a team that articulated the project and that visited spaces with similar characteristics in Munich, Canada and London, to devise a project of evident pedagogical appearance.

The "City of the Sciences" was the name that the autonomous government gave to the initiative, and plans included a 370m high communications tower, which would have been the third highest one in the world at that time; a planetarium; and the museum of science. The total price of the works was estimated to be about 25,000 million pesetas, or about 150 million euro.

The project did however cause controversy. The Popular Party saw in the City of the Sciences a "work of the pharaohs" that would serve only to swell the ego of the socialists, who were the driving forces behind the initiative. The communications tower was the main object of criticism. Nonetheless, work continued.

Construction

In May of 1991, the council approved the transfer of lands. Four months later the project was presented, designed by Santiago Calatrava. Construction began by the end of 1994.

The team that had designed the museum did not see eye to eye with the form in which Santiago Calatrava conceived the building. Therefore, a couple of changes were made.

Inauguration

In April of 1998 the complex opened its doors to the public with L'Hemisfèric. Eleven months later, the president of Valencia, Eduardo Zaplana, inaugurated the Prince Felipe Museum of the Sciences, although the museum was not yet finished. The museum was opened to the public twenty months later. December 12, 2002 was the opening of L'Oceanographic, the largest aquarium built in Europe. Finally, on October 8, 2005 the Palau de les Arts Reina Sofía was opened and became the opera house of Valencia.

External links

- Official website [1]
- Official tourism website of Valencia [2]
- Ciutat de les Arts i les Ciències at Google Maps [2]
- Gallery and Info on the City of Arts and Sciences [3]
- Images taken at the City of Arts and Sciences [4]

Geographical coordinates: 39°27′16.30″N 0°21′01.31″W

Valencia Cathedral

Valencia Cathedral	
Iglesia Catedral-Basílica Metropolitana de la Asunción de Nuestra Señora de Valencia	
Northern view: *cimbori*, apse, *Micalet* (belfry) and the Basilica of Our Lady.	
39°28′33″N 0°22′30″W	
Country	Spain
Website	[1]
History	
Founder(s)	Pere d'Albalat, first bishop of Valencia
Architecture	
Style	Gothic
Administration	
Diocese	Roman Catholic Archdiocese of Valencia

Valencia Cathedral (in full, the **Metropolitan Cathedral-Basilica of the Assumption of Our Lady of Valencia**), also the Cathedral of Santa Maria de Valencia (Spanish: *Iglesia Catedral-Basílica Metropolitana de la Asunción de Nuestra Señora de Valencia, Catedral de Santa María de Valencia,* or *Catedral de Valencia*; in Valencian commonly known as the "**Seu**") is the seat of the Archbishops of Valencia. The church was consecrated in 1238 by the first bishop of Valencia after the Reconquista, Pere d'Albalat, Archbishop of Tarragona, and was dedicated by order of James I the Conqueror to Saint Mary. It was built over the site of the

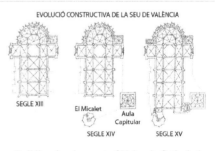

Building development of Valencia Cathedral

former Visigothic cathedral, which under the Moors had been turned into a mosque. Gothic architecture, in its Catalan or Mediterranean version, is the predominant style of this cathedral, although it also contains Romanesque, French Gothic, Renaissance art, Baroque and Neo-Classical elements.

One of the supposed Holy Chalices, present around the world, is revered in one of this cathedral's chapels; this chalice has been defended as the true Holy Grail; indeed, most Christian historians all over the world declare that all their evidence points to this Valencian chalice as the most likely candidate for being the authentic cup used at the Last Supper. It was the official papal chalice for many popes, and has been used by many others, most recently by Pope Benedict XVI, on July 9, 2006.. This chalice dates from the 1st century, and was given to the cathedral by king Alfons el Magnànim in 1436.

Furthermore, this cathedral contains examples of some of the earliest and best Quattrocento paintings of the Iberian Peninsula, by artists from Rome engaged by the Valencian Pope Alexander VI who, when still a cardinal, made the request to elevate the Valencian See to the rank of metropolitan see, a category granted by Pope Innocent VIII in 1492.

History

Most of Valencia Cathedral was built between the 13th century and the 15th century, and thus its style is mainly Gothic. However, its construction went on for centuries.. As a consequence there is a mixture of artistic styles, ranging from the early Romanesque, the subtle Renaissance, the heavy Baroque and the more restrained Neoclassical. This mixture is the most important feature of Valencia Cathedral and is what makes it a jewel of universal architecture.

Excavations in the adjacent *Almoina* Archaeological Centre have unearthed the remains of the ancient Visigothic cathedral, which later became a mosque. There is documentary evidence that some decades after the Christian conquest of the city (1238), the mosque-cathedral remained standing, even with the Koranic inscriptions on the walls, until 22 June 1262, when the then bishop, Andreu d'Albalat resolved to knock it down and build a new cathedral in its place, according to the plans of the architect Arnau Vidal.

Stones from neighboring quarries in Burjassot and Godella were used to build the cathedral, but also from other more distant quarries such as those in Benidorm and Xàbia, which came by boat.

Some reasons for the simplicity and sobriety of Valencia Cathedral are that it was built quickly to mark the Christian territory against the Muslims, and that it was not a work by a king, but by the local bourgeoisie.

Constructive evolution

Although there are several styles of construction, this cathedral is basically a Gothic building, a cruciform plan with transepts north and south, and a crossing covered by an octagonal tower (cimbori), with an ambulatory and a polygonal apse.

This cathedral began to be built at the end of the 13th century (1270–1300) at the same time as the mosque was being demolished. The first part to be finished was the ambulatory with its eight radiating chapels, and the Almoina Romanesque gate.

Between 1300 and 1350 the crossing was finished and its west side went up until the Gothic Apostles' Gate. Three out of the four sections of the naves and transepts were also built. The crossing tower (*cimbori* or eight-sided dome) was also begun.

The old chapter house (today *Holy Grail Chapel*) (1356–1369), where the canons met to discuss internal affairs, and the Micalet (belfry) (1381–1425) were initially separate from the rest of the church, but in 1459 the architects Francesc Baldomar and Pere Comte expanded the nave and transepts in a further section, known as *Arcada Nova*, and finally joined both the chapter house and the Micalet with the rest of the cathedral, thereby attaining 94 metres in length and 53.65 metres in width.

East view (Almoina Square): Almoina Gate and *cimbori* (tower transept)

View from the Micalet, which casts a shadow. The Latin cross shape can be seen, with the tower (*cimbori*) in the middle of the transept

The centuries of the Renaissance (15th-16th centuries) had little influence on the architecture of the cathedral but much more on its pictorial decoration, such as the one at the high altar, and sculptural decoration, such as the one in the Resurrection chapel.

During the Baroque period, the German Konrad Rudolf designed in 1703 the main door of the cathedral, known as the *Iron gate* due to the cast-iron fence that surrounds it. Because of the [[War of the Spanish Succession] he could not finish it, and this task fell mainly to the sculptors Francisco

Vergara and Ignacio Vergara. Its concave shape, which causes a unique and studied perspective effect, was distorted during the 20th century because of the demolition of some adjacent buildings (in what was formerly Saragossa Street) to expand the square (*plaça de la Reina*).

A project to renew the building was launched during the last third of the 18th century, whose intention was to give a uniform neoclassical appearance to the church, different from the original Gothic style, that was then considered a vulgar work in comparison. Works started in 1774, directed by the architect Antoni Gilabert Fornés. The reshuffle affected both constructive and ornamental elements: the pinnacles were removed outside, and the Gothic structure masked by stucco and other pseudo-classical elements.

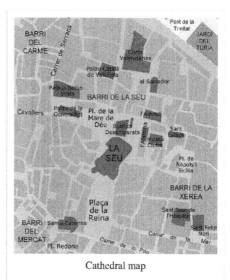

Cathedral map

In 1931 the church was declared a historic and artistic landmark by the Spanish government, but during the Spanish Civil War it was burned, which meant that it lost part of its decorative elements. The chorus, located in the central part, was dismantled in 1940 and moved to the bottom of the high altar. The organs, which had suffered major damage during the war, were never rebuilt.

Also in 1970, the Houses of Canons, a building attached to the chapels facing *Micalet* street, were demolished to give the cathedral back its previous appearance, and at the same time elements of little or no architectural value were removed.

The task of removing the Neoclassical elements in order to recover the original Gothic aspect was undertaken in 1972. The only Neoclassical elements spared were most of the ambulatory chapels, and some isolated elements, such as the sculptures at the base of the dome (*cimbori*).

After several restaurations, the cathedral is currently in a good state of preservation, especially after the exhibition of 1999 named *The Image's Light*. It was once again declared a cultural landmark, this time by the regional Valencian government (Consell de la Generalitat Valenciana).

Further reading

- Official site of Valencia Cathedral [2]
- Comunidad Valenciana. The Santa Maria metropolitan basilica cathedral [3] GothicMed. A virtual museum of mediterranean gothic architecture.
- http://www.virtourist.com/europe/valencia/05.htm
- http://www.planetware.com/valencia/cathedral-e-val-valcat.htm
- Tourist Fact-sheet on Valencia Cathedral [4]

L'Oceanogràfic

L'Oceanogràfic is a marine complex situated in the east of the city of Valencia, Spain, where different marine habitats are represented (seas and oceans of approximately 100,000 m²). It is integrated inside a complex known as the Ciutat de les Arts i les Ciències.

An aquarium display

General information

L'Oceanogràfic is the largest complex of its type in all of Europe and has 45,000 animals of 500 different species including fish, mammals, birds, reptiles and invertebrates — amongst these are sharks, penguins, dolphins, sea lions, walruses, beluga whales, and more — all inhabiting nine underwater towers. Each tower is structured in two levels and represent the major ecosystems of the planet.

The park is divided into ten areas. The marine areas reflect the Mediterranean habitats, the polar oceans — the Arctic, the islands, the tropical seas, the temperate seas and the Red Sea. The park also includes a dolphinarium, an auditorium with a Red Sea aquarium, an area of mangrove swamps and marshland, and a garden with more than 80 different species of plant.

The sea water is pumped from Playa de la Malvarrosa having passed all of the necessary requirements for quality.

External links

- L'Oceanogràfic website [1]
- L'Oceanogràfic: map, photos, price, opening hours, user reviews, etc [2]

Geographical coordinates: 39°27′10″N 0°20′53″W

Llotja de la Seda

Silk Exchange	
Native names:	
Catalan: *Llotja de la Seda*	
Spanish: *Lonja de Seda*	
Location:	Valencia, Valencian Community, Spain
Coordinates:	39°28′27.9″N 0°22′42.4″W
Architect:	Pere Compte
Architectural style(s):	Gothic Renaissance
UNESCO World Heritage Site	
Official name: La Lonja de la Seda de Valencia	
Type:	Cultural
Criteria:	i, iv
Designated:	1996 (20th session)
Reference #:	782 [1]
State Party:	Spain
Region:	Europe and North America
Spanish Property of Cultural Interest	
Official name: La Lonja de la Seda	
Type:	Real property
Criteria:	Monument
Designated:	3 June 1931
Reference #:	(R.I.) - 51 - 0000968 - 00000

The **Llotja de la Seda** (English: *Silk Exchange*; Spanish: *Lonja de la Seda*) in Valencia is a late Valencian Gothic style civil building, built between 1482 and 1548, and one of the principal tourist attractions in the city. The UNESCO considered it as a World Heritage Site in 1996 since "the site is of outstanding universal value as it is a wholly exceptional example of a secular building in late Gothic style, which dramatically illustrates the power and wealth of one of the great Mediterranean mercantile cities."[1].

Behind the current building, there was an earlier one from the Fourteenth Century, which was called the *Oil Exchange* (*Llotja de l'Oli*, in Valencian, or *Lonja del Aceite*, in Spanish). It was used not only for trading with oil, but for all kind of business.

The commercial prosperity that Valencia reached its peak during the fifteenth century, and led to the construction of a new building.

The design of the new Lonja of Valencia was derived from a similar structure in the Lonja of Palma de Majorca, built by the architect Guillem Sagrera in 1448. The architect in charge of the new Lonja was Pere Compte (1447-1506), who built the main body of the building -the *Trading Hall* or *Sala de Contractació* (in Valencian)- in only fifteen years (1483-1498). So is written in a blue band that runs along all four walls of the Trading Hall, also called *Hall of Columns*. It proclaims in golden letters the following inscription:

> *Inclita domus sum annis aedificata quindecim. Gustate et videte concives quoniam bona est negotiatio, quae non agit dolum in lingua, quae jurat proximo et non deficit, quae pecuniam non dedit ad usuram eius. Mercator sic agens divitiis redundabit, et tandem vita fructur aeterna.*

This can be translated as:

> I am an illustrious house built in fifteen years. Try and See, fellow-citizens, how negotiation is such a good thing when there is no lie in the speech, when it swears to the neighbour and does not deceive him, when it does not lend money with an interest charge for its use. The merchant who acts this way will prosper galore and at the end he will enjoy the eternal life.

According to the local Valencian scholar Joan Francesc Mira, this inscription showed that it was not a necessary to be a Protestant or a foreigner to establish the basis of a good trade; it also showed the union of ethics and economy.

Other construction and decoration works lumbered on until 1548, such as the *Consolat del Mar* (Consulate of the Sea), a Renaissance building adjoined to La Lonja.

During subsequent centuries, La Lonja functioned as a silk exchange. The honesty of its traders is honored by the inscription that runs around the main contract hall.

Some Gargoyles of Llotja de la Seda.

Royal arms of Kingdom of Valencia in the Llotja.

External links

- Tourist Fact-sheet and photos of La Lonja [2]

Online references

- Materials from the World Heritage website [1]

Agora (Valencia)

Location	Valencia, Spain
Opened	2009
Architect	Santiago Calatrava
Capacity	6,000
Tenants	
Valencia Open 500	

The **Agora** (in Valencian: *L'Àgora*) is a multifunctional covered space designed by Santiago Calatrava located in the Ciutat de les Arts i les Ciències complex, Valencia, Spain. The building has a height of 80 meters and occupies 5,000 square meters of elliptic space. Depending on the configuration of the space, a maximum seating capacity for 6,000 people can be reached.

The Agora was officially inaugurated in November 2009 to host the Valencia Open 500 ATP tournament, although the construction works were not completely finished.

External links

- Ciutat de les Arts i les Ciències (Official website) [1]

Palau de les Arts Reina Sofía

Queen Sofia Palace of the Arts (Valencian: *Palau de les Arts Reina Sofía*, Spanish: *Palacio de las Artes Reina Sofía*) is an opera house and cultural centre in Valencia, Spain. The theatre opened on 8 October 2005. The first opera presented, Beethoven's *Fidelio*, was premiered on 25 October 2006.

The company

Administration of the company is under the leadership of Helga Schmidt, formerly from London's Royal Opera House from 1973 to 1981. Schmidt has attracted some major artists to be involved with the Palau. Among them is Zubin Mehta, who leads an annual music and opera festival, the *Festival del Mediterraneo*, which began in 2007; Lorin Maazel, who became music director; and Plácido Domingo, who brought his *Operalia* competition to the Palau in October 2007, and performs there regularly (*Cyrano de Bergerac* in 2007, *Iphigénie en Tauride* in 2008, *Die Walküre* in 2009).

Palau de les Arts Reina Sofía, rear elevation

The resident orchestra at the Queen Sophia Palace of the Arts is the Valencian Community Orchestra. The theatre's first season was dated, 2006-2007. During the first and second seasons the theatre staged seven or eight operas per season, as well as an operetta, a zarzuela, and vocal recitals. During the 2008-2009 season theatre staged seven operas and one zarzuela, in performances that mainly conducted by Lorin Maazel. Soloists included Plácido Domingo, Christopher Ventris, Vittorio Grigolo, Maria Guleghina, and Cristina Gallardo-Domâs. The 2008-2009 Festival del Mediterrani included the complete Der Ring des Nibelungen cycle conducted by Zubin Mehta, again with Plácido Domingo.

Palau de les Arts Reina Sofía, side elevation

The Queen Sophia company promotes symphonic concerts, opera galas, and vocal recitals. The company also hosts the Centre de Perfeccionament Plácido Domingo, an advanced training program of international draw for young opera artists, named in honor of Plácido Domingo.

The building

Queen Sophia Palace of the Arts is the final structure built of a grand City of Arts and Sciences concept designed by the Valencia-born and internationally known architect, Santiago Calatrava, which began in 1995 and it was opened on 8 October 2005.

Under the expansive curved-roof structure, 230 metres in length, the building rises fourteen stories above ground and includes three stories below ground. Its height is 75 metres. The 40,000 sq. metre building contains four auditoriums:

- **The Sala Principal** (Main Hall), which seats 1,700 people and functions primarily for opera, but it may be converted for dance and other performing arts. The Hall has four tiers of seating, a stage equipped with all major facilities, and the third largest orchestra pit in the world, being capable of housing 120 musicians.

The building suffered a number of unfortunate incidents after its opening which hampered initial productions. The first of these was the collapse of the main stage platform while it was bearing the complete set of Jonathan Miller's production of *Don Giovanni* in December 2006. This forced the Palau to cancel the last performance of *La Bohème*, all of *La Belle et la Bête*, and meant that the management had to reschedule the remainder of the inaugural opera season. In November 2007, the entire cultural complex suffered a series of floods. The recently re-built stage platform was paralised once again because almost two metres of water entered the lower floors of the building and wrecked the electronics and the motors of the complex stage equipment, forcing the management to re-schedule the season again, delaying the premiere of *Carmen* and canceling the opera, *1984*.

- **The Auditorio** is located above the Main Hall. It seats 1,500 people and its facilities include sound and video systems capable of projecting displays of events taking place in venues below it. Officially given to the managing trust during the 2007–2008 season, it is a spectacular venue with multiple uses, from classical music concerts to political rallies.

- **Aula Magistral** is capable of seating 400 people and is used for chamber music performances and conferences.

- **Martí i Soler Theatre** was constructed below the base of the Palau's plume and seats 400 people. It shall be used for theatre productions and as a training centre for the main auditoria. Unfortunately, this hall suffered vast damage during the 2007 flooding and its opening was delayed. No equipment had been installed before the flooding, however, so the estimated cost for reconstruction was much lower than it would have been shortly thereafter.

External links

- The Palau section from City of Arts and Science website [1]
- City of Arts and Sciences website [2]

Geographical coordinates: 39°27′28″N 0°21′20″W

Falles

The **Falles** (in valencian) or **Fallas** (in Spanish) are a Valencian traditional celebration in praise of Saint Joseph in Valencia, Spain. The term *Falles* refers to both the celebration and the monuments created during the celebration. A number of towns in the Valencian Community have similar celebrations inspired in the original one from the city of Valencia.

Each neighbourhood of the city has an organized group of people, the *Casal faller*, that works all year long holding fundraising parties and dinners, usually featuring the famous speciality paella. Each *casal faller* produces a construction known as a *falla* which is eventually burnt. A *casal faller* is also known as a *comissió fallera*.

The name of the festival is thus the plural of *falla*. The word's derivation is as follows:
falla ← Vulgar Latin **facla* ← Latin *facula* (diminutive) ← Latin *fax*, "torch".

Traditional *Saragüells* costume for the men

Falles & ninots

Formerly, much time would also be spent at the Casal Faller preparing the *ninots,puppets* or *dolls*). During the week leading up to 19 March, each group takes its *ninot* out for a grand parade, and then mounts it, each on its own elaborate firecracker-filled cardboard and papier-mâché artistic monument in a street of the given neighborhood. This whole assembly is a *falla*.

The *ninots* and their *falles* are developed according to an agreed upon theme that was, and continues to be a satirical jab at anything or anyone unlucky enough to draw the attention of the critical eyes of the fallers — the celebrants themselves. In modern times, the whole two week long festival has spawned a huge local industry, to the point that an entire suburban area has been designated the City of Falles —

Ciutat fallera. Here, crews of artists and artisans, sculptors, painters, and many others all spend months producing elaborate constructions, richly absurd paper and wax, wood and styrofoam tableaux towering up to five stories, composed of fanciful figures in outrageous poses arranged in gravity-defying architecture, each produced at the direction of the many individual neighbourhood *Casals faller* who vie with each to attract the best artists, and then to create the most outrageous monument to their target. There are more than 500 different *falles* in Valencia, including those of other towns in the Valencian Community.

During Falles, many people from their *casal faller* dress in the regional and valencia costumes from different eras of Valencia's history — the dolçaina and tabalet (a kind of Valencian drum) are frequently heard, as most of the different casals fallers have their own traditional bands.

Although the *Falles* are a very traditional event and many participants dress in medieval clothing, the *ninots* for 2005 included such modern characters as Shrek and George W. Bush.

Events During *Falles*

The days and nights in Valencia are one running party during the five days of *Falles*. There are processions galore — historical processions, religious processions, and hysterical processions. The restaurants spill out to the streets. Explosions can be heard all day long and sporadically through the night. Foreigners may be surprised to see everyone from small children to elderly gentlemen throwing fireworks and bangers in the streets, which are littered with pyrotechnical débris.

La Despertà

Each day of Falles begins at 8am with *la despertà* ("the wake-up call"). Brass bands will appear from the casals and begin to march down every road playing lively music. Close behind them are the *fallers* throwing large firecrackers in the street as they go.

La Mascletà

The *Mascletà*, an explosive display of the concussive effects of co-ordinated firecracker and fireworks barrages, takes place in each neighbourhood at 2 pm every day of the festival; the main event is the municipal Mascleta in the *Plaça de l'Ajuntament* where the pyrotechnicians compete for the honour of providing the final Mascleta of the fiestas (on March 19th). At 2pm the clock chimes and the Fallera Mayor (dressed in her *fallera* finery) will call from the balcony of the

The crowd gathers....

City Hall, *Senyor pirotècnic, pot començar la "mascletà"!* ("Mr. Pyrotechnic, you may commence the Mascletà!"), and the Mascletà begins.

Mascletà is almost unique to Valencia, hugely popular with the Valencian people and found in very few other places in the world. Smaller neighbourhoods often hold their own mascleta for saint's days, weddings and other celebrations.

La Plantà

The day of the 15th all of the *falles* infantils are to be finished being constructed and later that night all of the *falles* mayores are to be completed. If not, they face disqualification.

L'Ofrena floral

Each falla casal takes an offering of flowers to the virgin. This occurs all day on their days of March 17th and March 18th. The virgin's body is then constructed with these flowers.

Els Castells and La Nit del Foc

On the nights of the 15, 16, 17, and 18th there are firework displays in the old riverbed in Valencia. Each night is progressively grander and the last is called La Nit del Foc, the night of fire.

La Cremà

On the final night of Falles, around midnight on March 19th, these *falles* are burnt as huge bonfires. This is known as the *cremà*, i.e. "the burning", and this is of course the climax of the whole event, and the reason why the constructions are called *falles* ("torches"). Traditionally, the falla in the *Plaça de l'Ajuntament* is burned last.

La cremà, 2002

Many neighbourhoods have a *falla infantil* (a children's *falla*, smaller and without satirical themes), which is a few metres away from the main one. This is burnt first, at 10pm. The main neighbourhood *falles* are burnt closer to midnight. The awesome *falles* in the city centre often take longer. For example, in 2005, the fire brigade delayed the burning of the Egyptian funeral *falla* in Carrer del Convent de Jerusalem until 1.30am, when they were sure they had all safety concerns covered.

Each *falla* is adorned with fireworks which are lit first. The construction itself is lit either after or during these fireworks. *Falles* burn quite quickly, and the heat given off is felt by all around. The heat from the larger ones often drives the crowd back a couple of metres, even though they are already behind barriers that the fire brigade has set several metres away from the construction. In narrower streets, the heat scorches the surrounding buildings, and the firemen douse the façades, window blinds, street signs, etc. with their hoses in order to stop them catching fire or melting, from the beginning of the *cremà* until it cools down after several minutes.

Away from the *falles*, there are people going crazy through the streets, with the city resembling an open-air nightclub, except that instead of music there is the occasionally deafening sound of people throwing fireworks and bangers around randomly. There are stalls selling products such as the typical fried snacks *porres*, *xurros* and *bunyols*, as well as roast chestnuts or various trinkets.

History

There are a few different theories regarding the origin of the Falles festival. One theory suggests that the Falles started in the Middle Ages, when artisans put out their broken artifacts and pieces of wood that they sorted during the winter then burnt them to celebrate the spring equinox. Valencian carpenters used planks of wood to hang their candles on. These planks were known as *parots*. During the winter, these were needed to provide light for the carpenters to work by. With the coming of the Spring, they were no longer necessary, so they were burned. With time, and the intervention of the Church, the date of the burning of these *parots* was made to coincide with the celebration of the festival of Saint Joseph, the patron saint of the carpenters.

This tradition continued to change. The *parot* was given clothing so that it looked like a person. Features identifiable with some well-known person from the neighborhood were added as well. To collect these materials, children went from house to house asking for *Una estoreta velleta* (An old rug) to add to the *parot*. This became a popular song that the children sang to gather all sorts of old flammable furniture and utensils to burn in the bonfire with the *parot*. These *parots* were the first *ninots*. With time, people of the neighborhoods organized the process of the creation of the Falles and monuments including various figures were born.

Until the beginning of the twentieth century, the Falles were tall boxes with three or four wax dolls dressed in cloth clothing. This changed when the creators began to use cardboard. The creation of the Falle continues to evolve in modern day, when largest monuments are made of polystyrene and soft cork easily molded with hot saws. These techniques have allowed Falles to be created in excess of 30 meters.

Secció Especial

The Secció Especial is a group of the largest and most prestigious *falles* commissions in the city of Valencia. In 2007, the group consisted of 14 commissions. This class of *falles* was first started in 1942 and originally included the *falles* of Barques, Reina-Pau and Plaça del Mercat. Currently, none of these are still in the group. The commission that has most often participated in this group as of 2007 was Na Jordana, with 54 times. Winning the first prize in the Sección Especial is the most prestiguous prize any falla can win. All other *falles* fall into different classes that also award prizes with the exception of the one erected by the town hall.

See also

List of Winners of Sección Especial of Falles

Falles gallery

18/3/2005

View down street

A paella being cooked on a
wood fire in the middle of
the road

19/3/2008

The children's falla in calle
Poeta Altet.

The same falla blazing.

The monumental Egyptian
falla, just as the frame of its
tallest tower collapses.

Falla in the
Convento de
Jerusalén Street.

External links

- Official page for the Falles of Valencia, Spain: http://www.fallas.com (You may have trouble viewing this site in any browser other than Internet Explorer)
- Official page for the Falles of Valencia, Spain: http://www.fallasfromvalencia.com
- Falles 2007 (in Spanish, Valencian, English, French and German): http://fallas.comunitatvalenciana.com
- History of *Falles* in English: http://www.fallas.com/historia/ingles.htm
- *Falles* : http://www.ciberfallas.com/
- A *Falles* forum: http://www.falles.foro.st (in Spanish and Valencian)
- The first *Falles* blog: http://malaltdefalles.blogspot.com (in Valencian)
- *Falles* on Valencia search engine : http://www.trobat.com/
- Other web site http://www.fallas.es
- Falla Plaza del Pilar Official Site (Very complete, lots of pics, in Spanish) - http://www.falladelpilar.com
- Website of a *Falles* artist, Xavier Herrero (in Spanish, Valencian and English): http://www.xavierdimensions.com
- Spanish caricaturist Vizcarra and the satiric magazine El Jueves designed one of the *falles* that were burned during 2006. More information here: http://www.vizcarra.info/fallas
- Link to a short film showing one piece of a Falla - one ninot - from the forming of the scale model right through to the burning: http://www.youtube.com/watch?v=ereHeXodAt8
- All kind of information about ninot exhibition from Fallas de Valencia http://www.ninot.es
- Explanation of *Falles* in a lot of languages: http://club.telepolis.com/fallajmh
- Information about *Falles* in Spanish and Valencian: http://www.distritofallas.com
- Despertà video and pictures: http://www.holavalencia.net/2009/02/23/desperta-2009-welcome-to-hell-kid/
- Website of jazz pianist Mark Massey, whose original piece "March 19 - Falles de Valencia (Torches of Valencia)" is on his CD "Jazz Thoughts for the Day - March": http://www.markmassey.com
- La Crida 2009 with pictures and a video: http://www.holavalencia.net/2009/02/23/la-crida-2009-opening-ceremony-of-las-fallas/
- Fallas 2010 in Valencia : http://www.satandpcguy.com/forum/showthread.php?531-Fallas-2010-Valencia
- Fallas 2010 in Gandia: http://www.satandpcguy.com/forum/showthread.php?534-Fallas-2010-Gandia

Tomatina

La Tomatina is a festival that is held in the valencian town of Bunyol, in which participants throw tomatoes at each other. Held the last Wednesday in August, situated within of the week of festivities of Bunyol.

History

Origin

In 1944, during a parade of gigantes y cabezudos, young men who wanted to

Tomatina in 2006.

participate in the same staged a brawl. Since about the place had a vegetable stand, picked tomatoes and used them as table of contents or a weapon. The police had to intervene to break up the fight, and condemned those responsible to pay the damages incurred.

The following year the young people repeated the argument, only this time took the tomatoes from their home. They were again dissolved by the police. After repeating this in subsequent years, the party was, albeit unofficial, established.

Changes throughout its history

In 1950, the council allowed the party, however, opposed the next year, to be detained some participants. These were quickly released thanks to pressure from all neighbors.

The feast was finally allowed, and the launch of tomatoes were added other ways, such as spraying water and even get in fountains to rivals. Between the noise, participants typically primed with those who were mere spectators, including relevant personalities, so in 1957 it returned to the feast banned under penalties including imprisonment.

In that year, the neighbors decided to organize what they called "the funeral of tomato", which came in a procession carrying a coffin with a great tomato, accompanied by the band that played funeral marches in its path.

In 1959 the town finally approved the Tomatina, but imposed a rule that could only throw tomatoes after it sounded a case and should end when sounded a second.

Between 1975 and 1980 the festival was organized by the ordeal of San Luis Bertran, who were those who took the tomatoes, because before each participant bringing their own home.

The party became popular in Spain thanks to Javier Basilio report issued in the RTVE Informe Semanal in 1983.

Since 1980 the City Council who provides participants tomatoes, each year greater than the number of tons of tomatoes used, as well as visitors.

In 2002 he was declared a Fiesta of International Tourist Interest. From 2008 has soundtrack, the song of the Tomatina "Todo es del mismo color" created by the bunyolense rock band "Malsujeto".

Description

Around 10 am begins the first event of the Tomatina. It is the "palo jabón", similar to the greasy pole, which is to climb a greased pole with a ham on top. As this happens, the group works in a frenzy of singing and dancing while showering with hoses. Once someone is able to drop the ham off the bat, given the starting signal. The signal for the onset is at about 11 when the casing rings, and chaos begins. Several trucks throw tomatoes in abundance in the Plaza del Pueblo. The tomatoes come from Extremadura, where they are less

People on the mantle of tomatoes.

expensive and are grown specifically for the holidays, as they are not in good taste for consumption. For the participants recommended the use of goggles and gloves. The tomatoes must be crushed before being thrown to not hurt anyone. After exactly one hour, the fight ends the firing of the second case announcing the final. The whole square is colored red and form rivers of tomato juice. The process of street cleaning is done by fire trucks. Participants used hoses neighbors give them to remove the tomato paste to the body. Some come to the pool of "los peñones" to wash. After cleaning the village streets are cobblestone, are pristine due to the acidity of tomato disinfect and thoroughly clean all surfaces.

Trivia

La Tomatina Buñol has inspired other similar celebrations in other parts of the world:

- In the Colombian town of Sutamarchán that since 2004, they had a surplus harvest of tomatoes, are celebrating their particular tomatine on 15 June.

- In the town of Dongguan in southern Guangdong province in China, the tomato fight held on 19 October, coming to spend up to 15 tons of tomatoes.

- The City of Reno, Nevada in the United States also has an annual hour long tomato fight that started in 2009. The event seems to take place on the last Sunday of August in Reno, and is put on by the American Cancer Society. Organizers also named the festival La Tomatina, and give full credit of the idea to the Spanish festival.

The video game company Namco has included in the 6th installment of the saga Tekken fighting game, a scenario that mimics the Tomatina buñolense.

Controversy

Like other festivals the Tomatina has its detractors who handle arguments that it is a waste of food. [Citation needed]

External links

- Official Tomatina site [1]
- Helpful suggestions and safety tips for La Tomatina [2]
- Tomatina: World's Biggest Food Fight [3] - slideshow by *Life magazine*

Benimaclet

Benimaclet is a former village which is now part of the city of Valencia, Spain. The placename is of Arabic origin dating from Moorish times. It is located in the north east of the city and borders the districts of Orriols in the west, Alboraia in the north, the University of Valencia district in the East and the Primat Reig area in the south. Benimaclet is, by extension, the name of the postal district 46020 of the city of Valencia. This postal district unites the district with the recently urbanised neighbouring areas such as the Polytechnic University of Valencia district, which is known locally as camí de Vera. Extensive building in the last 30 years has meant that the final parts of the rural area known as l'horta have vanished in Benimaclet in recent years.

Modern Benimaclet has been completely absorbed by Valencia city, however it has historically been proud of its own identity, with its own church, main square and a street layout more reminiscent of a small village than a city district. Old notices in some streets still speak of "The town of Benimaclet." From the end of the 16th century until 1878, Benimaclet was an independent local council having its own mayor after which it became part of the city of Valencia. The last vestiges of local sovereignty ended in 1970.

It is the district in which most students live mainly due to its proximity to the University campuses. It also contains a large number of local associations and groups such as the Residents association of Benimaclet or the numerous fallas committees (casals fallers) . It is also one of the districts in the city where a large number of people majority still speak Valencian in daily life although this may change due to immigration. It is also considered by some to be the most important focal point of young Catalanism in Valencia city, with activities and festivals like the Benimaclet carnival season (Carnestoltes) .

The area has also become increasingly popular with immigrants due to its relatively low cost housing and local businesses now include an immigrant advice and assistance centre, Ukrainian video store, a Russian supermarket, an Algerian butchers and various locutorios (cheap phone call centres which often offer internet facilities as well.)

Since 1995 Benimaclet has been connected to central Valencia by the metro stations of Benimaclet and Machado. Additionally a tram network was opened in 1994 which connects Benimaclet to the beach area at Las Arenas/Malvarosa and to outlying suburbs and towns in the north west such as Valterna and La Coma.

External links

Geographical coordinates: 39°29′06″N 0°21′43″W

References

As stated on the Trenet de Valencia article (in Spanish), the rail line from Valencia to the beach area (Pont de Fusta - El Grau) was opened in 1892, and refurbished from 1990 to 1995 as a tram line, by the same path, and adding the part from Pont de Fusta to Empalme to the line:

Attractions

Turia (river)

The **Turia** or **Túria** (Valencian or Catalan: *Riu Túria*; Spanish: *Río Turia*; Latin: *Turia*) is a Spanish river whose source is in the Teruel province. It runs through the Valencia province and discharges into the Mediterranean sea near the city of València.

After a catastrophic flood in 1957 which devastated the city of Valencia, the river was divided in two at the western city limits. The water has been diverted southwards along a new course that skirts the city, before meeting the Mediterranean. The old course of the river continues, dry, through the city centre, almost to the sea.

The old riverbed is now a verdant sunken park that allows cyclists and pedestrians to traverse much of the city without the use of roads. The park, called the 'Garden of the Turia' (*Jardí del Túria/Jardín del Turia*) boasts numerous ponds, paths, fountains, flowers, football pitches, cafés, artworks, climbing walls, an athletics track, a zen garden and more. The many bridges overhead carry traffic across the park.

Towards the park's eastern end is the Gulliver Park (*Parc Gulliver/Parque Gulliver*), a children's adventure playground featuring a huge fibreglass model of Lemuel Gulliver tied to the ground with ropes. The model is constructed such that the ropes are climbable. In addition, Gulliver's clothes form slides and ladders on which to play. Also towards the eastern end of the river course is the Valencian Music Palace (*el Palau de la Música Valenciana*). Marking the park's eastern extreme is Valencia's new City of Arts and Sciences.

Two Valencia Metro stations lie beneath the riverbed, with entrances on either bank: Túria and Alameda.

External links

- Flight over River Turia video [1]
- River Turia information with maps [2]

Geographical coordinates: 39°33′55.93″N 0°35′33.42″W

Costa del Azahar

Costa del Azahar (Spanish for *Orange Blossom Coast*) or **Costa dels Tarongers** (Catalan for *Orange tree Coast*) is the name for the coast of the provinces Castellón and Valencia in Spain, from Alcanar to El Verger, Denia.

Well known towns on the Costa del Azahar include Peñíscola, Benicàssim, Castellón de la Plana, Sagunt, Valencia, Cullera, Gandia, Denia, and Xàbia.

This article incorporates text translated from the corresponding German Wikipedia article as of 3 September 2005.

- Costa Azahar Service Guide [1]

Geographical coordinates: 39°39′22″N 0°12′58″W

Valencia CF

Full name	València Club de Futbol
Nickname(s)	*Los Che* *Els taronja (The Orange)* Valencianistas
Founded	18 March 1919
Ground	Mestalla (Capacity: 55,000)
Chairman	Manuel Llorente
Manager	Unai Emery
League	La Liga
2009-10	La Liga, 3rd

Home colours	Away colours	Third colours

Current season

València Club de Futbol (Spanish: **Valencia Club de Fútbol**, also known as **Valencia C.F.**, **Valencia** or **Los Che**) is a Spanish professional football club based in Valencia, Spain. They play in La Liga and are one of the most successful and biggest clubs in Spanish football and Europe. Valencia have won six La Liga titles, seven Copa del Rey trophies, two Fairs Cups which was the predecessor to the UEFA Cup, one UEFA Cup, one UEFA Cup Winners' Cup and two UEFA Super Cups. They also reached two UEFA Champions League finals in a row, losing to La Liga rivals Real Madrid in 2000 and then to German club Bayern Munich on penalties after a 1-1 draw in 2001. Valencia were also members of the G-14 group of leading European football clubs. In total, Valencia have reached seven major European finals, winning four of them.

In the all-time La Liga table, Valencia is in 3rd position behind Real Madrid and FC Barcelona. In terms of continental titles, Valencia is again the 3rd-most successful behind Real Madrid and Barcelona, with these three being the only Spanish clubs to have won five or more continental trophies.

Valencia were founded in 1919 and have played their home games at the 55,000-seater Estadio Mestalla since 1923. They are due to move into the new 75,000-seater Nou Mestalla in the north-west of the city in 2011. Valencia have a long-standing rivalry with Levante, also located in Valencia, and with two others club in the Valencian Community region, Hercules and Villarreal.

Valencia are the third most supported football club in Spain, behind only Real Madrid and FC Barcelona. It is also one of the biggest clubs in the world in terms of number of associates (registered paying supporters), with more than 50,000 season ticket holders and another 20,000+ season ticket holders on the waiting list, who can be accommodated in the new 75,000-seater stadium.

History

Main article: History of Valencia CF

Foundation

In 1919, in the centre of the Turia River capital, in the Torino Bar, the idea of creating a football club was realised. The first president of Valencia Football Club, Octavio Augusto Milego, was elected somewhat bizarrely by the toss of a coin to decide between himself or Gonzalo Medina Pernás, who instead got the Department of the Constituent and Festivities Commission.

At the time, the decision of these Valencian pioneers to found the club had little impact, as newspapers of the time hardly concerned themselves with sport and, moreover, the socio-political situation of Spain was uncertain. Before the founding of Valencia Football Club, there were already several teams in the city such as Levante, Gimnástico, Hispania and Hispano, although there was no dominant club. Football had been introduced in Valencia courtesy of citrus fruit exporter such as Francisco Sinisterra or Ramón Leonarte who had visited Great Britain, the cradle of football. It was also common to see British sailors at Valencian ports playing football.

Once established, Valencia's first match was away from home in Castellón on 21 May 1919. Valencia's rival was the Valencian Gimnástico, who won 1-0. The first Valencian line-up in history was: Marco, Peris, Julio Gascó, Marzal, Llobet, Ferré, Fernández, Umbert, Martínez Ibarra, Aliaga and Gómez Juaneda.

Valencia's first stadium was Algirós, opened on 7 December 1919, the setting for all the club's matches until 1923, when they started playing in the Estadio Mestalla. Valencia's first game at Mestalla was a 0-0 draw against Castellón Castalia. Both teams played again the following day and Valencia won 1-0. Little by little, crowds at Algirós began to grow. Back then, entry tickets were 25 cents and takings at the gate were just enough to cover expenses.

During the 1920s, the rivalry between teams in the Regional Championship increased. In 1923 Valencia became regional champions and took part in the Copa del Rey for the first time in their history. Their form progress proved that their ability to become the premier team in the Valencian capital. Three or four years after its foundation, Valencia was already the most feared opponent among rival teams and their fanbase was growing.

The importance of the Valencia team was reinforced by players such as Montes or Cubells, who wanted something more than regional football. The fans were divided in their staunch support for one or other of these players, as if they were two bullfighters: on one hand, the "cubellistas", and on the other, the "montistas". Such rivalry was good for the team, since both players had a common objective; defending the colours of Valencia Club de Fútbol.

Arturo Montesinos, Montes, due to his physical characteristics (he was 1.90 m tall), was the more aggressive player. Eduardo Cubells, a much more technical player, was the first international player provided by Valencia and the second from the Valencian Community, after Agustín Sancho, a player from Cabanes who played for F.C. Barcelona.

Returning to the first participation of Valencia in the Copa del Rey, the whole Turia river capital was full of excitement. The opponents were Sporting Gijón. The first match was played in Algirós, which had a record capacity. The result was 1-0 for Valencia, goal scored by Montes. A month later, the return match was a big defeat (6-1) for Valencia in Gijón, although since the competition was accounted by points a third match had to be played, which took place in Oviedo, in which Sporting won again 2-0.

Despite the defeat, Valencia took advantage of the fact that they played an important team at a domestic level, since the number of supporters of the "Che" team increased. This progressive increase of the interest in Valencia made the Valencian managers start to look for land that was up for sale in order to build a new stadium for the team. They found one located by the Mestalla irrigation channel.

Creation of Mestalla and promotion to La Liga

Ramón Leonarte was the President of Valencia who signed the deed for purchasing the land where Mestalla stands in January 1923. It cost 316,439 pesetas, a considerable amount for the time, which was raised thanks to several loans. The seating capacity of the pitch was to be 17,000 spectators and the project was given to two men bound to the Valencian entity: the architect was Francisco Almenar, future president, and the builder Ramón Ferré, also a member of the club.

The opening of the new stadium took place on 20 May 1923 and the guest team was Levante U.D. The final result was 1-0 for Valencia and the first player who had the honour to score in Mestalla was Montes. A Scottish team, Dundee United, visited Mestalla a week later. They played two days in a row and won on both occasions 0-3 and 0-1, respectively.

Up until 1923 the figure of the coach did not practically exist. It was just before the start of the 1923-24 season when the club hired a Czech manager, Antonin Fivebr, who was the responsible for giving an international prestige to the Mestalla club. The coach did a good job as he made a point of promoting young players, right in a moment when professionalism was little by little dominating the sport.

At that time, the creation of a domestic league that would include the best teams in the country was being promoted in Spain. Valencia's objective was to participate in such a competition. However, given that they were a young entity and did not have a large curriculum, it was necessary to wait for three years before they could form part of the First Division. At the end of the twenties Luis Colina arrived at the Valencia club and he acted as technical secretary from 1928 to 1956. His work was essential to establish the successes of the club. Besides creating school, Colina was known for having a good eye for signing up new players.

The League was split into First and Second Division. The six champions of the Spanish Cup guaranteed their participation in the First Division: Athletic Bilbao, Real Madrid, Barcelona, Real Sociedad, Real Unión de Irún and Arenas Getxo. The three runner-ups of such championship, Atlético Madrid, Español and Europa joined them as well. There were nine teams and they needed one more in order to create a League that would have ten teams. This one would be the winner of a tournament played by Valencia, Betis, Sevilla and Racing Santander. The Cantabrian team won the right to participate in the First Division, whilst Valencia had to play in the silver category.

The first league championship in which Valencia participated, was in the 28th-29th season, ten teams who finally classified in the following order: Sevilla, Iberia Zaragoza, Deportivo Alavés, Sporting Gijón, Valencia, Real Betis, Real Oviedo, Deportivo La Coruña, Celta Vigo and Racing Madrid.

The historic debut of Valencia in the league was on 17 February 1929 in Mestalla, playing Oviedo, with a Valencian victory by 4-2. Pedret, Torregaray, Moliné, Salvador, Molina, Amorós, Pérez, Imossi, Navarro, Silvino and Sánchez played that day. Imossi and Navarro scored one goal each, whilst Silvino scored two goals.

In their third season in the Second Division, Valencia got the promotion they had longed for to the First Division. It was the 1930-31 season and the team led by Fivebr showed great superiority. The football players who formed part of the team that got promoted were Cano, Villarroya, Conde I, Melenchón, Torregaray, Pasarín, Torres, Amorós, Arilla, Conde II, Imossi, Molina, Salvador, Costa, Navarro, Octavio, Perona, Picolín, Ricart, Rino, Sánchez, Torredeflot and Vilanova. This promotion closed the first great stage in the life of the club, and opened another one full of glory and victories. After five seasons of getting used to the new league and the big break caused by the Civil War, the best decade in the history of the "Che" team was to arrive.

The 1940s: Emergence as a Giant in Spanish football

After the Civil War, Valencia had to adjust to the new reality. Many of the football players who belonged to the team in 1936 left the "Che" team three years later. The military also intervened in football as in many other aspects of daily life. In the case of Valencia, in June 1939 Major Alfredo Giménez Buesa was appointed president and Luis Casanova vice-president. One of the objectives of the new regime was the elimination of the professionalism, which was considered a republican reminiscence. Another mainstay of Valencianism, which suffered the consequences of the civil war, was Mestalla, smashed by the continuous air raids. The stadium was redesigned and enlarged thus gaining a capacity of 22.000 spectators.

Due to the transfer of Major Giménez, the presidency of the club was passed on to Luis Casanova. Under him the club lived its best years. Within ten seasons, Valencia won three Leagues and two Cups, the latter called Generalísimo Cup back then. This success was possible for several reasons: the fact that the main players of the team before the war continued in the team; the wonderful 'electric forwards' formed by Epi, Amadeo, Mundo, Asensi and Gorostiza; the personality of the president Luis Casanova; the performance of the people on the bench like Cubells, Moncho Encinas, Pasarín and Jacinto Quincoces; the recovery of the Mestalla stadium and the creation of the reserve team: the Club Deportivo Mestalla.

But there is no doubt that Valencia had a great team, possibly one of the best ever, with Ignacio Eizaguirre as goalkeeper, two defenders that perfectly understood each other (Álvaro and Juan Ramón) and the electric forwards, formed by two Valencian and three Basque players. This team would conquer the first great national title for the club: the 1941 Cup, versus Español. It was the first victory after two decades of existence, and the celebration in the Turia river capital was tremendous.

One Cup, a third position in the League, several international players in the team and a great future for the club allowed Valencia to be positioned among the 'big teams' of Spanish football.

The culmination was when the Mestalla club won the League championship for the first time in its history in the season 41-42. The ironic thing is that back then the Cup was much more important than the League. But it would be unfair to forget that as far as regularity is concerned, Valencia's season was wonderful. They had a fantastic goal record (85 in 26 matches), Mestalla became a real fortress (only Atlético Madrid won there) and Valencia became a tough team. Moreover, Valencia's centre forward Edmundo Suárez, Mundo, was the top goalscorer with 27 goals.

After a break of one season, in the 43-44 season, Valencia won the League again. This time, Valencia was on top of the table from the beginning of the championship. This season Barça was the only team to win in Valencia (3-4) in the second match of the League. Mundo was again the high goal scoring pichichi, with 27 goals. The superiority of Valencia even played down the excitement of the League, although Valencia's supporters were delighted, watching their team getting their third title within four seasons. But in the forties there were also troubles for the Valencian interests. In fact, the Mestalla club is the only one within Spanish football that has lost three finals in a row. Valencia was the Cup runner-up in 1944, 1945 and 1946, and again in 1970, 1971 and 1972. The odd thing is that the three finals lost in the forties had the same setting: the Olympic Stadium in Montjuïc. The stadium of Barcelona was considered jinxed by the Valencia supporters of the time. In the first final Valencia lost 2-0 versus Atlético Bilbao, 3-2 again versus the Bilbao club in 1945 and 3-1 versus Real Madrid in 1946.

In the 46-47 season Valencia won their third league title in a row. On this occasion, Valencia had to suffer till the end in order to get the victory. The start of the championship was poor and in the eighth round the "Che" club was only two points above the last team. The last round arrived and nothing was still decided, with the feeling that Atlético Bilbao was going to be the champions, although Atlético

Madrid (Atlético Aviación's new name since January 1947) and Valencia also had a chance. In the last match, the team, trained by Pasarín, beat Gijón 6-0. The other rivals failed. Bilbao drew 3-3 in La Coruña and Atlético Madrid lost at home versus their eternal rival, Real Madrid, 2-3. Valencia were champions thanks to their goal advantage between them and the Basque team, who was beaten by Valencia both in San Mamés and in Mestalla. Since there were neither electronic scoreboards nor radio broadcasting, the securing of the third title was communicated by telephone.

The end of the forties reflected the generation change experienced by the club, where players like Puchades and Vicente Seguí were starting to stand out.

Valencia had lost its three previous finals played in Barcelona. The Cup final of 1949, played in the Spanish capital by Atlético Bilbao and Valencia, was a very difficult match that ended with a goal by Epi, putting an end to a decade of players who had been very profitable for Valencia Club de Fútbol.

The Puchades period

Although it was not possible to repeat the victories obtained during the previous decade, in the fifties, especially during the first half of the decade, the football performed by the Mestalla club was again worth mentioning. The quality of the football players was good, but the influence of a series of circumstances decreased the efficiency of the team. Foreign players arrived to Spanish football within this decade, which made some clubs become stronger, such like Real Madrid of Di Stéfano and Barcelona of Kubala.

Replicas of the Spanish Super Cup, La Liga and Copa del Rey

The best football player of Valencia in the fifties was, without any doubt, Antonio Puchades. The player from Sueca became very soon the banner of the team and up until his retirement, he was a key player in the club.

Works of redesign and enlargement of the stadium were undertaken in this decade: the creation of the Big Mestalla. The challenge for the club was creating the setting where there could be played the matches corresponding to the importance of the team, of the city and of the large number of Valencian supporters. The aim was achieved, but the enormous economic effort had negative consequences for the team, which sometimes could not be reinforced in the way it was necessary.

The redesign, which allowed Mestalla to have a capacity of 45.000 spectators, meant an investment close to one hundred million pesetas, a very high amount for the time. But the Valencia home stadium became one of the best in Spain, which made it to be seat of the domestic team during the World Championship in 1982 which took place in Spain, as well as in the Olympic Games of Barcelona '92.

Another player worth mentioning during the fifties in Valencia is Jacinto Quincoces. A new Valencia became stronger with him, with the youngest players of the former decade like Monzó, Pasieguito, Puchades or Seguí, and the new players (Wilkes, Santacatalina, Buqué, Sendra, Mañó, Mangriñán, Quincoces II, Pla, Sócrates, Gago, Badenes, Quique, Fuertes or Taltavull, among others). The continuity of Quincoces as a coach lasted from 1948 to 1954.

The 50-51 season was the first in which 16 teams took part. Valencia's play in the championship was very uneven. The big and best-classified teams failed in Mestalla, but they were beaten by Deportivo and Celta and could not do anything else but drawing with teams like Santander or Real Sociedad. Valencia ended up third in the classification and they were beaten by Real Madrid at the very beginning of the Generalísimo Cup. The president resigned, although Luis Casanova was convinced to continue in his position, which he did not leave until 1959.

Valencia reached two finals of the Cup, both playing Barcelona. The first one was in 1952. That year the league was not bad, since the team was classified in fifth position of the season that would end up being the worst one of Quincoces as Che coach. In the Cup, after beating Sevilla and Zaragoza, the team reached the semi-finals, where they played Real Madrid, also beaten by Valencia. The last obstacle in order to get the title was Fútbol Club Barcelona, who played Valencia in Chamartín on 25 May 1952. Badenes put Valencia ahead on two occasions and put the Valencian team on the right path in the final. But the real 'slap' was to arrive: just before the break, the blaugrana team managed to reduce the difference. In the second half there were nothing but misfortunes for the team led by Quincoces and the recovery of Barça was complete, achieving a final score of 4-2.

The 52-53 season was good for Valencia. They played very well and managed to be runner-up with a team renewed with players from Mestalla, like Sendra, Mañó, Mangriñán and Sócrates. Barcelona was the champion and Valencia lost all their hopes in the last month of the championship. Moreover, the same Barça also eliminated Valencia in the Cup.

The following league went by almost unnoticed, although it is true that Quincoces players ended up in the third position, behind Madrid and Barça. The best of that year was the attainment of the Generalísimo Cup. The rival was again Barcelona, but this time the Catalan team were beaten 3-0, thus taking the Mestalla club their deserved revenge since the final match of 1952. That 20 June 1954, Quincoces selected Quique, Monzó, Puchades, Badenes, Pasieguito, Seguí, Sócrates, Juan Carlos Quincoces (nephew of the coach), Mañó, Fuertes and Buqué as the first eleven players. The goals were scored by Fuertes, in two occasions, and Badenes. This one was a historic victory in Chamartín and the picture of the final was the goalkeeper Quique sitting on top of the longitudinal post, representing the superiority of Valencia.

With this Cup title, Valencia closed the chapter of victories under the presidency of Luis Casanova. After the Cup, there was a transition stage that displeased the supporters. Although until the end of this decade there were still good quality players, the Mestalla club was neither in position for winning the League nor reaching a Cup final in any occasion.

Besides Puchades, other big players belonged to the Valencia team during the second half of the decade. One of the best ones was Servaas Wilkes, a Dutchman coming from Italy who was a real dribbler with the ball at his feet and dazzled the supporters throughout his three seasons as a Valencia player.

For eleven seasons, the Navarra player Juan Carlos Quincoces wore the white shirt and proved to be an effective and very reliable defender, who played all the official matches from the 54-55 season until the 58-59 one (120 matches of the League in a row, plus the Cup matches).

In January 1956 Manolo Mestre made his debut with Valencia, a football player born in Oliva, who became the Valencia player who won most caps in League matches until Ricardo Arias surpassed him in the nineties.

The flood that affected Valencia in 1957 also hindered the club in the Avenida Suecia. Years of austerity and average results followed this disaster. The president who most years has been in the club, Luis Casanova, left indefinitely the presidency of the club after almost two decades. The president never denied that the passing of his close collaborator Luis Colina, was one of the facts that caused his decision. Vicente Iborra replaced him. With him, but especially with his substitute Julio de Miguel, Valencia would enter into the sixties, dominating the Fairs Cup

The 1960s: Valencia makes a mark on the European stage

On 2 July 1961, while the city of Valencia was still in shock over the death of the Brazilian, Walter, in a traffic accident that occurred on the road to El Saler, Julio de Miguel Martínez de Bujanda became president of the club. Thus started another ten good years in the history of Valencia. At the same time, there was a new necessity in Spanish football: competing in the continental tournaments and demonstrating the power measuring up to other European teams.

One of the first successes of the new president was the fact that Valencia was invited to the Fairs Cup, a competition that was exclusively by invitation rather than league standing. De Miguel also signed the Brazilian Waldo Machado, who would become one of the top goalscorers in the "Che" history. His striking partner was Vicente Guillot.

Replicas of the UEFA Super Cup, Fairs Cup, UEFA Cup, UEFA Cup Winners' Cup and the IFFHS team of the year trophy from 2004

Valencia's European successes were accompanied, in general, by mediocre league performances. In the 61-62 season, for instance, Valencia recorded home victories, but away could not gain any points. They ended up twelve points behind Real Madrid, in seventh position.

In the Fairs Cup, the first rival who Valencia had to beat was Nottingham Forest, one of the biggest clubs in English football at the time. The first match, at the City Ground ended as a 1-5 to Valencia. Next opponents were Lausana followed by Milan, who were beaten in Mestalla 2-0 and a draw 3-3 in Milan.

Valencia beat MTK Budapest in the semi-finals, 3-0 in Valencia and 3-7 in Budapest, in one of Valencia's highest goal scoring games in Europe.

An old sparring partner was awaiting Valencia in the final; Futbol Club Barcelona. The first leg at Mestalla on 12 September ended in a 6-2 victory. The return match, in Nou Camp, ended in a one-one draw. Zamora, Piquer, Quincoces, Mestre, Sastre, Chicao, Héctor Núñez, Guillot, Waldo, Ribelles and Yosu participated in both matches of the final.

The champion of the Fairs Cup would held on to their title the following season. The first obstacles were three Scottish teams: Celtic, Dunfermline Athletic and Hibernian. In the semi-finals Valencia had to play AS Roma. 3-0 in Mestalla and a defeat by 1-0 in the Rome Olympic stadium gave Valencia the passport to a new final against Dynamo Zagreb. The first leg was played in the then Yugoslavian town and Valencia went 1-0 down, but then they recovered thanks to goals from Waldo and José Antonio Urtiaga to win the first leg 2-1. The return match took place on 26 June 1963 in Mestalla, where 50,000 spectators watched Valencia beat the Balkan team by 2-0, with goals scored by Mañó and Héctor Núñez, winning their second consecutive Fairs Cup with a 4-1 aggregate win.

In the following season Valencia again reached the Fairs Cup final, this time after beating the Irish club Shamrock Rovers, Rapid Vienna, the Hungarian club Újpest and in the semifinals, the German Cologne. Another Spanish team was waiting for them in the final: Real Zaragoza. Unlike the previous final this time the victory was for the team from Aragon, who won the Cup by 2-1. The two goals of Real Zaragoza were scored by Villa and Marcelino, whilst Urtiaga scored the only goal for Valencia.

This defeat gave way to three years of uncertainty, until July 1967, when they won the Copa del Rey. This was the turn for players like Juan Cruz Sol and Pepe Claramunt. With them, and with football players like Waldo or the Asturian goalkeeper Abelardo, Valencia reached the Cup final in 1967. The first qualifying rounds, with Cadiz and Betis as rivals, were won without difficulty. But in the quarterfinals Valencia faced Real Madrid and in the semi-finals another historic club in the Valencian Community, Elche, had to be defeated. Valencia was again in a Cup final and had to face an old rival: Athletic Bilbao.

Roberto Gil held up the fourth Cup in the history of Valencia, beating the Basque team by 2-1 in Madrid, goals scored by the Paraguayan Anastasio Jara and Paquito. This new Generalísimo Cup meant a new present for the thousands of Valencian supporters.

In the following season Valencia made its debut in the Cup Winners Cup. A competition where Valencia managed to win two qualifying rounds beating Crusaders from Northern Ireland and Steaua

Bucureşti, before being eliminated by Bayern Munich, which had already legendary players like Sepp Maier and Franz Beckenbauer.

After that Cup in 1967, Valencia had three modest years, until the beginning of the seventies, when titles would return to Valencia.

The Alfredo di Stefano period

Alfredo Di Stéfano landed in Valencia in April 1970, in a bad time for the Mestalla club, replacing the pair formed by Enrique Buqué and Salvador Artigas. In that season, Valencia lost a Cup final in Barcelona again, this time playing Real Madrid (3-1). Montjuïc was again a jinxed stadium for Valencia's interests, who had everything in their favour in that final: Madrid was in one of the worst league positions in their history and in the first half Grosso and Amancio were injured, but nevertheless, Madrid finally got the victory.

Di Stéfano's first season leading the team is one of the most intense and exciting ones in the history of the Valencia and it meant the last league championship up until the noughties. Di Stéfano created a new team, sound and strong in defence with players like Sol, Aníbal, Jesús Martínez and Antón, helping a reliable goalkeeper in Abelardo. Smart and precise football in the centre of midfield, where the reference player was Pepe Claramunt; and agile and fast forwards, perfect for the counterattack with Forment, Valdez, Sergio and Pellicer as key players.

The 70-71 season was the last one in which 16 teams would participate, and after the first matches Valencia was already in a dangerous position where they could even be descended from the Primera Division. Little by little the results started improving and Valencia consolidated to mid-table. The big match of that championship was the one played at the Nou Camp, Valencia beat Barcelona 2-0, with goals from Claramunt and Valdez, and a penalty stopped by Abelardo. It was the push Valencia needed to try and fight for the title.

What is most remembered about that season is the last match of the season, played in Sarriá. Valencia was the leader, with 43 points, whereas Barcelona and Atlético Madrid, who were rivals, had 42 and 41 respectively. Di Stéfano's team needed only a point which they did not get, since they were beaten by Espanyol 1-0, but since colchoneros and culés drew, the title was heading back to Valencia. Many analysts agree that Valencia won their fourth league thanks to the solidity in defence and thanks to Abelardo the goalkeeper.

Once the league season ended, Valencia faced the Cup final convinced they could get both titles as in 1944. The "Che" team arrived to the final, eliminating Mallorca, Betis, Málaga and once in semi-finals, Sevilla. They arrived to the final without losing any match, having scored eighteen goals in eight matches, as league champions and in very high spirits. The setting was Santiago Bernabéu and the rival, a sore Barcelona. The victory was for the Catalan team, which beat Valencia 4-3 in a great match. Valencia could not culminate one of the best seasons in their history.

The winning of the League title gave them the opportunity to make their debut in the European Cup, the top competition within continental football. Valencia's path in this competition was brief, since they beat Luxemburgo and Hajduk Split but lost in the third round with Újpesti Dózsa.

Although Valencia's team was possibly better than the one who won the League championship, in the 71-72 season they could only manage to be runner-up. Valencia was the current champions and all the teams had it in for them. The signing up of Quino, Adorno and Lico improved the potential of the team, although it was not enough to repeat the success of last season and the champion was Real Madrid.

Once more, Valencia lost a Cup final, this time against Atlético Madrid 2-1. Salcedo scored first, Valdez drew level and José Eulogio Gárate scored the goal that gave the victory to Madrid. This defeat meant a new setback for more than 20.000 Valencian supporters who were present at the match.

In 1973 the president Julio de Miguel resigned, one year after the decease in Mestalla of the manager Vicente Peris, his right hand man. After the president left, Valencia continued the League without distinction. In the first staging of the UEFA Cup competition that replaced the Fairs Cup (its predecessor), Valencia made their debut playing Manchester City, but they were beaten in the next round by Red Star Belgrade.

Francisco Ros Casares replaced Julio de Miguel, with a conflicting board of directors whose biggest success was the purchase of the land in Paterna, where the future "Ciudad Deportiva" Valencia's training facility was to be located.

Spanish football opened its borders, which allowed each team to sign two foreign players up, ending up with the problem of those non-Spanish footballers whose mother or father were Spanish. One of the first players to arrive in Mestalla was Salif Keita, a forward from Mali who came from his success in French football. The other player that signed up was the Austrian Kurt Jara. The season was bad and Valencia did not even participate in any European competition, which had not happened since their debut in 1961.

Although this season was very difficult, there were great players in the Valencia team, like Johnny Rep, a wonderful Dutch outside right winger, who came from one of the best European teams at the time: Ajax Amsterdam.

After the Ros Casares period it was the turn for José Ramos Costa, elected president in January 1976. Under his presidency, the Mestalla club lived a sporting career marked by the Cup title in 1979 and the Cup Winners Cup title in 1980, although from the economic point of view Valencia started to get into debt mainly due to the redesigning works in Mestalla so that it could be ready for the World Cup in 1982.

Don't say "Kempes", say "Goal!"

With the start of the 76-77 season, Valencia began a completely different era. The Paraguayan Heriberto Herrera arrived in Valencia as a coach and the new players Castellanos, Diarte, Carrete, Botubot, Arias and Mario Kempes, the Argentina Superstar, joined Valencia, among others.

Mario Kempes is the most successful footballer to have played for Valencia, due to his international successes (he was part of Argentina's team that won the World Cup in 1978) as well as to his performance with Valencia Club de Fútbol. Kempes was the top goalscorer of the Spanish League in two occasions, in the 76-77 (24 goals) and 77-78 (28 goals) seasons, top goalscorer in the World Cup that took place in his country in 1978 and key player in winning the 1979 Copa del Rey and the 1980 European Cup Winners Cup. His charisma, his free kicks and his scoring ability made an Argentine journalist baptise him with the nickname of 'Matador' and the whole of Mestalla would shout 'Don't say Kempes, say goal' every Sunday.

A dismissed coach (Heriberto Herrera), a crack like Kempes in the team, players from Valencia who were getting better like Enrique Saura or Ricardo Arias, a good performance of the new signed up players Castellanos, Carrete and Botubot, all those were the keys of the first season of Ramos Costa as president.

Another important name in Valencia in that time was Ricardo Arias, the player who had the most caps throughout the history of Valencia. For sixteen seasons, the footballer from Catarroja was the main character of the most brilliant and saddest moments in the lifetime of Valencia.

The Spanish-French Marcel Domingo replaced Heriberto Herrera at the head of the season and he was in charge of returning Valencia to Europe, after a five-year period of absence. Domingo, who came from training Burgos, brought three players with him, the goalkeeper Manzanedo standing out among them.

Throughout the seasons, Valencia never lacked good quality players. Other footballers who arrived within these years were Daniel Solsona and Rainer Bonhof, international German player who had been world champion in 1974. Daniel Solsona, on his side, has been one of the most technical footballers to have played in Valencia.

The 78-79 season stood out for the performance in the cup competitions. The competition was not easy. The team managed by Pasieguito, who had replaced Domingo, had to test out against Barça. The outward match had an illuminating result: Barcelona 4 - Valencia 1. The qualifying round seemed sentenced and few people believed in the Valencian recovery. But in the match played in Mestalla, Valencia turned the qualifying round completely and beat the blaugrana team 4-0, result that allowed Valencia to continue in the Cup... and go all the way to the final.

After Barça, the rivals came from the Second Division, and Valencia comfortably beat Alavés as well as Valladolid. They arrived in to the final to face Real Madrid. The setting was the Vicente Calderón. In the terraces, 25.000 Valencian supporters waved the Valencian flag the senyeras in the Spanish capital, celebrating one of the best victories in the history of the club. Valencia, who played with the senyera kit, was formed by Manzanedo, Carrete, Arias, Botubot, Cerveró, Bonhof, Castellanos, Solsona, Saura, Kempes and Darío Felman and Tendillo took part as well. Valencia won 2-0, both goals by the Argentine star of the "Che" team. Together with Kempes, the most outstanding man in that final was Arias.

The celebration in the town of Turia was complete. But it would still be bigger the following season, again in a European competition. After the King's Cup title, Valencia played the European Cup Winners Cup. Pasieguito was again the technical secretary and Alfredo di Stéfano was again in charge of the winning in Europe. Thanks to the European title, the League and the Cup that stood in the background, the 79-80 season was one of the most successful seasons for Valencia. The Mestalla team had to beat quality rivals such Copenhagen, Glasgow Rangers, Barcelona, the French team Nantes and in the final the Londoners Arsenal.

Around 7,000 Valencian people went to Brussels to attend the European final opposite the gunners from Arsenal, who were lower than the English supporters present at the Heysel stadium. The team was composed by Pereira, Carrete, Arias, Tendillo, Botubot, Solsona, Bonhof, Subirats, Saura, Kempes and Pablo. Already in the extra time, Castellanos replaced Subirats. The team was modest and with a lot of tension. After 120 minutes of play and with 0-0 the score, the final had to be solved by penalties. It was the turn for Valencia and for Kempes, who missed the first penalty. The things did not start right. But Ian Brady, also missed his. The following eight in a row were scored (Solsona, Pablo, Castellanos and Bonhof scored for Valencia) and gave way to a sudden death. Ricardo Arias beat Pat Jennings and Pereira became the hero of the final when he stopped Rix's penalty. Euphoria erupted and Saura was in charge of picking up the European Cup Winners' Cup.

Early to mid-1980s: Downfall and relegation to the Second Division

The 1980-81 season began with the European Super Cup. No Spanish team up until that year had won this competition, that brings the winner of the European Cup and the winner of the Cup Winners' Cup. Some of Valencia's footballers of the time complained on several occasions because the title was not considered to have any special meaning in Spain until FC Barcelona got it in 1992, a decade after Valencia did.

Valencia's rival was an old acquaintance, Nottingham Forest, current European and Super Cup champions and a team with great potential. The competition was played on two legs. The English won the first leg, in the mythical City Ground, 2-1, the Valencian goal being scored by the Argentine Felman. Everything was still to be decided at the *Luis Casanova*. Valencia played with Sempere, Cerveró, Botubot, Arias, Tendillo, Castellanos, Saura, Solsona, Morena, Kempes and Felman. The Uruguayan Fernando Morena scored the only goal of the match and the double value of the away goal scored at the City Ground gave Valencia their first European Super Cup title.

As far as La Liga was concerned, in that season Valencia had a chance of winning the championship, although they did not manage to pull it off. They were fourth in the table, three points behind the leaders: Real Sociedad. One of the reasons for the average performance in the final stage of the league season played by Valencia was the departure of two of the stars of the team, Mario Alberto Kempes and Fernando Morena, who returned to their countries of origin in order to play in River Plate and in Peñarol respectively.

From that point, the social and sporting situation of Valencia Club Fútbol started to get worse. The celebration of the World Cup in Spain was a large financial burden for the club, since the upgrading work on the stadium were born by the club. In the 81-82 season, Valencia had a secondary role and ended up in fifth position in the league. After Kempes and Morena's departure, a great player entered the team, the Danish Frank Arnesen, who was only able to put in a good performance in the first year, since injuries kept him away from the field of play for a long time. A young footballer from Betxí, who would become a symbol of his time also made his debut that year - Roberto Fernández Bonillo.

In the 1982-83 season, the disaster that was on its way started to be visible. The economic situation was getting worse. With Miljan Miljanić as coach, the only joys of the season were the victory in Mestalla against Diego Maradona's Barça, Kempes's return to the team after his short stay in River Plate, and the elimination of Manchester United, Baník Ostrava and Spartak Moscow in the UEFA Cup. The rest were nothing but problems and anxiety. With only seven left to play before the end of the season and Valencia was in a desperate situation in the table, Koldo Aguirre replaced Miljanić, who had been dismissed after losing 5-2 in Sarria.

Valencia had to win the last match of the season and wait for the results of its rivals in order to avoid relegation to the Second Division and continue in the first division. In Mestalla, Valencia had to play Real Madrid, who was risking their League title. Valencia won 1-0, with a goal scored by Tendillo. The other results of that round of matches were also favourable for them: Atlético Madrid beat Racing Santander in Madrid and Celta Vigo lost to Real Valladolid, both by scores of 3-1, whilst UD Las Palmas was beaten 1-5 at the *San Mames* by Athletic Bilbao, who became champions of La Liga. Valencia had amazingly survived relegation.

The two following seasons (1983–84 and 1984–85) were a transition to even worse times. Ramos Costa had left the presidency, which was now taken by the cardiologist Vicente Tormo. The club's debt amounted to more than 2,000 million pesetas and the number of members had decreased a lot. In the face of the bad situation of the club, many footballers from the youth team started to play, among them it is worth mentioning a man who gave everything for Valencia CF: Fernando Gómez Colomer.

The situation became complicated to unexpected limits. Many footballers did not get paid and the club was up to its neck in debt. The responsibility for training the team fell on Óscar Rubén Valdez. The new signings did not turn out well, since Muñoz Pérez as well as Sánchez Torres went through Valencia without distinction. The relegation to the Second Division culminated in this fateful season: 85-86. The team did not have a bad start but the situation became more and more complicated. In the

22nd round of matches, Valencia lost 6-0 in Atocha, which caused the dismissal of Valdez and the return of Alfredo di Stéfano to the Valencian bench. With only four games left, Valencia were already relegated to the Second Division, although a victory in the *Estadio Ramón Sánchez Pizjuán* against Sevilla FC (0-2) and home against Hércules (3-1) gave some hope of returning to La Liga next season. The team confirmed the relegation by losing 3-0 at the *Camp Nou* and two draws with Cádiz CF and Real Betis. That draw put an end to 55 consecutive seasons in the elite of the Spanish football, with four League titles, five Copa del Reys, two European Fairs Cups, one Cup Winners' Cup, one Super Cup and a history full of great footballers of international standard. The relegation was the saddest day in the history of Valencia CF.

Mid to late-80s: Resurgence and back in the big League

In hindsight, Valencia's relegation was a blessing in disguise. Footballers, managers, and many supporters agree that the relegation to the Second Division helped Valencia to recover from their problems and to get back on course. 15 years later, the relegation is forgotten about and Valencia rubs shoulders with the best Spanish and European teams once again.

The president of Valencia after the relegation was Arturo Tuzón. The supporters, very much upset about playing in the Second Division, did not abandon Valencia and showed their love for the *Mestalla* club. In fact, the number of members increased. Valencia were champions of the Second Division and returned to the First Division only one year after the relegation.

The core of good Valencia players for the following years was created in the Second Division, with Fernando, Quique, Giner, Voro, Revert, Arroyo, Fenoll, Bossio and the players left from the relegated Valencia: Sempere, Subirats and Arias.

After the promotion, Valencia focused on consolidating their position in La Liga. In the 1987-88 season, Algerian Rabah Madjer played for six months, signed from F.C. Porto, it was a transition period and the team ended up in 14th position. That was the last season for Alfredo di Stéfano on the Valencia bench, at his third spell as the *Che* coach.

In order to face the following season, the board of directors, led by Tuzón, thought of Víctor Espárrago, who was currently managing Cádiz. The Uruguayan was a responsible man who transmitted his personality to the team, with him Valencia got back to contending for the La Liga crown, finishing third in 1989 and then second in 1990.

The 1989-90 season was brilliant for Valencia. The team played a wonderful league campaign and put in an acceptable Copa del Rey performance, plus they played two rounds of the UEFA Cup, against Victoria Bucureşti and Porto led by Rabah Madjer, which saw Valencia unfairly eliminated. The start of the league season was disappointing, although the team started improving as the season went on. When the league had already started, the Bulgarian forward Luboslav Penev arrived at Valencia from CSKA Sofia, known for his goal scoring. Moreover, this season saw the farewell of Javier Subirats after 12 years at Valencia.

The next season, the board of directors, led by Arturo Tuzón, bet on the same team that had got them second place the previous season, with the reinforcement of Roberto, who returned after playing for FC Barcelona. Nevertheless, in this season Valencia only got seventh position. In the UEFA Cup, A.S. Roma eliminated the *Che* team in the quarter-finals with a controversial refereeing decision that had an influence on the final result of the match. Valencia also lost in the Copa del Rey quarterfinals to RCD Mallorca.

In the 1991-92 season, Valencia invested heavily on reinforcing the team. After Víctor Espárrago's departure, Dutch coach Guus Hiddink arrived at Valencia, previously being European champion whilst managing PSV in the late 80's. In regards to the signings, the most remarkable ones were the Panamanian forward Rommel Fernández and the highly talented Brazilian Leonardo. In the league, Hiddink's team ended up fourth. Whilst in the Copa del Rey, Real Madrid eliminated Valencia in the quarterfinals.

There was a great hope for the possibilities of the new Valencia, which in that season lived important events, such as the opening of the *Ciudad Deportiva* training facilities in Paterna, the transformation of the club to a Sporting Limited Company and the presence of the Spanish Olympic football team that played their matches in Mestalla.

That season, Ricardo Arias, the footballer that had played most seasons and more official matches with Valencia in all its history, retired. The Valencian supporters lost one of the most reliable and classiest footballers of its history, but he was well replaced by another Valencian defender, Paco Camarasa.

The 1990s: Valencia stagnation

A new period for the Mestalla club started in 1992, when it became a Sporting Limited Company. There was a big social commotion during the following five years. After the indisputable success in the economic management led by Arturo Tuzón, the defeat by Karlsruher SC meant the beginning of the end of his period as president of Valencia.

The 1993-94 season started well for Valencia, who soon was first in the league and started the UEFA Cup eliminating the French team FC Nantes, who featured players such as Loko, Claude Makélélé, Karembeu and Pedros. That summer, Valencia bought Predrag Mijatović, who became one of the best players of Valencia in that decade, but left the club in a shocking way to rivals Real Madrid. As leader of the league on 2 November 1993, Valencia played against Karlsruher SC in Germany in the return match of the UEFA Cup second round. In the first match, Hiddink's team won 3-1, so it seemed likely that they would qualify for the next round. But a large defeat by 7-0 meant for Valencia the worst European defeat in its history. Guus Hiddink was sacked after losing to Sporting de Gijón the following weekend.

Francisco Real, who up until that moment was member of the technical team of the club, replaced Hiddink. He could raise neither the morale nor the results of the team and after five games was replaced by Héctor Núñez, a Uruguayan forward who had played for Valencia in the '60s. Meanwhile, the board of directors, led by Arturo Tuzón, started to crack. The resignations and internal scandals caused Tuzón's resignation, who was temporally replaced by Melchor Hoyos. An election process was opened that would bring Francisco Roig to the presidency, after beating the other candidate, Ramón Romero, in the polls. Meanwhile, Luboslav Penev, the star of the team, was diagnosed with testicular cancer that kept him away from football for a year, but from which he fortunately recovered completely. A very young Gaizka Mendieta started to play his first matches as well; he had signed coming from CD Castellón and became the big star of Valencia. Another personal tragedy happened in Valencia in September 1993: the Panamanian forward Rommel Fernández, on loan to Albacete Balompié, was killed in a car accident.

On 9 March 1994, Francisco Roig was elected president and in his first decision as president, only hours after winning the election, was to dismiss Héctor Núñez as manager and appointed Jesús Martínez as technical secretary. While they were deciding who would be the substitute for Núñez, the second coach José Manuel Rielo became main coach. Roig's decision for coach was surprising: Guus Hiddink was again chosen, only five months after his dismissal. Valencia straightened out their path, played better football and got better results at the end of the season.

Roig took advantage of the 1994 FIFA World Cup, which took place in the United States, to hire the person who would become coach of the world champions, the Brazilian Carlos Alberto Parreira. Other outstanding people that signed up for Valencia were Andoni Zubizarreta, the number one goalkeeper of the Spanish national team, and the Russian forward Oleg Salenko, who would end up being the top goalscorer of the World Cup. Unfortunately, Salenko did not shine in Valencia as much as he did in the United States. In the 1994-95 season, Valencia reached the final of the Copa del Rey, having previously dismissed the coach. Parreira was dismissed in the Cup semi-finals, against Albacete Balompié, and Rielo was in charge of the team again. In the final, Valencia played Deportivo La Coruña on 24 June 1995, the game was postponed due to a heavy downpour with the score at 1-1. They had to play the remaining time three days later, a goal scored by Alfredo prevented Valencia from getting the victory.

The 1995-96 season started with a new coach, the veteran Luis Aragonés who took Valencia to second place in the league within four points of the title with a team in which Zubizarreta, Camarasa, Fernando and Mijatović stood out. Atlético Madrid, who had hired Luboslav Penev, were the champions that season along with the King's cup to achieve the league and cup double. Predrag Mijatović, the Valencia star at the time, signed for Real Madrid who paid the minimum release clause in his contract, which was met with resentment from the Valencia faithful.

In the summer of 1996, Francisco Roig carried out his will of signing the Brazilian superstar Romário. Nevertheless, the brilliant and rebellious Brazilian forward clashed with Aragonés and was sold to Flamengo. His signing coincided with the signing of the Argentine winger Claudio López, another future idol of the Valencia supporters. The bad results obtained in the league caused the dismissal of the coach from Madrid and he was replaced by Jorge Valdano. The Argentine coach made his debut in

November 1996 and finished the new season without any titles, having been eliminated from the Cup by UD Las Palmas and beaten in the UEFA Cup by the German side Schalke 04, who would end up winning the competition. In December of the same year, Valencia signed another South American star, the Argentine Ariel Ortega.

Valdano started the 1997-98 season, but he was dismissed after three matches, after losing to RCD Mallorca, FC Barcelona and Racing de Santander. Jesús Martínez had also been dismissed as technical secretary, position that was now taken up by the Valencian Javier Subirats. Valdano's substitute was the Italian Claudio Ranieri, who quickly clashed with Romário - who was back from his loan to Flamengo - and Ortega, whose form was inconsistent. So much chaos caused the resignation of Francisco Roig as president, Pedro Cortés, vice-president up until that moment, accepted the club management on 2 December 1997. Valencia was in the relegation zone in the league and also had modest results in the Cup competitions. Valencia finished the league in ninth position, thus getting the right to participate in the Intertoto Cup, a new competition through which it was possible to enter the UEFA Cup competition. The only signing in the middle of the season was the Romanian forward Adrian Ilie, whose first months as a Valencia player were spectacular.

Claudio Ranieri started the 1998-99 season with the qualification of Valencia, through the Intertoto, for the UEFA Cup, where they were eliminated by Liverpool. In the league, Valencia finished fourth, qualifying for the UEFA Champions League. But the great success of this season happened in the Copa del Rey: Valencia won the competition in the Olympic stadium of Seville, by beating Atlético Madrid 3-0 on 26 June 1999, with a great goal by Mendieta and two by 'Piojo' López. The euphoria that the Valencia supporters experienced was indescribable, and the well-deserved festivities are still remembered. The heroes of the cup winning team were Cañizares, Angloma, Đukić, Roche, Carboni, Mendieta, Milla, Farinós, Vlaović, Ilie and Claudio López. Juanfran, Angulo and Björklund also played.

But Ranieri did not continue managing Valencia, the Roman coach had committed himself to Atlético Madrid in the spring of 1999, the same team he had beaten in the Copa del Rey. In order to replace him, the Argentine Héctor Cúper was chosen, who had arrived in RCD Mallorca two seasons before offering an incredible performance for the Balearic club: one Spanish Super Cup, one Copa del Rey final and one Cup winners' Cup final. The most notable signing that summer was of the Argentine left winger Kily González.

The 2000s: Valencia returns to the top of Spanish and European football

Valencia started the 1999–00 season by winning another title, the Spanish Super Cup, beating Barcelona. Valencia finished third in the league, behind the champions Deportivo La Coruña and level on points with second placed Barça. But the biggest success was in the UEFA Champions League; for the first time in its history, Valencia reached the European Cup final. However, in the final played in Paris on 24 May 2000, Real Madrid beat Valencia 3–0.

Cañizares

Angloma

Djukic

Pellegrino

Gerardo

Mendieta

Farinós

K. González

Angulo

Gerard

C. López

2000 UEFA Champions League Final starting
lineup

It was also Claudio López's farewell, as he had agreed to sign for the Italian side Lazio, also leaving was Farinós for Internazionale and Gerard for Barcelona. The notable signings of that summer were, the Norwegian John Carew, Rubén Baraja from Atlético Madrid, the Argentine Roberto Ayala and the Brazilian left back Fábio Aurélio. Baraja and Ayala would soon become a staple of Valencia's dominance of early 2000s in La Liga.

Valencia started the championship on the right foot and were top after 10 games, after the Christmas break Valencia started to pay for the top demand that such an absorbing competition like the Champions League requires. After passing the two mini-league phases, Cúper's team eliminated Arsenal in quarter finals and Leeds United in the semi-finals, and got ready to face Bayern Munich in the big final, Valencia had now reached two European Cup finals in a row. This time the final was to be played in Milan and at the San Siro, on 23 May. Gaizka Mendieta gave Valencia the lead by scoring from the penalty spot right at the start of the match, Cañizares then stopped a penalty from Mehmet Scholl, but Stefan Effenberg drew level after the break thanks to another penalty. After extra time, it was a penalty shoot-out to decide who would be European champions, Valencia, or Bayern Munich. Mauricio Pellegrino was the man who missed to give Bayern European glory and give Valencia heartbreak for the second season running in the biggest game in club football. For Valencia, it was difficult to recover from the blow in Milan, it culminated in Valencia finishing 5th in La Liga and out of the Champions League for the 2001–02 season, the final game of the season meant Valencia only needed a draw at the Nou Camp against Barcelona to seal Champions League qualification, unfortunately for Los Che they lost to Barcelona 3–2 at the Nou Camp, with a last minute goal from Rivaldo resulting in Barcelona qualifying for the Champions League and Valencia missing out, in a head-to-head tie.

The president, D. Pedro Cortés, resigned due to personal reasons and left the club in July, with the satisfaction of having won the King's Cup, one Spanish Super Cup and having been runners up in two

Champions League finals in a row. D. Jaime Ortí replaced him as president and expressed his intention on maintaining the good form that had made the club so admired on the European circuit. There were also some changes in the team and staff, Rafael Benítez, after helping Tenerife to promotion, replaced Héctor Cúper after the latter became the new coach at Internazionale. Among the footballers, Mendieta, Deschamps, Milla, Zahović and Gerard left, and Marchena, Mista, Curro Torres, Rufete, de los Santos, and Salva arrived.

> **Cañizares**
>
> **Angloma**
>
> **Ayala**
>
> **Pellegrino**
>
> **Carboni**
>
> **Mendieta**
>
> **Baraja**
>
> **K. González**
>
> **Carew**
>
> **Aimar**
>
> **Sánchez**
>
> 2001 UEFA Champions League Final starting lineup

From 1999 up until the end of the 2004 season, Valencia had one of the their most successful periods in the club's history. With a total of two La Liga titles, one UEFA Cup, one Copa del Rey and one UEFA Super Cup, in those six years, no less than five first class titles and two UEFA Champions League finals had been achieved.

The 2001–02 season brought Valencia a La Liga title, 31 years after the last title crown. There were new incorporations to the team, manager Rafael Benítez and the new players of Marchena, Mista, Curro Torres, Rufete, de los Santos and Salva.

That first game against fellow title rivals Real Madrid, produced a significant and important victory. This was followed by a record of eleven games won consecutively, breaking the existing one set in the 1970–71 season, the season they had last won the La Liga title under Alfredo di Stéfano.

After a defeat in La Coruña against Deportivo on 9 December 2001, the team had to win against Espanyol in the Estadi Olímpic Lluís Companys to prevent falling further behind the league leaders. Valencia were 2–0 down at half time, but a comeback in the second half saw Valencia win 3–2.

In the second part of the season, Benítez's team suffered a small setback after losing 1–0 in the Santiago Bernabéu to Real Madrid, but they recovered from this setback and achieved four victories and two draws in the following six games. The games against Las Palmas, Athletic de Bilbao, Deportivo Alavés, Real Zaragoza and Barça.

In one of those crucial games that they would come up against Espanyol, Valencia were trailing 1–0 half-time and a man down too with the dismissal of Carboni, but after two goals from Rubén Baraja, Valencia achieved a 2–1 victory. Furthermore, Real Madrid's defeat in Anoeta to Real Sociedad left Valencia with a three-point lead at the top of the table.

The final game of the season was at La Rosaleda to face Málaga, on 5 May 2002, a date that has gone down in Valencia's history. The team shut itself away in Benalmádena, close to the scene of the game, in order to gain focus. An early goal from Ayala and another close to half-time from Fábio Aurélio, assured them their fifth La Liga title, 31 years after their last title win.

The 2002–03 season was a disappointing one for Valencia, as they failed in their attempt to retain the La Liga title and ended up outside of the Champions League spots in fifth, behind Celta de Vigo. They were also knocked out in the quarter-finals of the Champions League by Internazionale on away goals. The 2003–04 season saw Valencia trailing the long time leaders Real Madrid. In February, after 26 games played, Real Madrid were eight points clear. However, their form declined in the late season and they lost their last five games of the campaign, allowing Valencia to overtake them and win the title. The club added the UEFA Cup to this success. Valencia had now been La Liga champions twice in three seasons.

In the summer of 2004, coach Rafa Benítez decided to leave the club stating he had had problems with the club president, he would soon become manager of Liverpool. He was replaced by former Valencia coach Claudio Ranieri, who had recently been sacked by Chelsea. However, his second reign at the club was a disappointment as Valencia harboured realistic hopes of retaining their La Liga crown but, by February, found themselves in 7th place. Valencia had also been knocked out of the Champions League group phase, with Ranieri being sacked promptly in February. The 2004-2005 season ended with Valencia outside of the UEFA Cup spots.

In the summer of 2005, Getafe coach Quique Sánchez Flores was appointed as the new manager of Valencia and ended the season in third place, which in turn gained Valencia a place in the Champions League after a season away from the competition. The 2006–07 season was a season with many difficulties, a season which started with realistic hopes of challenging for La Liga was disrupted with a huge list of injuries to key players and internal arguments between Flores and new Sporting Director Amedeo Carboni. Valencia ended the season in fourth place and were knocked out of the Champions League at the quarter-finals stage by Chelsea 3–2 on aggregate, after knocking out Italian champions Inter in the second round. In the summer of 2007, the internal fight between Flores and Carboni was settled with Carboni being replaced by Ángel Ruiz as the new Sporting Director of Valencia.

On 29 October 2007, the Valencia board of directors fired Flores after a string of disappointing performances and caretaker manager Óscar Rubén Fernández took over on a temporary basis until a full-time manager was found, rumoured to be either Marcello Lippi or José Mourinho. A day later, Dutch manager Ronald Koeman announced he would be leaving PSV to sign for Valencia. But there was still no improvement; in fact, Valencia even went on to drop to the 15th position in the league, just two points above the relegation zone. Although on 16 April 2008, Valencia lifted the Copa del Rey with a 3–1 victory over Getafe at the Vicente Calderón. This was the club's 7th Copa title. Five days later, one day after a devastating 5–1 league defeat in Bilbao, Valencia fired Ronald Koeman and replaced him with Voro, who would guide Valencia as Caretaker Manager for the rest of the season. He went on to win the first game since the sacking of Koeman, beating Osasuna 3–0 in his first game in charge. Voro would eventually drag Valencia from the relegation battle to a safe mid-table finish of 10th place, finally ending a disastrous league campaign for *Los Che*.

Highly-rated Unai Emery was announced as the new manager of Valencia on 22 May 2008. The start of the young manager's career looked to be promising, with the club winning four out of its first five games, a surge that saw the team rise to the top position of the La Liga table. Despite looking impressive in Europe, *Los Che* then hit a poor run of form in the league that saw them dip as low as seventh in the standings. Amid the slump emerged reports of a massive internal debt at the club exceeding 400 million Euros, as well as that the players had been unpaid in weeks. The team's problems were compounded when they were knocked out of the UEFA Cup by Dynamo Kyiv on away goals. After a run where Valencia took only five points from a possible ten games in La Liga, an announcement was made that the club had secured a loan that would cover the players' expenses until the end of the year. This announcement coincided with an upturn in form, and the club won six of its next eight games to surge back into the critical fourth place Champions' League spot. However, *Los Che* were then defeated by 4th place rivals Atlético Madrid and Villarreal in two of the last three games of the campaign, and finished sixth in the table, which meant they failed to qualify for a second successive year for the Champions League. No solution had yet been found to address the massive the debt Valencia were faced with, and rumours persisted that top talents such as David Villa, Juan Mata, and David Silva could leave the club to help balance the books. In the summer of 2010, David Villa and David Silva were sold to Barcelona and Manchester City, respectively, to reduce the club's massive debt.

Current stage

Current stadium

Main article: Mestalla

Valencia played its first years at the Algirós stadium but moved to the Mestalla in 1923. In the 1950s, Mestalla was restructured, which resulted in a capacity increase to 45,000 spectators. Today it holds 55,000 seats. However, Valencia is scheduled to move to a new stadium in the north-west of the city Valencia in 2010. The Nou Mestalla, as it will be called, will hold around 75,000 spectators and will be given a 5 star status by FIFA. It ranks as the fifth largest stadium in Spain. It is also renowned for its steep terracing and for being one of the most intimidating atmospheres in all of Europe to play.

Mestalla

On 20 May 1923, the Mestalla pitch was inaugurated with a friendly match that brought Valencia CF and Levante UD face to face. It was the beginning of a new era that meant farewell to the old place, Algirós, which will always remain in the memories of the Valencians as first home of the club. A long history has taken place on the Mestalla field since its very beginning, when the Valencia team was not yet in the Primera División. Back then, this stadium could hold 17,000 spectators, and in that time the club started to show its potential in regional championships, which led the managers of that time to carry out the first alterations of Mestalla in 1927. The stadium's total capacity increased to 25,000 before it became severely damaged during the Civil War.

Mestalla was used as concentration camp and junk warehouse. It would only keep its structure, since the rest was a lonely plot of land with no terraces and a stand broken during the war. Once the Valencian pitch was renovated, Mestalla saw how the team managed to bring home their first title, the 1941 Cup. An overwhelming team was playing on the grass of the redesigned Valencian stadium in that decade, team that conquered three League titles and two Cups with the legendary 'electric forwards' of Epi, Amadeo, Mundo, Asensi and Guillermo Gorostiza. Those years of sporting success also served as support to recover little by little the Mestalla ground.

During the decade of the fifties, the Valencia ground experienced the deepest change in its whole history. That project resulted in a stadium with a capacity of 45,500 spectators. It was a dream that was destroyed by the flood that flooded Valencia in October 1957 after the overflowing of the Turia River. Nevertheless, Mestalla not only returned to normality, but also some more improvements were added, like artificial light, which was inaugurated during the 1959 Fallas festivities. This was the beginning of a new change for the Mestalla.

During the sixties, the stadium kept the same appearance, whilst the urban view around it was quickly being transformed. Moreover, the Valencian domain became from that moment on, the setting of big European feats. Nottingham Forest was the first foreign team that played an official match in Mestalla with the "Che" club. They played on 15 September 1961 and it was the first clash of a golden age full of continental successes, reinforced with the Fairs Cup won in 1962 and 1963. Mestalla had just entered the European competitions as a stadium where the most important events were taking place.

Mestalla panoramic

From 1969, the expression "Anem a Mestalla" (Let's go to Mestalla), so common among the supporters, started to fall into oblivion. The reason was the change of name that meant a big tribute that the club paid to his most symbolic president that lasted for a quarter of a century. Luis Casanova Giner admitted that he was completely overwhelmed by such honour, and the president himself requested in 1994 that his name was again replaced by the name of Mestalla, as it happened. At the beginning of the seventies, the local bench of the back-then-called Luis Casanova stadium was occupied by Alfredo Di Stéfano, whose results were the winning of one League competition, one second place in the League and two Cup finals lost by the minimum difference. Moreover, Valencia participated for the first time in the European Cup and made their debut in the UEFA Cup. It all was a series of events that made that every match in the stadium located in Suecia Avenue turned into a big party.

In 1972, the head office of the club, located in the back of the numbered terraces, was inaugurated. It consisted of an office of avant-garde style with a worth mentioning trophy hall, which held the foundation flag of the club. In the summer of 1973 there was another new thing, the goal seats, which meant the elimination of fourteen rows of standing terraces providing more comfort and an adjustment to the new times. Valencia's management started to consider the possibility of moving Mestalla from its present location to some land in the outskirts of the town, but finally the project was turned down and some years later.

At that time, Mario Kempes, subsequently considered one of the greatest footballers in the world by Pele was playing for Valencia. With the Matador in its team, Valencia won the Copa del Rey, the Cup Winners Cup and European Super Cup in consecutive years. The "Che" team became continental superchampion in the last European final played in Mestalla. It was in 1980 against Nottingham Forest, which oddly enough was the first foreign team that had played an official match in the Valencian stadium.

Mestalla, which in 1925 had held the first match of the Spain national football team in Valencia, was chosen as the setting for the debut of Spain in the 1982 World Cup, although the performance of the combined national team was not finally what was expected. Ten years later, the Olympic team would look for support in the Valencian stadium, this time with a very different result, since the selected young footballers finally got the gold medal in the 1992 Summer Olympics held in Barcelona.

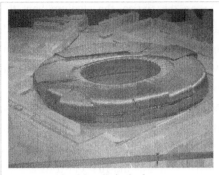

Nou Mestalla in the future

Mestalla has been the setting for important international matches, has held several Cup finals, has been seat for Levante UD, home of the Spanish national team and exile for Castellón and Real Madrid in the European Cup.

2008-2009 was to have been the last season at the Mestalla, with the club moving to their new 75,000-seater stadium Nou Mestalla in time for the 2009-2010 season. However, the club is in financial crisis, and work on the new stadium has stopped.

Kit and colours

Originally the kit was composed of white shirts, black shorts and socks of the same color. Although through the years these two have gone from alternating between white and black. Currently Valencia's main shirt sponsor is Swedish betting company Unibet

- *'First kit'*: White shirts with orange trim, black shorts, white socks with black trim.
- *'Second kit'*: Black shirts with orange trim, orange shorts and black socks.
- *'Goalkeeper Kit'*: Blue shirts with white trim, black shorts and black socks.

Kits and sponsors

1ˢᵗ Uniform Club Unión   Uniform season 2008-09   Uniform season 2009-10

Season	Manufacturer	Sponsor	Season	Manufacturer	Sponsor
1980-82	Adidas	None	1982-84	Ressy	None
1984-89	Ressy	Edesa	1989-93	Puma	Mediterrania Comunitat Valenciana
1993-94	Luanvi	Mediterrania Comunitat Valenciana	1994-95	Luanvi	Cip
1995-98		Ford	1998-00		Terra Mítica
2000-01	Nike	Terra Mítica	2001-02	Nike	Metrored
2002-03		Terra Mítica	2003-08		Toyota
2008-09		Valencia Experience	2009-	Kappa	Unibet

Hymn

The club assigned D. Pablo Sanchez Torella who composed the music of Valencia's anthem, named the "Pasodoble". The hymn was written by Ramon Gimeno Gil, in Valencian language. The anthem was premiered and had its official presentation at the 75th anniversary of Valencia Club de Futbol on September 21, 1993.

Valencia CF anthem

És un equip de primera
nostre València Club de Futbol
que lluita per a defendre en totes bandes nostres colors
En el Camp de l´Algirós ja començàrem a demostrar
que era una bona manera per a València representar
Amunt València, Visca el València, és el millor
Amunt València, Visca el València del nostre cor
Units com sempre els valencianistes et seguirem
en cada estadi per a què triomfes t´animarem
En la capital del Túria és el València qui vist de blanc
i defén la camiseta ple de coratge per a guanyar
En Mestalla continuarem sempre esforçant-se per a triomfar
i les glòries arribaren i en competència continuaran
Amunt València, Visca el València, és el millor
Amunt València, Visca el València, del nostre cor
Units com sempre els valencianistes et seguirem,
en cada estadi perquè triomfes t´animarem

Amunt València, Visca el València és el millooooooooor

The story of the bat

Valencia and the Balearic Islands were conquered by King James I of Aragon during the first half of the 13th century. After the conquest the king gave them the status of independent kingdoms of whom he was also the king (but they were independent of Catalan or Aragonese laws and institutions). The arms of Valencia show those of James I, King of Aragon.

The unique crowned letters L besides the shield were granted by King James. The reason for the letters was that the city had been loyal twice to the King, hence twice a letter L and a crown for the king.

Coat of arms of the city of Valencia.

There are several possible explanations for the bat; one is that bats are simply quite common in the area. The second theory is that on October 9, 1238, when James I was about to enter the city, re-conquering it from the Moors, one bat landed on the top of his flag, and he interpreted it as a good sign. As he conquered the city, the bat was added to the arms.

Current squad

The numbers are established according to the official website: www.valenciacf.com [1]

Note: Flags indicate national team as has been defined under FIFA eligibility rules. Players may hold more than one non-FIFA nationality.

No.		Position	Player
1		GK	César Sánchez *(4th captain)*
2		DF	Bruno Saltor
3		DF	Hedwiges Maduro
4		DF	David Navarro *(vice captain)*
5		MF	Mehmet Topal
6		MF	David Albelda
7		MF	Joaquín Sánchez *(3rd captain)*
8		FW	Chori Domínguez
9		FW	Roberto Soldado

10		FW	Juan Manuel Mata
11		FW	Aritz Aduriz
12		MF	Sofiane Feghouli
13		GK	Vicente Guaita

No.		Position	Player
14		MF	Vicente Rodríguez *(captain)*
15		DF	Ángel Dealbert
17		DF	Marius Stankevičius *(on loan from Sampdoria)*
18		MF	Manuel Fernandes
19		MF	Pablo Hernández
20		DF	Ricardo Costa
21		MF	Éver Banega
22		DF	Jérémy Mathieu
23		DF	Miguel Monteiro
24		MF	Tino Costa
25		GK	Miguel Ángel Moyà
28		MF	Jordi Alba

Out on loan

Note: Flags indicate national team as has been defined under FIFA eligibility rules. Players may hold more than one non-FIFA nationality.

No.		Position	Player	No.		Position	Player
		GK	Renan *(at Internacional)*			MF	Nacho González *(at Levante)*
		DF	Asier del Horno *(at Levante)*			MF	Aarón Ñíguez *(at Recreativo)*
		MF	Míchel *(at Deportivo)*				

Recent seasons

See also: Valencia CF seasons

Season	League									Cup	Europe		Other Comp.		Top scorer	
	Division	Pos.	Pl.	W	D	L	GS	GA	Pts						Name	Goals
2005–06	La Liga	3rd	38	19	12	7	58	33	69	QF			UEFA Intertoto Cup	RU	David Villa	28
2006–07	La Liga	4th	38	20	6	12	57	42	66	R16	Champions League	QF			David Villa	20
2007–08	La Liga	10th	38	15	6	17	48	62	51	W	Champions League	GS			David Villa	22
2008–09	La Liga	6th	38	18	8	12	68	54	62	QF	UEFA Cup	R32	Supercopa de España	RU	David Villa	31
2009–10	La Liga	3rd	38	21	8	9	59	40	71	R16	Europa League	QF			David Villa	28
2010–11	La Liga	1st	6	5	1	0	11	4	16		Champions League					

Last updated: 25 Sep 2010

Pos. = Position; **Pl** = Match played; **W** = Win; **D** = Draw; **L** = Lost; **GS** = Goal Scored; **GA** = Goal Against; **Pts** = Points

Technical staff

- **Coach**: Unai Emery
- **Assistant coach**: Juan Carlos Carcedo
- **Goalkeeping coach**: José Manuel Ochotorena
- **Physical coach**: Julen Masach
- **Delegator**: Jesús Paniagua
- **Head of Medical**: Antonio Giner Marco
- **Club Doctor**: Miguel Frasquet
- **Assistants**: Bernardo España, Vicente Ventura Deval, Jorge Vicente Ramón Donat, Vicente Navarro Navarro, José Manuel López.
- **Physiotherapists**: José de los Santos, Andreu Gramaje, Ximo Galindo, Álvaro Ortiz, Luis Baraja, David Ponce, Jordi Sorli.

Manager Unai Emery

Statistics and records

Main article: Valencia CF statistics

- **Average Attendance:** 46,894
- **Socios:** 45,116
- **Seasons in First Division:** 75
- **Seasons in Second Division:** 4
- **Historical classification in La Liga:** 3rd place.
- **Highest position in League:** 1st place
- **Lowest position in League:** 16th place
- **Games played:** 2,284
- **Games won:** 1,017
- **Games drawn:** 529
- **Games lost:** 738
- **Goals for:** 3,810
- **Goals against:** 2,973
- **Goal difference:** 837
- **Overall points:** 2,789
- **Biggest home win:** Valencia 18–0 Sporting de Gijón (29/11/1953)
- **Biggest away win:** Lleida 1–6 Valencia (04/02/1951) and Málaga 1–6 Valencia (31/01/2004)
- **Biggest home defeat:** Valencia 1–5 Athletic Bilbao (15/01/1933) and Valencia 1–5 Real Madrid (31/10/2007)
- **Biggest defeat:** Sevilla 10–3 Valencia (13/10/1940)
- *Pichichi*'s won: Mundo (2): 1941–42, 27 goals; 1943–44, 27 goals; **Ricardo Alos**: 1957–58, 19 goals; Valdo: 1966–67, 24 goals; Mario Kempes (2): 1976–77, 24 goals; 1977–78, 28 goals.
- **Zamora's won:** Ignacio Eizaguirre (2): 1943–44, 32 goals conceded; 1944–45, 28 goals conceded; **Goyo**: 1957–58, 28 goals conceded; **Angel Abelardo**: 1970–71, 19 goals conceded; **José Luis Manzanedo**: 1978–79, 26 goals conceded; José Manuel Ochotorena: 1988–89, 25 goals conceded; Santiago Cañizares (3): 2000–01, 34 goals conceded; 2001–02, 23 goals conceded; 2003–04, 25 goals conceded.
- **Most games played:** Fernando (542), **Árias** (500), Santiago Cañizares (416), Miguel Ángel Angulo (411)
- **Most goals scored:** Mundo (260), Waldo (147), Mario Kempes (145), Fernando (140), David Villa (129)

Managerial Information

Main article: Valencia CF managers

The following managers have all won at least one major trophy when in charge.

Name	Period	Trophies								Total
		Domestic			International					
		LL	CdR	SC	UCL	UCWC	UEL	UIC	USC	
Ramón Encinas Dios	1939–42	1	1	-	-	-	-	-	-	2
Eduardo Cubells	1943–46	1	-	-	-	-	-	-	-	1
Luis Casas Pasarín	1946–48	1	-	-	-	-	-	-	-	1
Jacinto Quincoces	1948–54	-	2	1	-	-	-	-	-	3
Alejandro Scopelli	1962–63	-	-	-	-	-	2	-	-	2
Edmundo Suárez	1966–68	-	1	-	-	-	-	-	-	1
Alfredo di Stéfano	1970–74, 1979–80	1	-	-	-	1	-	-	-	2
Bernardino Pérez	1979, 1980–82	-	1	-	-	-	-	-	1	2
Claudio Ranieri	1997–99, 2004–05	-	1	-	-	-	-	1	1	3
Héctor Cúper	1999–01	-	-	1	-	-	-	-	-	1
Rafael Benítez	2001–04	2	-	-	-	-	1	-	-	3
Ronald Koeman	2007–08	-	1	-	-	-	-	-	-	1
Total	**1919–2010**	**6**	**7**	**2**	**0**	**1**	**3**	**1**	**2**	**22**

Honours

Main article: Valencia CF honours

Main article: Valencia CF in Europe

Domestic competitions

- **La Liga**
  - *Winners (6):* 1941-42, 1943-44, 1946-47, 1970-71, 2001-02, 2003-04.
  - *Runners-up (6):* 1947-48, 1948-49, 1952-53, 1971-72, 1989-90, 1995-96.
- **Copa del Rey**
  - *Winners (7):* 1940-41, 1948–49, 1953–54, 1966–67, 1978–79, 1998-99, 2007-08.
  - *Runners-up (10):* 1933-34, 1936–37, 1943–44, 1944–45, 1945–46, 1951–52, 1969–70, 1970–71, 1971–72, 1994-95.

- **Supercopa de España**
  - *Winners (1):* 1999.
  - *Runners-up (3):* 2002, 2004, 2008.
- **Copa Eva Duarte (Predecessor to the Supercopa de España)**
  - *Winners (1):* 1949.
  - *Runners-up (1):* 1947.
- **Segunda División**
  - *Winners (2):* 1930-31, 1986-87.

▪ Major European competitions

- **UEFA Champions League**
  - *Runners-up (2):* 1999-00, 2000-01.
- **UEFA Cup Winners' Cup**
  - *Winners (1):* 1979-80.
- **UEFA Cup**
  - *Winners (1):* 2003-04.
- **Fairs Cup (Predecessor to the UEFA Cup)**
  - *Winners (2):* 1961-62, 1962-63.
  - *Runners-up (1):* 1963-64.
- **UEFA Super Cup**
  - *Winners (2):* 1980, 2004.
- **UEFA Intertoto Cup**
  - **Winners (1):** 1998.

See also

- Valencia CF Mestalla
- Orange Trophy
- Richest football clubs
- European football records
- List of UEFA club competition winners

Sources

- *Valencia Club de Fútbol (1919–1969), Bodas de Oro*, de José Manuel Hernández Perpiñá. 1969, Talleres Tipográficos Vila, S.L.
- *Historia del Valencia F.C.*, de Jaime Hernández Perpiñá. 1974, Ediciones Danae, S.A. ISBN 84-85.184
- *La Gran Historia del Valencia C.F.*, de Jaime Hernández Perpiñá. 1994, Levante-EMV. ISBN 84-87502-36-9
- *DVD Valencia C.F. (Historia Temática). Un histórico en la Liga.". 2003, Superdeporte. V-4342-2003*

External links

- Official website [2] (Spanish) (Catalan) (English) (Japanese)
- The New Stadium [3]

Valencia CF Mestalla

Full name	Valencia Club de Fútbol Mestalla
Nickname(s)	*Los Che*
Founded	1944
Ground	Paterna, Valencia, Spain
Chairman	Manuel Llorente
Manager	Vicente Mir
League	3ª - Group 6
2009–10	2ªB - Group 3, **18th**

Home colours	**Away colours**

Valencia Club de Fútbol Mestalla or **Valencia CF B** is a Spanish football team. It is the reserve team of Valencia CF. Reserve teams in the Spanish football league system play in the same football pyramid as their senior team rather than in a separate league. However, reserve teams cannot play in the same division as their senior team. Therefore the team is ineligible for promotion to the Primera División. Reserve teams are also no longer permitted to enter the Copa del Rey. In the past the reserve teams of both FC Barcelona and Real Madrid have blurred the lines between being a reserve team and a separate entity.

The team is officially known as **Valencia CF Mestalla** on the club's official promotion and website, but LFP rules prohibit B clubs from having different names to their parent club, except Real Madrid B and Sevilla B, which currently plays/once played in Segunda División.

History

In 1952 they were slotted to join the top division however they were not allowed due to the fact that the senior team was already in the top division.

Current squad

Note: Flags indicate national team as has been defined under FIFA eligibility rules. Players may hold more than one non-FIFA nationality.

No.	Position	Player
	GK	Salva
	GK	Sergio Garabato
	DF	Jaume
	DF	Ángel
	DF	Alexis
	DF	Lillo
	DF	Manu Micó
	DF	Arturo
	MF	Míchel

No.	Position	Player
	MF	David Tímor
	MF	Carlos David
	MF	Carles
	MF	Ximo Forner
	FW	Daniel Olcina
	FW	Pablo Morgado
	FW	Joaquín Calderón
	FW	Alexander Olsen

Season to season

Season	Division	Place	Copa del Rey
1944/45	Regional	—	
1945/46	Regional	—	
1946/47	3ª	2nd	
1947/48	2ª	8th	
1948/49	2ª	12th	
1949/50	2ª	6th	
1950/51	2ª	8th	
1951/52	2ª	2nd	
1952/53	2ª	6th	
1953/54	2ª	15th	
1954/55	3ª	2nd	
1955/56	2ª	6th	
1956/57	2ª	17th	
1957/58	3ª	1st	
1958/59	3ª	2nd	
1959/60	2ª	11th	
1960/61	2ª	10th	

Season	Division	Place	Copa del Rey
1961/62	2ª	12th	
1962/63	2ª	9th	
1963/64	2ª	4th	
1964/65	2ª	8th	
1965/66	2ª	6th	
1966/67	2ª	9th	
1967/68	2ª	8th	
1968/69	2ª	17th	
1969/70	3ª	2nd	
1970/71	3ª	1st	
1971/72	2ª	13th	

1972/73	2ª	20th	
1973/74	3ª	2nd	
1974/75	3ª	5th	
1975/76	3ª	18th	
1976/77	Regional	—	
1977/78	3ª	6th	

Season	Division	Place	Copa del Rey
1978/79	3ª	10th	
1979/80	3ª	5th	
1980/81	3ª	8th	
1981/82	3ª	3rd	
1982/83	3ª	1st	
1983/84	3ª	3rd	
1984/85	3ª	1st	
1985/86	3ª	5th	
1986/87	3ª	5th	
1987/88	2ªB	16th	
1988/89	3ª	3rd	
1989/90	3ª	2nd	
1990/91	3ª	4th	
1991/92	3ª	1st	
1992/93	2ªB	12th	
1993/94	2ªB	13th	
1994/95	2ªB	3rd	

Season	Division	Place	Copa del Rey
1995/96	2ªB	4th	
1996/97	2ªB	14th	
1997/98	2ªB	14th	
1998/99	2ªB	10th	
1999/00	2ªB	17th	
2000/01	3ª	2nd	
2001/02	2ªB	2nd	
2002/03	2ªB	6th	
2003/04	2ªB	17th	
2004/05	3ª	1st	
2005/06	3ª	2nd	
2006/07	2ªB	16th	
2007/08	3ª	2nd	
2008/09	2ªB	12th	
2009/10	2ªB	18th	
2010/11	3ª	—	

- **21** seasons in *Segunda División*
- **15** seasons in *Segunda División B*
- **27** seasons in *Tercera División*
- **3** seasons in *Categorías Regionales*

Managerial history

- 2006-07: Luis Sánchez Duque
- 2007-08: Óscar Rubén Fernández

External links

- (Spanish) (Catalan) (English) Official Site [1]
- Futbolme.com profile [2]

Valencia Street Circuit

Not to be confused with Circuit de Valencia

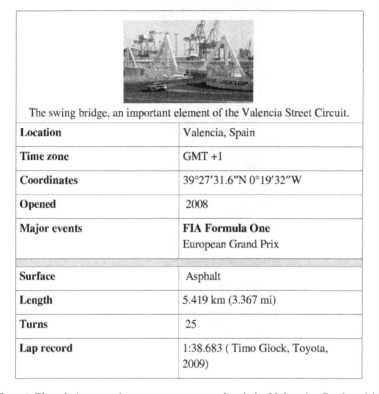

The swing bridge, an important element of the Valencia Street Circuit.

Location	Valencia, Spain
Time zone	GMT +1
Coordinates	39°27′31.6″N 0°19′32″W
Opened	2008
Major events	**FIA Formula One** European Grand Prix
Surface	Asphalt
Length	5.419 km (3.367 mi)
Turns	25
Lap record	1:38.683 (Timo Glock, Toyota, 2009)

The **Valencia Street Circuit** is a semi-permanent street circuit in Valencia, Spain which will host the Formula One European Grand Prix for seven years. The first race meeting on the circuit was held over the 23/24 August 2008 weekend, with Felipe Massa winning the main event, the European Grand Prix, after starting from pole position. The circuit utilizes the roads skirting around the city's harbour and America's Cup port area – including a section over a 140 metre long swing bridge, and also includes some roads designed exclusively for racing purposes by the German architect Hermann Tilke who also designed the infrastructural buildings for the circuit.

History

The deal to host the Valencia race was signed on June 1, 2007 and is for seven years. The deal was made between Formula One supremo Bernie Ecclestone and the Valmor Sport group, which is led by former motorcycle rider Jorge Martinez Aspar and Villarreal football club's president Fernando Roig. This deal goes back on comments made by Ecclestone previously stating that no European country should hold more than one race each year as Barcelona currently holds the Spanish Grand Prix each year.

Although now confirmed, the deal was rumored to be conditional on People's Party winning regional elections on 27 May 2007. However, Ecclestone had clarified his comments on May 16, 2007: "I said I wouldn't formalise a contract until after the elections because I didn't know who I would be signing it with." He said his statements were taken out of context. Ecclestone has since been cleared of influencing the election by the Valencian Electoral Commission.

The official track layout was unveiled by Valencia councillor and transport minister, Mario Flores, on 19 July 2007. The track was first used in the last weekend of July 2008, as the circuit hosted a round of the Spanish F3 Championship and International GT Open. It was first used for the European Grand Prix on August 24, 2008.

Layout

The track is 5.419 kilometres (3.367 mi) long and incorporates a total of 25 turns – 11 right-handers and 14 left-handers. It is estimated that the track has a top speed of around 323 kilometres per hour (201 mph), with a lap record of 1:38.683, held by Timo Glock, which he set during the 2009 European Grand Prix. Valencia is not as tight as Circuit de Monaco but overtaking opportunities are still relatively few, due to the straights not being straight and the dust off line. Nico Hülkenberg noticed quite a bit of space for a street circuit and some corners have a lot of run-off area. Robert Kubica suggested that good traction and good braking stability are crucial to win at this circuit because there is a lot of long straight lines ending with heavy braking.

The circuit has been criticised by the drivers for its lack of overtaking opportunites. There have only been 4 recorded overtakes since the race was first held in 2008, with none of them in 2009. There is little space for improvements to the circuit to address this problem.

2008 European Grand Prix

Main article: 2008 European Grand Prix

The 2008 European Grand Prix was held on August 24, 2008. It was the 12th race of the 2008 Formula One season. The race, contested over 57 laps, was won by Felipe Massa for the Ferrari team after starting from pole position. Lewis Hamilton finished second in a McLaren car, with Robert Kubica third in a BMW Sauber.

During the race Massa was reprimanded by the stewards and fined €10,000 for nearly colliding with Adrian Sutil's car in the pits, but the Brazilian kept his victory.

This was Bridgestone's 200th and Massa's 100th entry, and this makes Massa the only driver to date to win his 100th race.

2009 European Grand Prix

Main article: 2009 European Grand Prix

The 2009 European Grand Prix was held on August 23, 2009. It was the 11th race of the 2009 Formula One season. The race, contested over 57 laps, was won by Rubens Barrichello for the Brawn team after Lewis Hamilton took pole in the McLaren. Hamilton came second, while Kimi Räikkönen took third in the Ferrari car. It was notable for there not being one single on track overtaking manouvere, the first time since the controversial 2005 United States Grand Prix. It marked the first race of Frenchman Romain Grosjean in the Renault. Barrichello's victory was the 100th for a Brazilian driver.

See also

- List of Formula One circuits
- Circuit de Valencia − another motor racing circuit in Valencia used for MotoGP Valencian Community motorcycle Grand Prix.

External links

- The F1 Valencia Street Circuit Guide Site [1]
- The F1 Valencia Street Circuit Official Site [2]
- Valencia Street Circuit guide from Official F1 Site [3]
- BBC's circuit guide [4]
- More Monza than Monaco − why Valencia's no ordinary street circuit [5]
- City limits: Toyota on what to expect in Valencia [6]
- A lap of Valencia with Honda's Mike Conway [7]
- Facts and figures − Valencia and its new street circuit [8]
- Valencia − the technical requirements [9]
- Valencia F1 Street Circuit in Google Maps [10]

Circuit Ricardo Tormo

Location	Cheste, Valencia, (Spain)
Time zone	GMT +1 (DST: +2)
Major events	**FIM MotoGP** Valencian Community motorcycle Grand Prix WTCC; DTM; F3; GP2;SBK
Length	4.051 km (2.517 mi)
Turns	14
Lap record	1:23.489 (Marc Gené, LMS, 2007)

Circuit Ricardo Tormo (also known as **Circuit de Valencia** and officially named "**Circuit de la Comunitat Valenciana Ricardo Tormo**") is a motorsport race track located in Cheste (Valencia, Spain) and built in 1999. It has a capacity of 120,000 spectators and seating for 60,000. It is often used as a test track by the Formula One teams, because of the mild temperatures in winter. Anthony Davidson holds the unofficial lap record, set in 2006 while testing a Honda, with a time of 1 m 08.540sec.

The track hosts the MotoGP Valencian Community Grand Prix.

The track is named after Spanish Grand Prix motorcycle racer Ricardo Tormo (September 7, 1952 – December 27, 1998).

External links

- Circuit de Valencia [1] – Official website
- Trackpedia's guide to driving the Circuit de Valencia [2]

Geographical coordinates: 39°29′9″N 0°37′41″W

Transportation

Valencia Airport

Valencia Airport	
IATA: VLC – ICAO: LEVC	
Summary	
Airport type	Public
Operator	Aena
Serves	Valencia
Location	Manises
Hub for	• Air Nostrum • Ryanair (from 2 November) • Vueling • Wondair
Elevation AMSL	73 m / 240 ft
Coordinates	39°29′22″N 00°28′54″W

Runways			
Direction	**Length**		**Surface**
	m	**ft**	
12/30	3,215	10,548	Asphalt

Statistics (2008)	
Passengers	5,779,336
Passenger growth 07-08	-2.6%

Source: Passengers from AENA
Spanish AIP at EUROCONTROL

Valencia Airport in Manises (IATA: **VLC**, ICAO: **LEVC**), also known as **Manises Airport**, is the 8th busiest Spanish airport in terms of passengers and second in the region after Alicante. It is situated 8 km (5.0 mi) west of the city of Valencia. The airport has flight connections to about 15 European countries and 5.7 million passengers passed through the airport in 2008. The airport has one terminal and one runway. The former runway 04/22 is not in use and has no ILS but has a helipad at the southwestern end.

Valencia airport is situated adjacent to the Autovía A-3 highway which connects Valencia with Madrid and is also close to the Autovía A-7 coastal route to Barcelona. It is also well served by public transport. It is connected to Valencia by a regular bus line (MetroBus) which takes 45 minutes, while the shuttle service (Aerobus) to city centre takes only 20 minutes. The metro network (lines 3 and 5) also connect the airport to the city centre (15 minutes), the Railway Station and the Port.

A new regional terminal, expanded car parking facilities and apron area have been recently constructed in time for the 2007 America's Cup. The runway has been also lengthened by 50 m (160 ft).

It is the main base of Iberia's regional carrier Air Nostrum. Irish low-cost airline Ryanair used the airport as a hub since 2007 but decided to close it in November 2008 following a row over subsidies by the airport authorities. Since then the airline has continued to operate out of Valencia but as a relatively large destination airport, and not a base. Ryanair since announced on 23 June 2010, that it would re-open its Valencia base with 2 based aircraft and 10 new destinations from November 2010.

Airlines and destinations

Airlines	Destinations
Air Berlin	Cologne/Bonn, Palma de Mallorca, Stuttgart [ends 30 October]
Air Europa	Arrecife, Palma de Mallorca, Paris-Charles de Gaulle, Tenerife-South
Alitalia	Rome-Fiumicino
Baboo	Geneva
Blue Air	Bucharest-Băneasa, Sibiu
Delta Air Lines	New York-JFK [seasonal]
EasyJet	London-Gatwick
Iberia	Madrid
Iberia operated by Air Nostrum	A Coruña, Badajoz, Barcelona, Bilbao, Casablanca, Dubrovnik [seasonal], Funchal [seasonal], Huesca, Ibiza, Las Palmas de Gran Canaria, León, Lisbon, Madrid, Málaga, Marrakech [seasonal], Melilla, Minorca, Oveido, Palma de Mallorca, Santander, Santiago de Compostela, Seville, Tenerife-North, Valladolid, Vigo
Iberworld	Arrecife, Tenerife-South
Lufthansa	Düsseldorf
Lufthansa Regional operated by Eurowings	Düsseldorf
Niki	Vienna [begins 3 February]

Royal Air Maroc	Casablanca [begins 18 December]
Ryanair	Barcelona, Bari, Bologna, Bournemouth [ends 28 October], Bristol, Brussels South-Charleroi, Cagliari, Dublin [seasonal], East Midlands, Fuerteventura [begins 5 November], Hahn, Ibiza [begins 2 November], London-Stansted, Madrid, Malaga, Malta, Milan-Orio al Serio, Marrakech [begins 2 November], Marseille [begins 2 November], Memmingen [begins 3 November], Oslo-Rygge, Palma de Mallorca [begins 2 November], Paris-Beauvais [begins 3 November], Pisa, Porto [begins 2 November], Rome-Ciampino, Santiago De Compostela [begins 3 November], Seville [begins 2 November], Trieste [begins 2 November], Trapani, Venice-Treviso, Weeze
Spanair	Algiers [begin 31 October],Arrecife, Barcelona, Madrid, Tenerife-South
Swiss International Air Lines	Zürich
TAP Portugal operated by Portugália	Lisbon
TAROM	Bucharest-Otopeni
Turkish Airlines	Istanbul [begins 2011]
Transavia.com	Amsterdam
Travel Service Airlines operated by Smart Wings	Prague [seasonal]
Vueling Airlines	Amsterdam, Brussels, Milan-Malpensa, Paris-Orly, Rome-Fiumicino
Wizz Air	Bucharest-Băneasa, Cluj-Napoca, Sofia, Timişoara

External links

- Aena.es Valencia Information [1] Official Airport Website (in English)
- [2] Flightaware
- [3] Flight tracker
- Current weather for LEVC [4] at NOAA/NWS
- Accident history for VLC [5] at Aviation Safety Network

Ferrocarrils de la Generalitat Valenciana

Ferrocarrils de la Generalitat Valenciana or **FGV** is a Spanish railway company which operates several metre gauge lines, in the Autonomous Community of Valencia, in Spain.

The company operates a non-electrified 92 km (55 mile) long line, between Alicante, Benidorm, and Denia.

And also operates the city tram and metro system of Valencia (Valencia Metro) and Alicante (Alicante Tram).

The company is owned by the Generalitat of Valencia (government of the Valencian Community).

History

Establishment of FGV

FGV was founded as a company in 1986, and on 1 January 1987 took over all remaining narrow gauge railways in the Valencian Community. These had previously been part of the nationally owned FEVE system.

The newly formed railway system consisted of various electrified suburban lines around Valencia and the diesel-worked Alicante to Denia railway. Much of the infrastructure was in a poor state following neglect by the FEVE administration and patronage was consequently low.

Investment in the Valencia system

The early years of FGV saw much investment in the Valencia suburban system. The lines to the north and south of the city were connected by cross-town tunnels which were developed into the current metro system. FGV also introduced the first modern tram in Spain, partly running on the alignment of narrow gauge railways.

Both the metro and trams systems are being developed through the addition of new lines. Projects are also in hand to modernise the classic parts of the system through realignments and new rolling stock.

Investment in the Alicante system

In Alicante too, the narrow gauge railway is being developed into a modern tramway. It has been extended through a tunnel to Mercado and will ultimately reach the RENFE railway station through an extension of this tunnel. The tram system is also being extended in other directions.

The Alicante to Denia railway line is being electrified as far as Altea and will be served by tram-trains (vehicles that can run on both railway and tramway infrastructure). The remaining section to Denia will continue to be diesel-worked for the time being and trainsets have been modernised for this purpose.

In Benidorm, a local tram service is also being planned. This will branch off the main railway line and serve the centre of this town.

Future projects

FGV is seeking to take over the Xativa to Alcoi railway from Renfe. The mountain railway is currently in a poor state and served only by three trains per day and direction.

External links

- FGV Official website [1]

Valencia Metro (Spain)

metrovalencia	
Info	
Owner	Ferrocarrils de la Generalitat Valenciana
Locale	Valencia, Spain
Transit type	Rapid transit Tram
Number of lines	5
Number of stations	169
Chief executive	Mario Flores Lanuza
Operation	
Began operation	October 8, 1988 (as FGV) May 5, 1995 (as MetroValencia)
Number of vehicles	82
Technical	
System length	175.34 km (108.95 mi)
Track gauge	1000 mm (3.3 ft)
Minimum radius of curvature	0 feet 0 inches (0 mm)
Electrification	50 V DC 1500 V DC, overhead wire
Average speed	0 mph (0 km/h)
Top speed	0 mph (0 km/h)

Map of MetroValencia

The Valencian narrow gauge railway, or **metrovalencia**, is a modernised amalgamation of former FEVE diesel operated suburban/regional railways. It is a large suburban network that crosses the city of Valencia, with all trains continuing out to far-flung suburbs. It also has destinations on lines that make it more closely ressemble commuter train evidence of its history - there is no street running. A tramway system north of the Túria riverbed park is considered Line 4 of the MetroValencia.

This network consists of more than 134 kilometres (83 mi) of track, of which around 19 kilometres (12 mi) is below ground.

The system authority *Ferrocarrils de la Generalitat Valenciana* uses bilingual signage in Valencian (also known as Catalan elsewhere) and Spanish.

Lines

Line	Terminals	Length		Number of stations	Passengers in 2008
		km	mi		
1	Llíria/Bétera - Torrent Avinguda/Villanueva de Castellón	95.2	59.5	59	20.650.928
	Tavernes Blanques - Natzaret	Under construction. Completion expected 2011-2012.			
	Rafelbunyol - Aeroport	19.8	12.4	27	27.306.347
	Mas del Rosari/Ll. Llarga/Fira – Dr. Lluch	9.8	6.1	33	4.506.164
5	Neptú ~ Marítim-Serreria - Aeroport/Torrent Avinguda	24.1	14.9	31	15.057.074
	Tossal del Rei - Marítim Serrería	10.8	6.7	21	432.654

Technical data

- Gauge width: 1000 mm
- Current system: 750 V DC / 1500 V DC, overhead wire

History

First four lines

On 8 October 1988 the tunnel through which line 1 crosses Valencia was opened between Sant Isidre and Ademuz (now Empalme), which connected the line with southbound trains from València-Jesús to Castelló de la Ribera (now Villanueva de Castellón) at Sant Isidre. Line 2 went from València-Sud to Llíria, with some trains terminating in Paterna.

In May 1994 the *tranvia* line 4 opened. Valencia was the first city in Spain to use this mode of transport in modern era. Originally line 4 was 9.7 kilometres (6.0 mi) long and had 21 stations. The line connected the suburban lines with high demand zones such as the Polytechnic University, the new university campus and the Malvarosa beach, which the former line Empalme - Pont de Fusta - El Grau had connected before. One year later, in May 1995, line 3 was extended from El Palmaret in Alboraria to Alameda. The extension reused the older railway line Pont de Fusta-Rafelbunyol, of which part

Many stations have an artistic exhibit in the entrance hall. This one is in Benimaclet.

was scrapped (between Pont de Fusta - Sant Llorenç - El Palmaret), and the rest was switched from 750 V to 1500 V.

Further alterations followed five years later. On 16 September 1998, line 2 was merged with line 1, and Line 3 was extended from Alameda to Avinguda del Cid in the west and Torrent in the south with some trains only going as far as Jesús. Half a year later, on 20 May 1999, line 3 was extended from Avinguda del Cid to Mislata-Almassil

Lines 5 and 6, and more extensions

In April 2003, the new line 5 was opened. This line took over the previous line 3 connection from Alameda to Torrent, together with a newly constructed branch from Alameda to Ayora 2.3 kilometres (1.4 mi). (Although some very early morning trains still travel from Machado to Torrent, this is not represented on maps.) One year later, the new line 5 was extended, together with line 1, from Torrent to

Torrent Avinguda, a distance of 2.3 kilometres. On October 3 2005, Bailén station was opened on line 5. This station is between Colón and Jesús, and has connections with València-Nord, the main railway station of València. Furthermore, Bailen is close to the Plaça d'Espanya station on line 1. In October 2005, line 4 was extended to Mas del Rosari, and on 20 December 2005 to Lloma Llarga-Terramelar.

2 April 2007 - Line 5 was extended to the East to a new station Marítim-Serrería (originally planned as Jerónimo Monsoriu).

18 April 2007 - Line 5 extended to the Airport (Aeroport Station) in the west and to the Port (Neptú Station) in the east, this last section from Marítim-Serreria to Neptú is a tram section; the trains go from Aeroport to Marítim-Serrreria and then a tram operates between Marítim-Serreria and Neptú. Line 3 was extended to the Airport as well to cover the schedule limitations of line 5 to Aeroport station.

22 September 2007 - Line 6 was opened, linking the neighbourhoods of Orriols and Torrefiel to the metro system for the first time. Additionally a new station "Torre del Virrei" was added to Line 1. It is situated between the stations of "L'Eliana" and "La Pobla de Vallbona".

Future lines

Four more lines are planned to be inaugurated in upcoming years. Line 2 is under construction, and its inauguration is expected to be in 2011. Line 7, without new stations, will be inaugurated in 2011. It will be a new connection with stations from lines 3,4,5,6 and a future eighth line.

Accidents

On 9 September 2005, two trains crashed into each other on Line 1. Nobody was killed, but according to early reports 35 people were injured, 4 of whom were taken to hospital, their condition described as serious. The first train had been stationary waiting for a red signal. The second used its emergency brakes to avoid a collision, but was hit by a third train. The force of the impact severely damaged the drivers' cabs at the front of the last train and at the rear of the second train. The crash occurred between Paiporta and Picanya about 5 km south-east of the city centre. The 3729 and 3730 EMUs

Accident occurred on 9th September 2005

are now a single EMU with 3729A and the 3730A cars, the 'B' cars were severely damaged and are currently at València-Sud workshop, waiting to be scrapped.

3 July 2006 was a black day for the Valencia metro. In a severe accident, a two-car EMU derailed between Jesús and Plaça d'Espanya stations. At least 43 people were killed and 52 injured. It was the worst metro accident in Spanish history.

External links

- Metrovalencia [1]
- Information, images and maps [2]

See also

- Madrid Metro
- Barcelona Metro
- Bilbao Metro
- List of Valencia, Spain metro stations
- List of metro systems

Article Sources and Contributors

History of Spain *Source*: http://en.wikipedia.org/?oldid=390148277 *Contributors*: 1 anonymous edits

Geography of Spain *Source*: http://en.wikipedia.org/?oldid=389453690 *Contributors*: Grondemar

Politics of Spain *Source*: http://en.wikipedia.org/?oldid=389383487 *Contributors*: NerdyScienceDude

Economy of Spain *Source*: http://en.wikipedia.org/?oldid=389986308 *Contributors*: 1 anonymous edits

Foreign relations of Spain *Source*: http://en.wikipedia.org/?oldid=390048604 *Contributors*: John of Reading

Culture of Spain *Source*: http://en.wikipedia.org/?oldid=390533295 *Contributors*: 1 anonymous edits

Burgos Cathedral *Source*: http://en.wikipedia.org/?oldid=390571411 *Contributors*: 1 anonymous edits

El Escorial *Source*: http://en.wikipedia.org/?oldid=384323083 *Contributors*: Entirelybs

Poblet Monastery *Source*: http://en.wikipedia.org/?oldid=387216406 *Contributors*: Venerock

Palmeral of Elche *Source*: http://en.wikipedia.org/?oldid=373744041 *Contributors*: TDogg310

Valencia, Spain *Source*: http://en.wikipedia.org/?oldid=390672480 *Contributors*: Diplomatiko

El Museu de les Ciències Príncipe Felipe *Source*: http://en.wikipedia.org/?oldid=384098700 *Contributors*:

Valencian Museum of Ethnology *Source*: http://en.wikipedia.org/?oldid=306305978 *Contributors*: Rosiestep

Ciutat de les Arts i les Ciències *Source*: http://en.wikipedia.org/?oldid=390636488 *Contributors*: Look2See1

Valencia Cathedral *Source*: http://en.wikipedia.org/?oldid=384507500 *Contributors*:

L'Oceanogràfic *Source*: http://en.wikipedia.org/?oldid=385442636 *Contributors*: Polydeuces

Llotja de la Seda *Source*: http://en.wikipedia.org/?oldid=382938592 *Contributors*: Prof saxx

Agora (Valencia) *Source*: http://en.wikipedia.org/?oldid=384605413 *Contributors*: Xelaxa

Palau de les Arts Reina Sofía *Source*: http://en.wikipedia.org/?oldid=380464614 *Contributors*: Mauliddin mutz

Falles *Source*: http://en.wikipedia.org/?oldid=389770492 *Contributors*: 1 anonymous edits

Tomatina *Source*: http://en.wikipedia.org/?oldid=390573601 *Contributors*: Venerock

Benimaclet *Source*: http://en.wikipedia.org/?oldid=306464233 *Contributors*: Valenciano

Turia (river) *Source*: http://en.wikipedia.org/?oldid=380888768 *Contributors*: Woohookitty

Costa del Azahar *Source*: http://en.wikipedia.org/?oldid=354067306 *Contributors*: Pmmollet

Valencia CF *Source*: http://en.wikipedia.org/?oldid=390359147 *Contributors*: 1 anonymous edits

Valencia CF Mestalla *Source*: http://en.wikipedia.org/?oldid=381986663 *Contributors*: Keith D

Valencia Street Circuit *Source*: http://en.wikipedia.org/?oldid=390504427 *Contributors*: DH85868993

Circuit Ricardo Tormo *Source*: http://en.wikipedia.org/?oldid=390151664 *Contributors*:

Valencia Airport *Source*: http://en.wikipedia.org/?oldid=390499470 *Contributors*: MKY661

Ferrocarrils de la Generalitat Valenciana *Source*: http://en.wikipedia.org/?oldid=374386967 *Contributors*:

Valencia Metro (Spain) *Source*: http://en.wikipedia.org/?oldid=382923218 *Contributors*:

Image Sources, Licenses and Contributors

CPSIA information can be obtained at www.ICGtesting.com
Printed in the USA
LVOW03s1404161213

365558LV00004B/63/P